AGS

United States Government

by
Jane Wilcox Smith
Carol Sullivan

American Guidance Service, Inc.
Circle Pines, Minnesota 55014-1796
800-328-2560

About the Authors

Jane Wilcox Smith received her Master of Arts in teaching as a reading specialist from Emory University in Atlanta, Georgia. She taught basic reading skills at the Schenck School in Atlanta, and remedial English and reading skills at Forsyth Central High School in Atlanta.

Carol Sullivan received her Bachelor of Science degree from Jersey State College of New Jersey. She teaches special education at Sandburg Junior High School in Elmhurst, Illinois, in the content areas of English, social studies, and science.

Printed in the United States of America

ISBN 0-7854-0882-7 (hardcover)

ISBN 0-7854-0883-5 (softcover)

Product Number 90400 (hardcover)

Product Number 90401 (softcover)

A 0 9 8 7 6 5 4 3 2

Contents

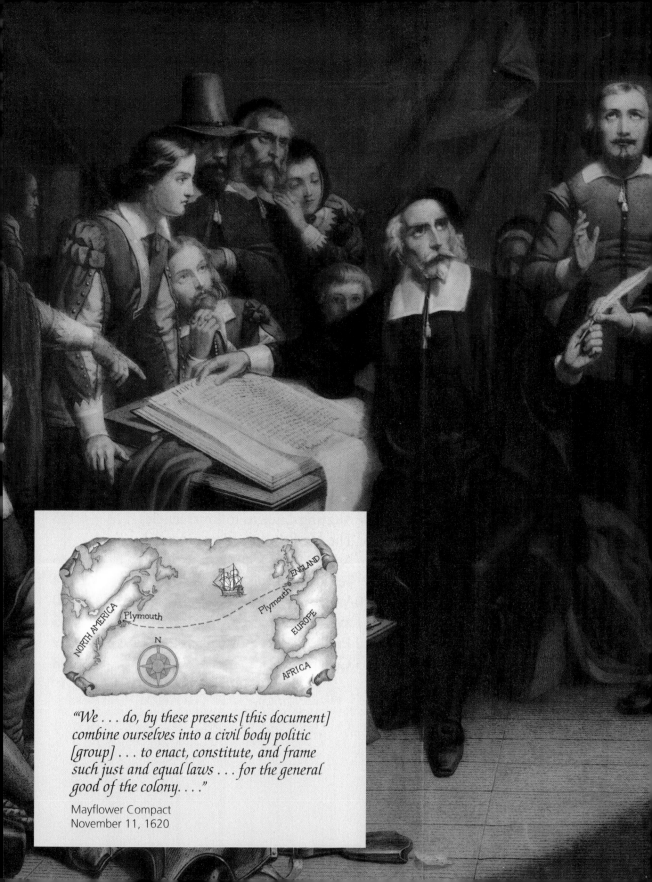

"We . . . do, by these presents [this document] combine ourselves into a civil body politic [group] . . . to enact, constitute, and frame such just and equal laws . . . for the general good of the colony. . . ."

Mayflower Compact
November 11, 1620

Chapter

1

Beginnings of American Government

The first ideas for government in America came from the Pilgrims. Before they landed, they wrote a contract. In the contract, they agreed to make laws and rules "for the general good of the colony." As the colonies grew, many rules and laws were needed.

In Chapter 1, you will learn about events that shaped our country and the rules and laws we have today.

Goals for Learning

★ To describe the reasons for forming the American government

★ To identify ways the American government was influenced by the governments of ancient Greece and Rome

★ To identify principles from English government that influenced American government

★ To describe the political ideas from the original thirteen colonies that became part of the American government

★ To describe the events that led to the American colonies' decision to fight for independence

★ To name the basic rights stated in the Declaration of Independence

Words to Know

Ancient
Many years ago; belonging to early history

★Colonist
Person that settles in a new country

Combination
A grouping of people, things, or ideas that are joined together for a special reason

★Community
The people living together in an area; a group of people who have a common interest

Complicated
Difficult

Consider
To examine or think over carefully

★Custom
A common practice observed by many people

★Government
Laws and customs people live by

★Political
Having to do with government or the actions of the government

Many people live in large cities that are crowded and busy. Others live far out in the country, where they can go for days without seeing another person. In between are the people who live in towns and small **communities.** All of these people share a common need—the need for rules and laws to help them live peaceful and safe lives. Families have rules for their children. Schools have rules for their students. **Governments** have rules for their citizens.

A government is a **combination** of laws and **customs** that people live by. Governments developed as the needs of people grew. Early groups of people lived simply. Simple rules were all they needed. They shared food, punished people who did wrong, and joined together for protection. As these groups grew into larger communities, life became more **complicated.** Governments grew in size and power in order to meet the needs of the new communities. As land and property became more important to people, rules were needed to protect their possessions.

How Did the United States Government Begin?

The government of the United States was formed because the early settlers, or colonists, did not like the way they were treated by England. Thirteen of the American colonies belonged to England and were ruled by English law. Many things happened under these laws that upset the **colonists.** They felt they were taxed unfairly and could not choose their own leaders. Soon the colonists decided to form their own government. They broke away from England.

The American colonists wanted to make rules and laws that were fair. The rights of people were also **considered** and written into the law. All **political** ideas used by the colonists had their roots in older forms of government. **Ancient** civilizations such as Greece and Rome had an influence. The greatest influence, however, came from the governments in England and Europe at that time.

SECTION 1 REVIEW Complete the sentences below using the words from the Word Bank. Write your answers on a separate sheet of paper.

WORD BANK

ancient
combination
community
complicated
considered
customs
political

1) People in a ___ need rules and laws to live peaceful lives.

2) A government is a ___ of laws and ___.

3) Governments grew in size and power when life became more ___.

4) The colonists ___ the rights of the people when they made rules and laws.

5) Many ___ ideas used by the colonists had their roots in ___ governments.

What do you think

Why are rules and laws needed to protect people's possessions?

Words to Know

★**Appoint**
To name or choose a person for an office, but not by election

★**Assembly**
A group gathered to discuss and pass laws

★**Democracy**
A form of government in which citizens take part

★**Dictator**
A person ruling with total control, power, and authority

★**Representative**
A government in which officials are elected by people

★**Republic**
A government in which citizens elect people to speak and act for them

★**Revolt**
To take a stand against a government or a cause

★**Senate**
A governing body that makes rules and laws

★**Veto**
The power of a person or group of people to reject or forbid a rule or law

The word **democracy,** which comes from the Greek language, means "rule by the people." The idea of a democratic government began in Greece in 700 B.C., about twenty-five hundred years ago. Greece was made up of city-states. These were cities with large amounts of land around them. In the beginning these city-states were ruled by kings, and then they were ruled by landowners. Some were even ruled by **dictators.** Dictators can rule any way they please, no matter what the people want. Some dictators became unpopular with the people. The people **revolted** against them. The people wanted to govern themselves, so they formed democracies.

How Did Democracy Work in Greece?

This "rule by the people," or democratic rule, did not mean that all people could take part in running the city-states. The people were divided into four groups. There were free men, women, young males, and slaves. Only free men were members of the ruling body, called an **Assembly.** They ran the government and took turns holding office. The Greek city-state, Athens, had the best-run government.

The city-states of Greece were always at war with one another, and they became weak. Rome, another great power, soon took over the weakened Greek city-states.

How Did Democracy Work in Rome?

Because Rome had such a large population, all of the free men could not take part in running the government. The citizens elected people to speak and act for them. The people they chose were their representatives. This representative type of government was called a **republic.** Rome was a republic.

Philosophers were important political thinkers in ancient Greece. Aristotle was a Greek philosopher who lived between 384 and 322 B.C.

Rome, like Greece, did not give slaves, women, or young males a part in running the government. The free men who ran the government were divided into two groups: wealthy men and common people. The wealthy, or rich, men had more power than the common people, or workers. Two wealthy consuls, or leaders, were chosen. These consuls in turn **appointed** senators, also from the wealthy class. When a man became a senator, he remained a senator for the rest of his life. The **Senate** was the most powerful part of the government. It made rules and laws. The common people had some say in government. They could **veto** any rule or law made by the Senate.

The United States government used many ideas from these ancient civilizations. The United States has a **representative** form of government with elected representatives who make laws and rules. Many words that came from ancient Greece and Rome are still used to describe government processes today. Some of these words are *Senate, veto, republic, representative,* and *democracy.*

SECTION 2 REVIEW Decide if each statement below tells about the Roman government or the Greek government. Write *Greece* or *Rome* beside each sentence number on a separate sheet of paper.

1) Its representative form of government was known as a republic.

2) The ruling body was called an Assembly.

3) All free men took turns holding office.

4) The citizens elected people to represent them.

5) The city-states of this country were always at war.

What do you think

How do you think the right to veto rules or laws helped the common people of Rome?

Words to Know

Decision
Act of making up one's mind; judgment

Generation
The people in each stage or step in a family's history. For example, a grandfather, a father, and a son are three generations

★Jury
A group of citizens chosen in a court to listen to both sides in a case and to make a decision

★Lawsuit
A question or case that is decided in a court of law

★Legislature
A group of people in a country or state with power to make laws

★Monarchy
Rule by a royal family; the rulers are called king, queen, empress, or emperor

★Parliament
A legislative body in England and some other countries

★Petition
A written document or legal paper asking for a right or benefit from someone in authority

Some early forms of government did not have rule by the people. Two common forms of government were **monarchy** and dictatorship.

In a monarchy, the country is ruled by one family, **generation** after generation. The leadership is usually passed down to the monarch's oldest son or daughter. The rulers have titles like king, queen, empress, or emperor. In a dictatorship, a dictator rules alone. A dictator does not pass the rule down to the next generation. No limit is placed on how long a dictator can rule.

How Was England Governed Under King Henry II?

During the late 1000s and early 1100s, the government of England changed form many times. The constant changing of power was very confusing for the people. The rights of the common person were not considered. In 1154 Henry II became king. He was a strong monarch who made changes that did consider the rights of the common person.

Henry II appointed judges. These judges traveled throughout the country to hold court. They decided how to punish people who disobeyed the law. Soon the judges' **decisions** became rules and were followed as law. These laws were divided into two types. The first type included rules that everyone must obey. The second type had to do with rights and duties between individuals. For example, if a person borrowed money and did not pay it back, he could face a **lawsuit.**

As the judges for King Henry II traveled from place to place, they were told of all the crimes committed in an area. The king had appointed special people to inform the judges when a crime had been committed. Today we have

Henry II was a twelfth-century monarch who considered the rights of common people when he made changes in England's system of law.

a grand **jury** in the United States. The grand jury tells our officials if a crime has been committed and if it should be brought to trial. Our trial-by-jury system is much like the system Henry II used.

How Did the English Parliament Begin?

In very early times only the English king and his lords could make laws. In the 1200s, the nobles and King John agreed to limit the king's power and grant rights to the common people. They signed a paper called the *Magna Carta.* The common people were allowed to elect people to represent them in government. This type of lawmaking body in England was called **Parliament.**

By the mid-1300s Parliament had two parts: the House of Lords, which included nobles and church leaders, and the House of Commons, which included knights and common people.

Parliament was used by some rulers and ignored by others. Finally the Parliament was allowed to make laws on its own. The system that Parliament used to make laws worked very well. The colonists followed the same system. Today the United States Congress and state **legislatures** are based on this system.

How Did Parliament Protect Basic Rights?

By 1628 the members of Parliament felt that the power of the kings had become too strong. In the **Petition** of Right they listed the things that a king could not do. The Petition said that a king could not force rich people to make loans and that people could not be put in prison without a jury trial.

In 1689, during the rule of William and Mary, Parliament passed the English Bill of Rights. It stated the powers that a king or queen had. Under this Bill of Rights, Parliament had to approve all taxes. The king was not allowed to suspend, or stop, the work of Parliament. The people could ask the government for help, and a person accused of a crime had the right to a jury trial.

The settlers who came to America knew about the rights that were included in the English Bill of Rights. When the settlers wrote a plan for their own government, they added a Bill of Rights that was similar to the English Bill of Rights and the earlier Petition of Right.

SECTION 3 REVIEW Write the answers to these questions on a separate sheet of paper.

1) Which form of government has a ruler who does not have to pass the rule on to the next generation?

2) What system of justice that we use today was based on a system used during the reign of Henry II?

3) Parliament is made up of the House of Lords and which other house?

4) What part of our government today is based on the English Parliament?

5) Name one English paper that influenced the American settlers when they wrote the Bill of Rights.

What do you think

What part of English government do you think had the most influence on American government? Explain your answer.

The Magna Carta

The king of England in 1199 was King John. He was an unfair king who made many enemies. He taxed the people very heavily. The people did not want to pay all the taxes. They believed that the king was spending the money on himself.

The nobles (rich people of the country) decided that something had to be done to check the king. They planned very carefully. Together with town leaders and church officials, they presented King John with a petition known as the Magna Carta. *Magna Carta* means *great charter*. A *charter* is a written agreement. In June of 1215, King John finally agreed to the demands and put his seal on the paper.

The Magna Carta gave certain rights to the English people and limited the king's power. It stated that the king must ask advice of the nobles in important matters. It also said that no special taxes could be raised without the nobles' consent. No free man could be put in prison without first being judged by his peers (equals). Judges and other officials were to be appointed to serve the kingdom.

The important ideas written in the Magna Carta were used by many people for hundreds of years. For example, one complaint the American colonists had against England was that they were being taxed without their consent and that they had "taxation without representation." This charter helped rulers recognize the wants, needs, and rights of the common people.

Review Answer the following questions on a separate sheet of paper using complete sentences.

1) Which three groups of people developed the petition that became known as the Magna Carta?

2) Why did they send the petition to King John?

3) Explain one way the power of the King was limited by the Magna Carta.

4) Name one important idea that developed from ideas written in the Magna Carta.

5) Why is the Magna Carta considered an important document?

Words to Know

★Constitution
A plan for government

Contract
An agreement made by two or more persons

Criticize
To put down or find fault with

Loyal
Faithful; true to a country or belief

★National
Having to do with the whole country or nation

★Press
Newspapers, magazines, and the people who work for them

Publish
Print information, such as a newspaper, magazine, or book

★Puritan
A member of a religious group

★Religious
Having to do with church practices

Strict
Stern; not changing

The early English settlers in America had ideas about forming a new government. One group of settlers, the Pilgrims, left England because they did not want to belong to the Church of England or pay taxes. On their way to America, they wrote a **contract** for all to sign. This contract, called the Mayflower Compact, said that these settlers would write fair laws and choose leaders. They would do these things but remain **loyal** to the king. As their colony in Massachusetts grew, each church became a meeting place, and each man had a vote.

In other English colonies people did not all vote, as they did in Massachusetts. The Jamestown, Virginia, colony was the first to have an assembly of representatives. This assembly, called the *House of Burgesses,* made decisions for the people. The people elected the representatives. The plan for the assembly did not come from the settlers, but was set up by England. England also sent a governor to rule Jamestown.

The ideas of voting and electing representatives that began in these colonies were later used in the American government. Today we elect representatives at all levels of government: city, county, state, and **national.**

Which Colony Had the First Constitution?

Some of the people who were living in Massachusetts decided that the **religious** rule there was too **strict** for them. They moved away and settled in the Connecticut area. The leader of this group was Thomas Hooker. He believed in a more democratic government that would give more control to the people. Hooker and his followers drew up a **constitution.**

A constitution is a written plan for government. It lists the powers of the government, as well as the rights of the people. In its constitution, the Connecticut group agreed to create an assembly with elected representatives. The group agreed to elect a governor and judges.

This first constitution set an example. Soon other colonies were writing constitutions of their own. Massachusetts' constitution even set up a public school system which was paid for with tax money.

Years later, in 1787, the writers of the United States Constitution took many ideas from these early colonial constitutions.

Could Newspapers Speak Against England?

In colonial times there was a law in the New York area that said no one could **publish** anything that spoke out against the English government. John Peter Zenger, a newspaper publisher, broke this law. Zenger was arrested and tried. The jury found him innocent. This trial was a big step toward the idea of a free **press** as we know it. In the United States, it is not against the law to **criticize** the government or its leaders in a newspaper or on radio or television.

Could Colonists Worship Freely?

Many colonists came to America to worship as they pleased. The **Puritans** came for this reason, but they would not give religious freedom to people living in their colony. People who disagreed with the Puritans were sent away or left the Puritan colony in Massachusetts.

These people then set up colonies that did allow a few different religions. This idea of religious freedom soon spread throughout the colonies. It led to our system today, which gives people the right to worship as they please.

Public Schools Began in Massachusetts

In the early colonial days, children were educated at home or in private schools. Only the wealthy colonists were able to send their children to private schools. Children of poor parents were required to work at an early age. In 1647, the colony of Massachusetts passed a law establishing public schools. All towns of fifty or more people were told to set up a school and hire a teacher. The money for the school came from the town's taxes. The Puritans of this colony felt that all children should learn to read the Bible in order to avoid evil ways. Even though these first schools were set up for religious reasons, it was an important step in the country towards free public education. The responsibility for education was shifted from the home to the community.

Other colonies were slow to follow the example set by Massachusetts. It was not until the early 1800s that a system of free public education was widespread throughout the country. Even then, children were only educated through elementary school. Later, after the Civil War, a system of high schools was set up in many states.

SECTION 4 REVIEW Write the answers to these questions on a separate sheet of paper.

1) What did the Pilgrims agree to do in the Mayflower Compact?

2) Why did the Puritans leave England?

3) Who set up a colony with a more democratic rule than the Puritan colony?

4) What is a written plan for government called?

5) Which colony set up the first public school system?

What do you think

What ideas from the colonies are still part of our government today?

John Peter Zenger

In 1733, William Cosby, the royal governor of New York, suspended a judge who ruled against him in a salary dispute. The only newspaper, *The New York Gazette,* supported the government. The judge and his friends started an opposition newspaper, the *New York Weekly Journal,* to oppose the governor.

John Peter Zenger was the publisher of the *New York Weekly Journal.* The *Journal* accused Cosby of breaking both English and American law and of trying to destroy the court system. Zenger was arrested. He was charged with seditious libel. *Libel* is a written or spoken statement that is unfair or untrue. *Seditious* libel suggests that Zenger's statements were made to resist lawful authority.

Zenger was jailed for ten months. Mrs. Zenger kept the newspaper going and visited him in jail. She had to talk to him through a keyhole. During his trial in 1735, Zenger's lawyer argued that Zenger had printed the truth. The jury decided that Zenger was not guilty.

This case was important to freedom of the press in the United States. In honor of John Peter Zenger, the Zenger Memorial Room was dedicated in 1953. It is located in the Federal Hall Memorial Museum in New York City.

Review

1) In a democracy, why is it important to be able to criticize government leaders without being punished?

2) What are some ways you use a newspaper to get information?

Words to Know

Interfere
To meddle in the business of others

★Legal document
An official paper having to do with rules and laws

★Minutemen
A group of armed men who fought in the Revolutionary War

Organize
To arrange or set up a group effort

Pamphlet
A printed paper

England did not **interfere** with the government in the colonies for nearly a century. Then England needed money to pay its debts and tried to raise money from the colonies. By the middle 1700s, the colonists felt that England was trying to gain control. The colonists did not like the high taxes collected on certain goods. Then England passed the Stamp Act. It forced the colonists to pay a tax on all newspapers, **pamphlets, legal documents,** calendars, and playing cards. In order to end this taxation, representatives from the colonies began to meet in 1765. Gradually feelings against English rule increased.

What Action Did the Colonists Take?

In 1774 a large meeting, called the *First Continental Congress,* was held in Philadelphia. At this meeting the colonists decided to take action against England. They sent the king of England a list of the rights they demanded. They also said that they would refuse to buy all British goods, including tea.

This action of the First Continental Congress made no difference in the way England treated the colonists. Trouble continued between the colonists and England and finally resulted in a war.

The Revolutionary War between the English colonists and England started on April 19, 1775. The first battle of the war took place in Massachusetts. It started at Lexington when British soldiers ordered the colonists to lay down their guns. When they would not, the British fired on them. The armed colonists were called **minutemen** because they had promised to be ready to fight at a minute's notice. Eight minutemen were killed. The British then marched on to Concord where they burned buildings until the minutemen forced them to retreat. Many more battles were fought that spring. In May, the *Second Continental Congress* met.

Who Ran the Country During the War?

The Second Continental Congress ran the government of the colonies and supported the colonists' cause during the war. The Congress met a few weeks after the shooting began. They **organized** an army to be led by George Washington. Not all Americans supported the war. It was difficult to get soldiers to join the army. Other countries, such as Spain, the Netherlands, and France, helped the Americans.

The Continental Congress realized that the trouble with England would not end peacefully. They wanted to end British rule and to have a government run by the people. They asked Thomas Jefferson to write down all their ideas to send to the king. The document Jefferson wrote was called the *Declaration of Independence.* It was the greatest contribution of the colonial period to the future form of democratic government in America.

Thomas Jefferson wrote the Declaration of Independence. Later Jefferson became the third President of the United States.

The Declaration of Independence

The first part of the Declaration of Independence states that all people have certain rights, including "life, liberty, and the pursuit of happiness." It goes on to say that if a government denies these rights to the people, then that rule must end.

The middle section of the Declaration lists all the grievances, or complaints, the colonists had against the king of England, George III.

The last paragraph of the Declaration says, in part:

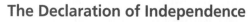

"...That these united colonies are, and of right ought to be, free and independent States; that they are absolved from all allegiance to the British Crown, and that all political connection between them and the state of Great Britain, is and ought to be totally dissolved...."

The Declaration of Independence was approved by Congress on July 4, 1776. Five years later, in October 1781, the British surrendered at the Battle of Yorktown. This marked a turning point in the war. By 1783, the war was over, but many lives had been lost on both sides.

SECTION 5 REVIEW Write the correct phrase to complete each sentence on a separate sheet of paper.

1) The Stamp Act
    (a) helped the colonies.
    (b) forced the colonists to pay taxes on newspapers and pamphlets.

2) At the First Continental Congress, the colonists
    (a) decided to take action against England.
    (b) organized an army to fight the British.

3) The colonists sent England a list of the rights they demanded and said that they
    (a) would not buy British goods.
    (b) wanted to fight a war.

4) The group that ran the government of the country during the war between the colonists and the English was the
    (a) First Continental Congress.
    (b) Second Continental Congress.

5) The Declaration of Independence
    (a) listed the grievances the colonists had against the king.
    (b) was a new plan of government for the colonies.

What do you think

Why do you think some Americans did not support the war?

★ Ideas from the ancient governments of Greece and Rome were used by the American colonists when they formed their own government.

★ King Henry II of England appointed judges and used a jury system.

★ The Magna Carta limited the power of the king and gave certain rights to common people.

★ The English Parliament was the basis for the American Congress and the individual state legislatures.

★ Political ideas for American government also came from the English colonies.

★ In the 1700s, England began to force the colonists to pay high taxes. The First Continental Congress sent the King of England a list of rights the colonists demanded. England ignored their demands.

★ The Revolutionary War, between the colonists and the British, began in 1775.

★ The Second Continental Congress ran the government during the Revolutionary War and wrote the Declaration of Independence in 1776. The Revolutionary War lasted eight years. The Americans won the war in 1783.

Main Events of Colonial Times

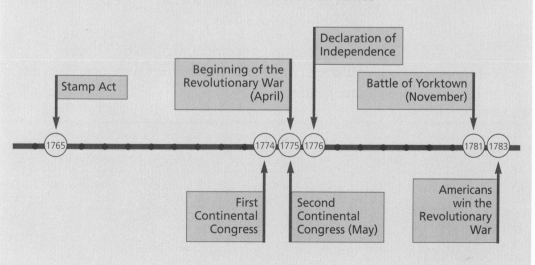

Stamp Act — 1765

First Continental Congress — 1774

Beginning of the Revolutionary War (April) — 1775

Second Continental Congress (May) — 1775

Declaration of Independence — 1776

Battle of Yorktown (November) — 1781

Americans win the Revolutionary War — 1783

CHAPTER 1 REVIEW

Comprehension: Identifying Facts

On a separate sheet of paper, write the correct word or words from the Word Bank that match each statement.

WORD BANK

Declaration of Independence

democracy

Henry II

Jamestown

John Peter Zenger

Magna Carta

Mayflower Compact

monarchy

senate

Second Continental Congress

1) This Greek word means "rule by the people."

2) This group in ancient Rome made the rules and laws.

3) In this type of government the rulers have titles such as king, queen, or emperor.

4) King John agreed to the demands written into this document.

5) When this king came into power, he considered the rights of the common people.

6) This important document was written by the Pilgrims before they left the Mayflower.

7) This early colony had an elected assembly called the House of Burgesses.

8) This man wrote a newspaper article criticizing the governor.

9) This group ran the government of the colonies during the Revolutionary War.

10) This important document, written by Thomas Jefferson, stated that the colonies were now "free and independent."

Comprehension: Understanding Main Ideas

Write the answers to the following questions on a separate sheet of paper using complete sentences.

1) Give two reasons why the English colonies broke away from England.

2) What ideas from Greece and Rome influenced the development of democracy in England and America?

3) How did the trial-by-jury system help people who were accused of a crime?

4) What rights did the Petition of Rights give to English Citizens?

5) Name three ideas from the English Bill of Rights that the Americans wanted in their government.

6) What was the Stamp Act?

7) After the Revolutionary War began, the colonists sent the English king a document. What was this document called? Why did the colonists feel English rule of the colonies should end?

Critical Thinking: Write Your Opinion

1) What are the benefits of using ideas from ancient civilization in our government?

2) Which idea from English government do you think had the greatest influence on American government?

3) Why do you think England did not want to give up the American colonies and was even willing to go to war to keep them?

Test Taking Tip | Before you begin a test, look over it quickly. Try to set aside enough time to complete each section.

"If men were angels, no government would be necessary. . . ."

James Madison
Constitutional
Convention, 1787

"It is probable that no plan we propose will be adopted. . . ."

George Washington
Constitutional
Convention, 1787

Chapter 2

Creation of American Government

The Articles of Confederation was the first plan of government for the colonies. When the Congress decided the Articles of Confederation were too weak, they met again to revise the plan. This meeting became known as the Constitutional Convention. It was held in Philadelphia in 1787. The United States Constitution was written at this meeting. George Washington, who was a hero of the Revolutionary War, was chosen to lead the convention. Washington knew it would be difficult to form a plan that all states would accept.

Our Constitution became a model for democratic government that has worked with only a few changes for over two hundred years. In Chapter 2, you will learn how the Constitution was created.

Goals for Learning

★ To explain why the Articles of Confederation didn't work and why a stronger plan was needed

★ To identify and describe the compromises made at the Constitutional Convention

★ To name the four guiding principles used to write the Constitution

★ To describe the process used to ratify the Constitution

★ To describe the Federalist and the Anti-Federalist points of view

★ To explain why the Bill of Rights was needed

Words to Know

★Delegate
A person chosen to speak or act for another person or group

Financial
Having to do with money

★Justice
Fair and equal treatment under the law; the use of authority to uphold what is right and lawful

Limited
Restricted; kept within a boundary

Revise
To improve; to bring up to date

★Treaty
An agreement between two or more countries or states about trade, peace, or other matters

At the end of the Revolutionary War, all ties between the colonies and England were broken. A new nation was formed, but it was a nation of separate and individual colonies. These colonies needed a form of government to join them together as a country.

What Was the First Plan of Government?

At the Second Continental Congress a committee wrote a plan for joining the states together. This plan was called the Articles of Confederation. It gave the thirteen states a plan for government. It was popular with the states because it did not make the national, or central, government too strong. The colonists remembered their dislike for strong English rule. The Articles were quickly approved by all the states.

The Articles of Confederation set up a national Congress made up of **delegates** from the thirteen states. This Congress could make war, agree to **treaties** with other countries, and take care of **financial** needs. Each state sent one delegate to the Congress. The Articles did not provide for a president as a national leader or for a system of **justice.**

At first most people were satisfied with the Articles of Confederation because they allowed the states to control most of their own affairs. The Articles **limited** Congress's power over the states. However, as time went on, the states saw that the Articles were too weak.

Why Didn't the Plan Work?

The war with England had cost a great deal of money. The country owed 40 million dollars to foreign governments alone. Congress had no money of its own, and no way of raising money. Most of the money needed should have come from the states, but many states refused to pay. The Articles of Confederation had no system of law to force the

ARTICLES *of* CONFEDERATION

★ ★ ★ ★ ★ ★ ★ ★

Articles allowed Congress to:
- ☑ make war
- ☑ agree to treaties with other countries
- ☑ take care of the country's financial needs

Articles did not allow for:
- ☐ a president or national leader
- ☐ a way for Congress to raise money
- ☐ a system of law or justice

states to pay. In addition the Articles of Confederation did not provide for a system of law or justice.

Other financial problems, besides the war debt, were also facing the new nation. Businesses and farmers were out of money. Congress had no funds to pay an army and navy to defend the nation. Also, the soldiers who fought in the Revolutionary War had not yet been paid. Individual states were printing their own money. A better government was needed to make the new nation a strong, rich country. Finally, a meeting was called to **revise** the Articles of Confederation. This meeting was held in Philadelphia in 1787. It became known as the Constitutional Convention.

SECTION 1 REVIEW Choose the correct word or words in parentheses that make each statement true. Write your answers on a separate sheet of paper.

1) The Articles of Confederation (set up, did not set up) a system of justice.

2) At first the Articles of Confederation were (unpopular, popular) with the people in the colonies because the Articles gave the states control over their own affairs.

3) The Articles of Confederation (did, did not) make the national government strong.

4) The Articles of Confederation (did, did not) provide for a president of the new country.

5) Congress (had, did not have) money to pay for an army and navy to defend the nation.

What do you think **?**

What problems might be caused by each state printing its own money?

Words to Know

★**Executive**
A person or group having the power to carry out the plans and duties of a group; for example, a president

★**Federal**
A system of government in which power is divided between a central government and state governments

Responsibility
An activity or task that is assigned to a person or group

★**Voting power**
The right to vote

The delegates who attended the convention in Philadelphia in 1787 were well-educated men, mostly from the cities. They shared the same ideas about government. The delegates were important people in their own states. George Washington was the leader at the convention.

At first the delegates worked to revise the Articles of Confederation. Soon they saw that a new plan for government was needed. The colonists knew what they did *not* want. They did not want the states to lose control of the government. They did not want a king or a strong central government. The delegates worked for four months in secret to create a new plan for the country. They discussed many different plans.

What Plans Were Considered?

The plans that were considered were based on the idea of a **federal** government. A federal government is one in which states join together to form a country. Some, but not all, power is given to a central government. The states are equal to each other in **voting power.** They are also given some **responsibility** to govern themselves. The convention delegates finally worked out a federal type of government for the new nation.

Several forms of federal government were suggested at first, but two plans were finally presented for discussion:

Virginia Plan. This plan, suggested by the larger states, favored a strong central government. It called for one **executive,** and a two-part lawmaking body (legislature). The people would elect members of the legislature.

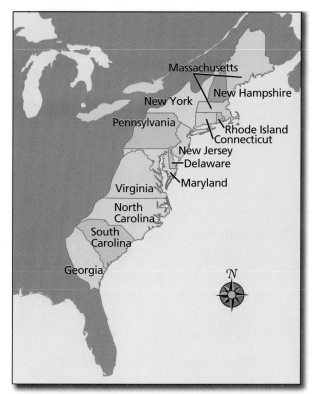

Original 13 colonies.

New Jersey Plan. This plan, suggested by the smaller states, favored greater power for the states. It called for a one-part legislature and two or more executives. All members of the legislature would be chosen by the states. The presidents would be chosen by the legislature.

Both plans provided for the federal government to be in charge of admitting new states to the union. Both plans favored a supreme court that would make final decisions concerning the law. The delegates finally decided to use parts of both plans.

SECTION 2 REVIEW Match the definitions with the words in the Word Bank. Write your answers on a separate sheet of paper.

WORD BANK
delegates
federal government
George Washington
New Jersey Plan
revise Articles of Confederation

Definitions:

1) Leader of the delegates at the Constitutional Convention.

2) Original purpose of convention in Philadelphia.

3) The people who attended the Constitutional Convention.

4) Type of government that does not give all power to a national, or central, government.

5) Plan that favored greater power to the states.

What do you think

How might the government be different today if the New Jersey Plan had been chosen?

The Philadelphia Convention

The Constitutional Convention began in the early summer of 1787. The doors to Philadelphia's State House, where the Constitutional Convention was held, were

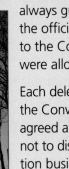

always guarded. Only the official delegates to the Convention were allowed inside.

Each delegate at the Convention had agreed ahead of time not to discuss Convention business with outsiders. They knew they were facing difficult decisions. The delegates wanted to meet in private to settle their differences and form their ideas for the new government. They did not want the public to be allowed to judge their ideas until they were finished.

Although official records of the Convention proceedings were kept, James Madison kept his own notes. The notes were kept secret until after his death in 1836. From his notes, we know much about the Convention. Although the delegates represented different sections of the country with different interests, they did agree on the following issues:

★ The Articles of Confederation could not be revised to solve all the problems.

★ The country needed a strong central government.

★ The power of the government must rest with the voters who would elect representatives to run the government.

★ The powers of government needed to be separated.

★ The new government must be able to tax, raise an army, and regulate trade.

Finally, as the summer ended, the hard work of the Convention also came to a close. All that remained was for the states to agree to the new document.

Review Answer the following questions on a separate sheet of paper using complete sentences.

1) Where was the Constitutional Convention held?

2) Why did the delegates want their discussions to be private?

3) Name two issues concerning the new government which all of the delegates agreed upon.

4) After the Convention was over, what did the delegates do with the new plan for government?

5) If the Convention were held today, do you think the delegates could have met in as much privacy? Explain your answer.

At the Constitutional Convention, each side had to **compromise,** or give up, some of its plan in order to reach an agreement. Four major compromises were made.

How Would the States Be Represented?

The most important compromise was about how to create a legislature (lawmaking body) for the new government. A group of delegates from Connecticut suggested a two-part legislature. The delegates said it should be a two-part legislature in order to please both the larger and smaller states. The members of one part of the legislature would be chosen according to population. The other part would have two representatives from each state, no matter how large or small the state was. This became known as the Connecticut Compromise.

How Would Slaves' Votes Be Counted?

The second compromise settled a problem about slaves. The problem was whether the slaves should be counted the same as free men for tax collection and population purposes. The compromise said that every five slaves would count the same as three free men. This was called the Three-Fifths Compromise.

Who Would Control Trade Among the States?

The third compromise had to do with **interstate** trade. The delegates debated how much power Congress should have over trade. They decided Congress would control trade between states. The states were given control of trade within their own borders.

Who Would Control Trade Between Countries?

The northern and southern states did not agree on the issue of foreign trade. The northern states wanted Congress to control all foreign trade. The southern states sold large amounts of rice and tobacco to foreign countries. They were afraid they would lose this trade if Congress taxed these goods. The northern and southern states also disagreed about slaves. The southerners worried that Congress would stop slave trade.

The two sides compromised. The delegates gave Congress the power to control foreign trade. Congress could tax **imports** but not **exports.** The delegates said that Congress could not end slave trade for twenty years.

By September 17, 1787, the delegates agreed on all the compromises, and the Constitution was signed. The country had a new plan for government.

SECTION 3 REVIEW Select the correct ending for each sentence. Write your answers on a separate sheet of paper.

1) A compromise is a system
(a) of give and take by each side to end a disagreement.
(b) of rules and laws to run a country.

2) The delegates from Connecticut tried to settle the problems about
(a) a legislature.
(b) the slaves.

3) Everyone at the Convention agreed that the states should control
(a) trade within a state.
(b) all foreign trade.

4) One compromise that the delegates agreed on was that slave trade could
(a) never be ended.
(b) not be ended by the federal government for twenty years.

5) On September 17, 1787, the compromises were agreed upon by
(a) all delegates.
(b) only some of the delegates.

Words to Know

★Checks and
Balances
*A plan to keep any
part of government
from becoming too
powerful*

★Judicial
*Having to do with
courts of law and
justice*

★Limited
Government
*All parts of
government must
obey the law*

★Popular
Sovereignty
*People elect their
leaders*

★Separation
of Power
*Government power
is divided between
the executive,
legislative, and
judicial branches*

Principle
*A basic truth, law,
or ideal of behavior*

★Unconsitutional
*Not following the
Constitution*

The writers of the Constitution were careful to base this new plan on certain **principles** they felt were necessary for a democratic government. These principles were **Popular Sovereignty, Limited Government, Separation of Powers,** and **Checks and Balances.**

Popular Sovereignty

Popular Sovereignty is when all power is held by the people because they elect the leaders of the national and state governments.

Limited Government

The Constitution set limits on the power the government has. Government must obey the law and conduct business according to the principles of the Constitution. The government and its officers are never above the law.

Separation of Powers

The Constitution put the power into three different departments. The Congress is the legislative or lawmaking branch. The executive branch applies or enforces the laws. The **judicial** branch interprets the laws made by Congress.

Only Congress can make laws. It cannot give anyone else the power to do so. It also must approve appointments made by the President. The President and the executive branch see that the laws are carried out. The President can veto bills and appoint officials, such as ambassadors and judges.

The courts, with the United States Supreme Court as the most powerful court, can settle disagreements or disputes brought to them by the government or by any person. The judicial branch interprets the laws (tells what they mean) and decides whether a law agrees with the Constitution.

How does the system of checks and balances work?

Limits of Branches of Government

Presidential Limits

★ Congress can remove the President by impeachment.

★ Congress can pass a bill even if the President vetoes it.

★ Congress must approve how money is spent.

★ Only Congress can declare war.

Congressional Limits

★ The President can veto bills of Congress.

★ The Supreme Court can say a law is unfair.

Judicial Limits

★ The President appoints federal judges.

★ Congress must approve the President's appointments of judges.

★ Congress can remove a judge.

Checks and Balances

The three branches of government have separate duties, but they must act together in some cases. Limits are placed on each branch to prevent one branch from becoming too powerful.

The Supreme Court cannot make laws, but it can decide if a law is **unconstitutional.** Congress then has to change the law or write a new law. The President cannot make laws, but the President must approve the laws Congress passes. In turn Congress must approve all money spent by the country. Congress must also approve the President's appointments of people to important government jobs.

SECTION 4 REVIEW Match the basic principle of the Constitution in the Word Bank with the statements below. Write your answers on a separate sheet of paper.

WORD BANK

Checks and Balances

Limited Government

Popular Sovereignty

Separation of Powers

Statements:

1) The power of the federal government is shared by three groups: Congress, the President, and a system of courts.

2) The three branches of the government work together and each branch must approve certain actions of other branches.

3) The government and its officers must always obey the law. They cannot take away the rights of the people as guaranteed in the Constitution.

4) The people elect the leaders of the national and state governments.

What do you think ?

Why do you think Popular Sovereignty is a needed part of our government system?

Once the Constitution was completed, it had to be approved by the states. Most of the delegates at the Constitutional Convention had signed the Constitution. These delegates worked hard to **persuade** the states to **ratify** it. Each state held a convention to study the Constitution. The approval of nine of the thirteen states was needed before the Constitution could be put into use.

Did People Want the New Constitution?

It had been eleven years since the Declaration of Independence was signed. The people of the country were divided in their ideas about the Constitution. Some people, called **Federalists,** favored the Constitution because it provided for a strong national government. The Federalists believed a strong central **authority** was necessary to defend the nation and keep it united. Alexander Hamilton, James Madison, and John Jay were three well-known Federalists. They sent their messages to the people of New York by writing **essays** in the New York newspapers.

Another group was known as the **Anti-Federalists.** They favored stronger state governments than the Constitution permitted. They were opposed to the Constitution because they thought it would take away many state and individual rights.

How Did They Reach Agreement?

The Federalists agreed to add amendments to the Constitution to protect peoples' basic rights. Many Anti-Federalists then favored it. This addition was made two years later. It is known as the Bill of Rights. It **guarantees** such rights as freedom of speech, of religion, and of the press.

Discussions continued throughout the winter at the state conventions. Finally, by June of 1788, nine states had ratified the Constitution. This was enough to allow the

Ratifying the Constitution

	Accept	Reject
Dec. 7, 1787 Delaware	30	0
Dec. 12, 1787 Pennsylvania	43	23
Dec. 18, 1787 New Jersey	38	0
Jan. 2, 1788 Georgia	26	0
Jan. 9, 1788 Connecticut	128	40
Feb. 6, 1788 Massachusetts	187	168
April 28, 1788 Maryland	63	11
May 23, 1788 South Carolina	149	73
June 21, 1788 New Hampshire	57	46
June 25, 1788 Virginia	89	79
July 26, 1788 New York	30	27
Nov. 21, 1789 North Carolina	194	77
May 29, 1790 Rhode Island	34	32

How many votes could have kept the Constitution from being ratified by Pennsylvania, Maryland, Virginia, and New York?

Constitution to become the new plan for government. By 1790 all thirteen states had ratified the Constitution.

Where Was the Constitution Put in Action?

Congress began putting the Constitution into use as soon as it was ratified. The first action Congress took was to name New York as the **temporary** capital. Later it was moved to Philadelphia and by 1800, to Washington, D.C. The first elections were held, and George Washington was the popular choice for President. John Adams was elected Vice President. Twenty-six senators and sixty-five representatives were elected from the states to serve in the new Congress. They met for the first time on March 4, 1789, in Federal Hall in New York.

SECTION 5 REVIEW Choose the answer from the three choices given that best completes the sentences. Write your answers on a separate sheet of paper.

1) The (Anti-Federalists, Federalists, Congress) favored the new Constitution.

2) The Constitution had to be ratified by (eight, nine, ten) of the thirteen states in order to be put into use.

3) The (Anti-Federalists, Federalists, Constitution) favored strong state governments.

4) The (Federalists, senators, Anti-Federalists) agreed to approve the Constitution after the Bill of Rights was added.

5) By 1790 (all, some, ten) states had ratified the Constitution.

What do you think

What do you think people were afraid might happen if the Bill of Rights wasn't added to the Constitution?

The Federalist Papers

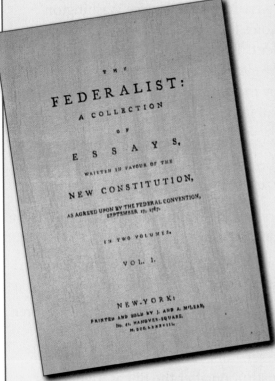

The Federalists used the press to persuade people to ratify the United States Constitution. They wrote essays that were published in the New York newspapers. They wrote eighty-five essays that became known as "The Federalist Papers." George Washington and Benjamin Franklin were both on the side of the Federalists. The success of The Federalist Papers helped convince people to ratify the Constitution.

The Anti-Federalists wrote letters and pamphlets to respond to The Federalist Papers. The Anti-Federalist arguments were not as widely read as The Federalist Papers.

Review

1) The Federalist Papers persuaded people to vote for the new Constitution. What methods could be used today, besides the newspaper, to influence people about a certain point of view? Give an example of how another method might be used.

2) Why are newspapers, radio, and television important in a democratic form of government?

3) How might the support of George Washington and Benjamin Franklin for the Federalists have convinced people to ratify the Constitution?

Newspapers, radio, and television are important in a democracy. Candidates for political office use the media to persuade American citizens to vote for them. When a bill is before Congress, special interest groups sometimes print editorials or buy advertising time to promote their view. Often, they encourage Americans to ask their representatives in Congress to vote for or against a certain bill.

★ Under the Articles of Confederation, the government did not have the power to raise money needed to pay the nation's war debt, or to force the states to pay their share of the debt.

★ A convention was called to revise the Articles of Confederation. The delegates at this convention decided that a new, stronger plan for government was necessary.

★ The larger states favored a strong central government (Virginia Plan), while the smaller states wanted more power to go to the states (New Jersey Plan).

★ The Constitution was written based on four principles, or ideals. These principles are Popular Sovereignty, Limited Government, Separation of Powers, and Checks and Balances.

★ After the Constitution was finished it had to be approved, or ratified, by the states. Each state held a convention.

★ The Federalists, who favored a stronger central government, approved of the Constitution. They were opposed by the Anti-Federalists, who said the states should have more power.

★ The Federalist Papers helped convince many Anti-Federalists to vote for ratifying the Constitution.

★ By 1790, every state had ratified the Constitution.

★ The Bill of Rights was added after the Constitution was ratified.

The Path to the Constitution

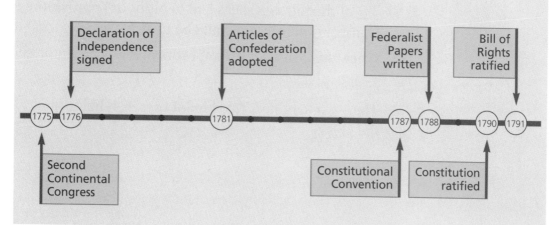

Comprehension: Identifying Facts

Complete the sentences below using the words from the Word Bank. Write your answers on a separate sheet of paper.

WORD BANK

Bill of Rights

compromises

federal

first plan of government

national leader

Nine

Popular Sovereignty

Revolutionary War

right away

smaller

three

1) The ___ broke all ties between the English colonies and England.

2) The Articles of Confederation were written as the ___ for the new country.

3) The Articles of Confederation did not provide for a ___ or a system of law or justice.

4) In a ___ form of government, some power is given to a central government, and some power is given to the states.

5) The ___ states at the Constitutional Convention favored more power for the individual states.

6) Many ___ were made at the Constitutional Convention before the delegates approved the Constitution.

7) ___ means that power is in the hands of the people because they elect the leaders.

8) The separation of powers among the ___ branches of the government was provided for by the Constitution.

9) ___ of the thirteen states had to ratify, or approve, the Constitution before it could be used.

10) When the Constitution was ratified, it was put into use ___.

11) The ___ guarantees freedom of speech, religion, and the press.

Comprehension: Understanding Main Ideas

Write the answers to the following questions on a separate sheet of paper using complete sentences.

1) Why were the Articles of Confederation accepted at first by all the states as a plan for the new government?

2) Name one reason the Articles of Confederation were considered to be too weak.

3) How did delegates at the Constitutional Convention compromise on the issue of trade?

4) Before the Bill of Rights was added, why did the Federalists and Anti-Federalists disagree about the Constitution?

5) When the new Constitution was finally agreed upon, why did the plan for a two-part legislature please the smaller states?

6) Why did the southern states want to control their own foreign trade?

Critical Thinking: Write Your Opinion

1) In writing the Constitution the New Jersey plan was rejected by the delegates at the convention. Why do you think the delegates rejected this plan?

2) Which of the four guiding principles of the Constitution do you think is most important and why?

3) Why is the Bill of Rights important?

Test Taking Tip | When studying for a test, you will remember the facts and definitions better if you write them down.

The United States Constitution is ". . . The most wonderful work ever struck off at a given time by the brain and purpose of man."

William Ewart Gladstone
Nineteenth Century British statesman

We the People

Chapter 3

A Look at the Constitution

The Constitution became the new plan for government for the United States of America. It explained how the new government should be set up and run. Amendments, or written changes, were added to the Constitution as they were needed. The first ten amendments, known as the Bill of Rights, were added two years after the Constitution was approved.

The Constitution has been in use for over two hundred years. It has worked even though the country has changed from a small farming nation to a powerful, modern nation. When we celebrate Independence Day on July 4, we are celebrating the success of our Constitution. In Chapter 3, you will learn about the parts of the Constitution.

Goals for Learning

★ To name the goals described in the Preamble to the United States Constitution

★ To explain the power given to each of the three branches of government in the first three articles

★ To name the rights given to the states in Article Four

★ To describe the process for amending the Constitution in Article Five

★ To identify the rights and freedoms guaranteed to American citizens by the Bill of Rights

★ To identify the changes made in the Constitution in Amendments 11 - 27

Words to Know

★Ambassador
A person appointed by the President to represent the United States in a foreign country

★Article
One of the parts of a written document

★Congress
The legislative branch of the United States government; it includes the Senate and House of Representatives

★Preamble
An introduction or short statement of purpose

The **Preamble** is a short introduction to the Constitution. It states:

"We the people of the United States, in order to form a more perfect Union, establish justice, insure domestic tranquility, provide for the common defense, promote the general welfare, and secure the blessings of liberty to ourselves and our posterity, do ordain and establish this Constitution for the United States of America."

The Preamble explains the goals and purpose of the Constitution: The people of the United States could expect justice, peace, and safety at home. The government will provide protection from other countries.

Following the Preamble are three **articles** that explain the principle of separation of powers. Three branches of the federal government would be set up. Each branch would have certain powers and duties.

Article I (One): The Legislative Branch
Section 1. *All legislative powers herein granted shall be vested in a Congress of the United States, which shall consist of a Senate and House of Representatives.*

This article gives **Congress** the power to make laws. It further says that the Congress has two parts—a Senate and a House of Representatives.

Powers of Congress

The legislative branch

★ makes laws

★ collects taxes and borrows money

★ regulates commerce with foreign nations

★ sets rules for citizenship

★ provides for the country's defense and declares war

★ sets up lower courts (lower than the Supreme Court)

Article II (Two): The Executive Branch

Section 1. *The executive power shall be vested in a President of the United States of America. The President shall hold office for a term of four years, and together with the Vice President, chosen for the same term, be elected. . . .*

The many duties of the President are explained in this article. They include the power to appoint **ambassadors** to foreign countries and judges to the Supreme Court.

Executive Powers

The executive branch

★ carries out laws made by Congress

★ makes treaties

★ appoints ambassadors, some judges, and other public officials

★ leads the armed forces

Article III (Three): The Judicial Branch

Section 1. *The judicial power of the United States, shall be vested in one Supreme Court, and in such inferior courts as the Congress may from time to time ordain and establish. . . .*

The types of cases that come under the federal courts are outlined in Article III.

Judicial Powers

The judicial branch

★ decides whether laws follow the Constitution

★ decides appeals from lower courts

Article IV (Four): The States and the Federal Government

The laws and other legal rulings of one state must be recognized by all other states. Article IV also says that the rights a citizen has in one state will be respected in all states. Finally, this article states that the federal government guarantees each state a republican form of government.

The Constitution of the United States

Preamble	—	Goals and Purpose
Article I	—	The Legislative Branch
Article II	—	The Executive Branch
Article III	—	The Judicial Branch
Article IV	—	The States and the Federal Government
Article V	—	Amending the Constitution
Article VI	—	Supreme Law of the Land
Article VII	—	Ratifying the Constitution

SECTION 1 REVIEW Read each statement. Decide which one of the first four articles of the Constitution it matches. Write the article number (I, II, III, or IV) beside the sentence number on a separate sheet of paper.

1) A Congress is established or set up.

2) A citizen's rights are respected in all states.

3) Congress shall consist of a Senate and House of Representatives.

4) Each state has a republican form of government.

5) A President's term of office is four years.

6) The highest judicial power of the United States shall be given to the Supreme Court.

7) The President has the power to appoint ambassadors to foreign countries.

What do you think

Why are the first three articles of the Constitution so important?

Words to Know

★Amendment
A change or correction made by a certain process

★Convention
A formal meeting called for a special purpose

★Majority
The greater number or part of something; more than one-half of the total

★Prohibition
The Twenty-First Amendment to the Constitution; it made production and sale of alcoholic beverages illegal

Any change to the Constitution is called an **amendment.** The writers of the Constitution knew that changes might have to be made from time to time.

Article V (Five): Amending the Constitution

Article V was added so that changes could be made when necessary. Amendments are proposed in order to make corrections or to add something new. Changes to the Constitution are not made easily.

First, an amendment is voted on by Congress. It must be approved by a two-thirds (2/3) **majority** vote in both the Senate and House of Representatives. Then the amendment is sent to all the states. There are two ways the states can ratify, or approve an amendment. In the first way, three-fourths (3/4) of the state legislatures must approve the change. If this happens, the change is added to the Constitution as an official amendment. The second way an amendment can be approved is for Congress to order special state **conventions.** Three-fourths of these conventions must vote yes to approve a new amendment. If special conventions are called, the state legislatures do not have to approve the amendment.

Through the years, more than 9,000 amendments have been suggested, but only twenty-seven have been added to the Constitution since it was written in 1787.

Article VI (Six): Law of the Land

Article Six of the Constitution declares that the Constitution is the supreme, or highest, law of the land. All officials of both the federal and state governments are sworn under oath to support and obey the Constitution.

The Twenty-First Amendment

All but one of the amendments have been approved by state legislatures. The one exception was the Twenty-First Amendment. This amendment ended **Prohibition,** the law that banned the manufacture, use, and transportation of alcoholic beverages. In this case, Congress called for state conventions to approve the amendment.

To vote on this amendment, state-wide elections were set up to choose delegates for the state conventions. Delegates had to say ahead of time if they would vote to keep or to end Prohibition.

By December, 1933, the amendment was ratified by constitutional conventions in three-fourths of the states, and Prohibition ended.

Article VII (Seven): Ratifying the Constitution

Article Seven tells how the Constitution will be ratified. It says that the thirteen states should hold conventions. If at least nine of the states approve the Constitution, it would become law.

SECTION 2 REVIEW On a separate sheet of paper, write answers to the following questions using complete sentences.

1) Why was Article V added to the Constitution?

2) After an amendment is passed by a two-thirds majority in both houses of Congress what is the next step?

3) In what two ways can the states ratify an amendment to the Constitution?

4) Who decides how an amendment will be ratified by the states?

5) Why was the Twenty-First Amendment different from all other amendments?

What do you think

Why do you think so few amendments that have been suggested have atually been added to the Constitution?

The Equal Rights Amendment

The Nineteenth Amendment gave women the right to vote. After it was passed, women began to work for an amendment that would give them equal rights in all areas. In 1972, Congress approved an equal rights amendment. The amendment said, "Equality of rights under the law shall not be limited . . . because of a person's sex." The amendment became known as the ERA.

The ERA was sent to the states for approval. Twenty-two states had ratified it by the end of 1972. Thirty-eight states were needed to ratify it.

In 1972, a group called "Stop ERA" was formed by Phyllis Schlafly, a woman from St. Louis, Missouri. Schlafly wanted to defeat the ERA because she believed it would mean women would no longer be protected by existing laws. For example, some laws limited the number of hours women could work. She believed that women would not be protected by these laws if the ERA were passed. Schlafly's arguments against the ERA caused many people to think that the amendment might not be a good idea.

Congress extended the deadline for approval of the ERA until 1982. By then, only thirty-five states had ratified it. Five states that had previously ratified the ERA wanted to change their vote. The equal rights amendment was not approved. Today, some people feel that the amendment is no longer needed because women have equal rights in most areas of public life.

Review

1) How would an equal rights amendment have protected women from job discrimination?

2) Why do you think the Stop ERA message caused people to change their minds about approving the ERA?

Words to Know

★**Assemble**
To come together as a group

Express
To make known one's thoughts, ideas, or feelings; to put an idea into words

★**Militia**
An organized group of citizens who serve as soldiers during times of state or national emergency

Opinion
A belief or judgment of an individual or group

Some people were opposed to the new Constitution because it did not guarantee individual rights. A promise was made at the Constitutional Convention to add a part that would give people the rights they wanted. People wanted a guarantee that they would have the right to worship as they pleased and the right of free speech. This promise caused many people to vote in favor of the Constitution.

It took two years for the states to ratify the new amendments.

These first ten amendments, known as the Bill of Rights, were added to the Constitution. They guaranteed basic freedoms to the people, including freedom of religion, freedom of speech, and the right to trial by jury.

The First Amendment

The purpose of the First Amendment is to allow people to **express** themselves. This right of free expression is considered by many to be the most important freedom guaranteed by the Constitution.

"Congress shall make no law respecting an establishment of religion, or prohibiting the free exercise thereof; or abridging the freedom of speech, or of the press; or the right of the people peaceably to assemble, and to petition the Government for a redress of grievances."

The First Amendment guarantees people the right to worship as they please, or not to worship at all. Also, the government may not give public tax money or other support to any one religion. The First Amendment also guarantees all people the right to express themselves in speech or writing, even if the words offend others. The writers of the amendments felt that by allowing freedom

Bill of Rights *(1791)*

1. Freedom of religion, speech, press, petition, and assembly

2. Right to keep and bear arms; states' right to have **militia**

3. Freedom from having to allow soldiers to stay in citizens' homes in times of peace

4. Freedom from unreasonable searches and seizures

5. Freedom from being accused of crime except by grand jury indictment and from being tried twice for the same offense; right to due process

6. Right to a fair trial in criminal cases

7. Right to jury trial in most civil cases

8. Right to reasonable bail, fines, and punishment

9. Protection of rights not written in Constitution

10. Powers not given to federal government reserved for states or people

of speech, many different **opinions** would be heard. They believed that the best opinions would be accepted by the people.

Freedom of the press is the third guarantee of the First Amendment. This means that not only can people speak freely, they also can write down their opinions. These opinions can then be circulated in newspapers, magazines, pamphlets, and on radio and television. People also have the right to be informed. In the United States, the government does not own the press. It is owned by private individuals or groups of persons. The press can print what it believes to be true and fair.

The fourth guarantee of the First Amendment is the right to **assemble** in groups in a peaceful way and for peaceful purposes. In some countries this is not allowed. Any group in the United States has the right to hold meetings, whether its ideas are popular or not. Outdoor or indoor meetings and demonstrations are permitted.

The Supreme Court has ruled that people may assemble in public places, such as parks, sidewalks, state capitol buildings, and national monuments. These assemblies can be stopped only if there is a danger to citizens. State and local officials can make rules for such gatherings, but they cannot stop them. A city usually requires people to get a permit to hold a march or parade.

The fifth and last guarantee in the First Amendment is the right to petition. This means that people can ask government officials to do something or to stop doing something. These petitions, or requests, may come from individuals or from groups. They may be letters or formal written requests. Group petitions may also be prepared and signed by many people and sent to government officials. For example, people often send petitions to ask that the building of a highway or a shopping center be stopped.

SECTION 3 REVIEW On a separate sheet of paper, write the correct word to complete each sentence.

1) The government (may, may not) favor one religion over another.

2) The press (is, is not) owned by the government in the United States.

3) Groups in the United States (can, cannot) hold meetings if their ideas are unpopular.

4) Group petitions (may, may not) be sent to government officials.

5) Many people consider the First Amendment to be the (most, least) important amendment to the Constitution.

What do you think

Why is it important for the government to not own the press?

Media & Government

First Amendment Rights

The Bill of Rights protects American citizens' individual rights and gives us important freedoms. When there is a question about these rights, the Supreme Court has the job of interpreting the amendments. Freedom of the press is guaranteed in the First Amendment. Sometimes freedom of the press and individual rights are in conflict.

In August 1972, an Ohio TV station filmed the performance of Hugo Zacchini, a "human cannonball." Zacchini was shot from a cannon into a net 200 feet away. The station broadcast the entire fifteen-second act without Zacchini's permission. Zachinni sued the station saying that it had taken away his right to control advertising about his performance. The Ohio Supreme Court ruled in favor of the TV station. It said that the broadcast of the performance was protected under the First and Fourteenth Amendments. They said the station didn't intend to harm Zacchini or to use the film for a private purpose.

In 1977, the United States Supreme Court overturned the Ohio Supreme Court ruling by a 5 to 4 vote. The decision said the First and Fourteenth Amendments did not protect the TV station's right to broadcast an entire act without the performer's consent. They said the same rules that require the media to get permission to use a play apply to this man's performance.

Review

1) How might the TV station's broadcast of the act have affected Zacchini's show?

2) How was Zacchini deprived of his rights?

Words to Know

★**Civil**
Having to do with citizens; a civil law case does not involve a crime

★**Convict**
To find guilty of a crime

★**Due process**
Right to a fair trial according to rules and procedures

★**Evidence**
The objects and statements gathered and used to judge a person of a crime

★**Grand jury**
A group of people who decide if there is enough evidence against an accused person to conduct a trial

★**Indict**
To accuse or charge with a crime, usually done by a grand jury

Witness
Someone who has seen or heard something; a person who is called to testify, or tell what he or she knows, in court

The First Amendment of the Bill of Rights guaranteed basic freedoms of expression and religion to American citizens. There were many other rights the colonists felt were important. Amendments 2 to 10 protected these individual rights.

The Second Amendment: The Right to Bear Arms

During the Revolutionary War, the British tried to take weapons away from the colonists. This made the colonists feel helpless. They needed the guns to serve in their state militias.

The Second Amendment gives people the right to bear arms (weapons) and the right to use them when serving in an organized militia. This amendment permits a state to train and keep a militia for protection in time of need.

Most states have a National Guard that is organized to serve the state in an emergency. National Guard units from the states are sometimes used in national emergencies, too. For example, National Guard units from some states were called into duty to help enforce the peace in Bosnia in 1996.

The Third Amendment: Housing Soldiers in Homes

The British forced the colonists to allow soldiers to stay in their homes. Many colonists did this against their will. The Third Amendment protects people from having to let soldiers stay in their homes.

The Fourth Amendment: Searches and Seizures

In colonial days, people in authority felt free to enter and search private homes. Sometimes the searchers were looking for stolen or smuggled goods. Many times they had no real reason to search a home. The Fourth Amendment makes it illegal, except in certain cases, to search a home.

Gun Control

The Second Amendment to the U.S. Constitution says: "A well-regulated militia, being necessary to the security of a free state, the right of people to keep and bear arms shall not be infringed."

In colonial America, guns were used to hunt for food and in fighting wars. Today many Americans use guns for hunting and other recreational purposes. Because many people are hurt and killed by guns each year, there is a national movement promoting gun control laws. Gun control laws have been proposed to

ban the sale and use of handguns or, at least, to make it more difficult for people to buy them. In 1994, the Brady Handgun Violence Prevention Act went into effect. This national law requires a

five-day waiting period to buy a handgun. It also requires local law enforcement agencies to check the backgrounds of people who want to buy handguns. **Convicted** criminals, minors, drug abusers, and illegal immigrants cannot buy handguns in the United States.

The "Brady Law" is named for Jim Brady, who was President Ronald Reagan's press secretary. Brady was shot when someone tried to kill President Reagan in 1981. Brady and his wife, Sarah, campaigned very hard for Congress to pass this law.

In 1967, the Supreme Court ruled that this amendment protects people from listening devices. It is illegal to install a hidden listening device in telephone lines or offices without a special court order.

The Fifth Amendment: Rights in Criminal Cases

The Fifth Amendment protects Americans from being unfairly accused of committing a crime. It requires certain steps to happen before a person is accused or **indicted.** A person accused of a capital (serious) crime, must be brought before a **grand jury.** This jury listens to the charges and studies the **evidence** given. If the citizens serving on the grand jury decide there is enough evidence, the person is indicted and stands trial for the crime. A person cannot stand trial without being indicted by a grand jury.

The Fifth Amendment also guarantees **due process** of law. This means that a person must be given a fair trial according to all the rules and procedures set down in the Constitution.

The Sixth Amendment: Right to a Fair Trial

The Sixth Amendment protects people's right to defend themselves in a federal court trial. An accused person has the right to:

- Be told of the crime of which he or she is accused.

- Be given a speedy public trial before a fair jury in the state where the crime took place.

- Have a lawyer to argue the case.

- Have witnesses appear, by legal force if necessary, to tell the accused person's side of the case.

- Hear and question what **witnesses** have to say.

The Seventh Amendment: Rights in Civil Cases

The Seventh Amendment applies to **civil** lawsuits. A civil case does not involve a crime. It is usually a dispute between two or more parties over rights or duties. According to this amendment, if the value being disputed is more than twenty dollars, the civil lawsuit is brought to trial before a jury.

The Eighth Amendment: Bails, Fines, and Punishments

The Eighth Amendment was added to limit the amount of bail set by a judge, or the fines a person must pay for breaking certain laws. Bail is a sum of money that an accused person must deposit for the privilege of staying out of jail while waiting for the case to come to trial. The judge decides on the amount of bail, usually according to the seriousness of the crime and the reputation of the accused. The reason for bail is to be sure that the person will appear for his or her trial. This money is returned to the person when the trial begins. This amendment also states that punishments such as torture are not allowed.

The Ninth and Tenth Amendments: Individual and States Rights

Amendments Nine and Ten were added so that all rights not listed directly in the Constitution would belong to the people or to the states.

SECTION 4 REVIEW Match the beginning of the sentence in Part 1 with the correct ending in Part 2. Write the complete sentences on a separate sheet of paper.

Part 1, Beginning of Sentences

1) A person accused of a serious, or capital, crime . . .

2) Due process of law means . . .

3) A militia is an . . .

4) The Third Amendment protects people from . . .

5) The Sixth Amendment says an accused person may defend himself or herself . . .

Part 2, Ending of Sentences

a) is first brought before a grand jury.

b) housing soldiers in their homes during peacetime.

c) organized group of citizens who serve as soldiers.

d) an accused person must be given a fair trial.

e) in a court of law and have a lawyer.

What do you think **?**

Why should a person accused of a crime be given rights listed in the Sixth Amendment?

Words to Know

★Candidate
A person who hopes to be elected to a public office

Debate
An argument or discussion between persons with different views

Sue
To bring legal action against a person to satisfy a claim or complaint

Between 1791, when the Bill of Rights was ratified, and 1860, only two amendments were added to the Constitution.

The Eleventh Amendment

The Eleventh Amendment denied the federal courts, including the Supreme Court, the right to make rulings in state affairs. The matter arose when the state of Georgia was **sued** by two citizens of South Carolina. The federal government stepped in to force Georgia to pay. Georgia refused to pay. The state said that the federal government was taking away some of its power by ruling in the case.

The Twelfth Amendment

The Twelfth Amendment changed the system for electing a President and Vice President. In earlier elections, all the **candidates** ran for the office of President. The candidate getting the highest number of votes was elected President. The second-place candidate was elected Vice President. Problems arose with this system, and one election resulted in a tie. This amendment states that separate candidates have to be chosen to run for each office. A candidate for President chooses a running mate for Vice President. If the candidate for President is elected, the running mate becomes Vice President. The House of Representatives chooses a winner if no candidate receives a majority of votes.

The Civil Rights Amendments

Both in 1863, and at the end of the Civil War, President Lincoln declared that the slaves were free people. The document that gave slaves freedom is called the *Emancipation Proclamation*. After the Civil War ended, Congress passed the Thirteenth Amendment to end slavery. The issue of slavery had been one of the causes of trouble between

Amendments 11 through 15

11. States can't be sued by federal government, other states, or foreign governments *(1798)*

12. Separate ballots for President and Vice President *(1804)*

13. End of slavery in all states *(1865)*

14. Citizenship for African-Americans *(1868)*

15. Voting rights for African-American males *(1870)*

the North and South. Congress wanted to end the dispute once and for all.

Slaves were now free, but there was still a **debate** over whether the slaves and other African-American people could be citizens. Passing the Fourteenth Amendment settled this debate. The amendment says that all people born in the United States and under its rule are citizens. Foreign-born persons who live in the United States can become citizens by following certain steps. The Fourteenth Amendment also says that the states must follow due process and give all citizens equal protection, just as the federal government does.

The Fifteenth Amendment was the last of the amendments that was passed soon after the Civil War ended. It gave all male Americans the right to vote. The Northern states approved the amendment right away, but the Southern states, except for Tennessee, would not obey the amendment. Congress, using military force, made the Southern states hold conventions. They had to rewrite their state constitutions so that African-American men were guaranteed the right to vote.

SECTION 5 REVIEW Complete the sentences below using words from the Word Bank. Write your answers on a separate sheet of paper.

WORD BANK

affairs

citizens

Civil War

Constitution

courts

ended

President

slavery

Vice President

vote

1) Until 1860 only slight changes were made to the _____.

2) The Eleventh Amendment said the federal _____ could not make rulings in state _____.

3) The Twelfth Amendment changed the system for electing a _____ and _____.

4) After the _____, three amendments were added, having to do with _____.

5) The Thirteenth Amendment _____ slavery in all states.

6) The Fourteenth Amendment said all slaves and black persons could be _____.

7) The Fifteenth Amendment gave the right to _____ to all males, even former slaves.

What do you think

Why do you think only African-American males, but not females, were given the right to vote from the Fifteenth Amendment?

After the Fifteenth Amendment, forty-three years passed before any more changes were made to the Constitution. From 1913 to 1992, twelve amendments were added. Since 1971, several amendments have been proposed but have failed to pass. For example, the Equal Rights Amendment was approved by Congress in 1972. This amendment would have guaranteed equal rights to women in all areas. It failed, by three states, to win approval.

An amendment that made it illegal to burn the American flag was proposed by Congress in 1989. The Supreme Court ruled that this amendment would be unconstitutional. It said that people's right to burn the flag was a form of free speech that was protected by the first amendment. In 1992, the Twenty-Seventh Amendment, which tells how salary increases for members of Congress will take effect, was passed.

These amendments were passed in the 1900s:

Amendments 16 through 27

16. Allows Congress the power to pass income tax laws and to collect taxes. (1913)

17. Allows direct election of senators by the people of their states. (1913)

18. Bans the making and selling of alcoholic beverages. This was called Prohibition. (1919)

19. Gives women the right to vote. (1920)

20. Sets new dates for Congress to begin; sets January 20 as the day the President takes office. (1933)

21. Ends Prohibition; gives states the decision on whether to ban liquor. (1933)

22. Limits the term of President to two elected terms. (1951)

23. Allows citizens of Washington, D.C., to vote for national officials. (1961)

24. Ends the poll tax (a tax paid to vote) in federal elections. (1964)

25. Identifies who will fill the positions of President and Vice President if these persons leave office or become disabled. (1967)

26. Sets the voting age at 18 in all states. (1971)

27. Says that any pay raise Congress votes for itself will not take place until after the next Congressional election. (1992)

On a separate sheet of paper write the correct word from the Word Bank to complete each sentence.

WORD BANK

18
20
27
alcoholic
poll
Sixteenth
Twenty-One
Twenty-Third
two
vote

1) The Twenty-Sixth Amendment set the voting age in all states at ____.

2) A person may be elected President no more than ____ times.

3) The Nineteenth Amendment gives women the right to ____.

4) The ____ Amendment allowed the citizens of the nation's capital to vote in national elections.

5) Prohibition banned the making and selling of ____ beverages.

6) Amendment Twenty-Four put an end to the ____ tax in federal elections.

7) Amendment ____ put an end to Prohibition.

8) Because of the ____ Amendment, Congress has the power to pass income tax laws.

9) January ____ is the day the President takes office.

10) The Constitution has been changed, or amended, ____ times.

What do you think

Why do you think the Twenty-Seventh Amendment was added to the Constitution?

Chapter Summary

★ The Preamble states the purpose and goals of the Constitution.

★ The first three articles tell how the federal, or national, government is set up with legislative, executive, and judicial branches.

★ Article Four explains how the states should treat each other.

★ Article Five describes how the Constitution can be amended, or changed.

★ The Bill of Rights include the first ten amendments that guarantee individual rights.

★ The First Amendment through the Fourth Amendment allow people
  • freedom of religion, speech, and press

  • the right to keep and bear arms
  • to be protected against having soldiers stay in their homes
  • to be protected against unreasonable searches

★ Amendments Five through Eight have to do with the treatment of people accused of crimes.

★ The last two amendments of the Bill of Rights give to the states and the people any power not given to the national government.

★ After the Civil War, three important amendments dealing with slavery were approved.

★ Between 1913 and 1992, Amendments Sixteen through Twenty-Seven were added to the Constitution.

Amendments Sixteen Through Twenty-Seven

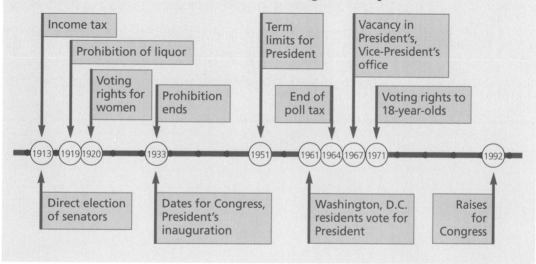

Comprehension: Identifying Facts

Complete the sentences below using the words from the Word Bank. Write your answers on a separate sheet of paper.

WORD BANK

accused

amendments

articles

Congress

freed

freedoms

Preamble

President

Rights

supreme

voting

women

1) The purpose and goals of the Constitution are stated in the ___.

2) The first three ___ tell how the federal government is set up.

3) Article V said that changes, or ___, could be made when necessary.

4) Article VI said that the Constitution is the ___ law of the land.

5) The first ten amendments are known as the Bill of ___.

6) The First Amendment of the Bill of Rights gave people many ___.

7) There are four amendments that have to do with how people ___ of crimes should be treated.

8) The Thirteenth Amendment ___ the slaves.

9) One important amendment gave ___ the right to vote.

10) An amendment was added that said the ___ may be elected to office for only two terms.

11) Amendment Twenty-Six sets the ___ age at 18.

12) Amendment Twenty-Seven affects pay raises for ___.

Comprehension: Understanding Main Ideas

On a separate sheet of paper, write the answers to the following questions using complete sentences.

1) According to the Preamble of the Constitution, what could people expect from their newly formed government?

2) According to Article II of the Constitution, whom may the President appoint?

3) According to Article IV of the Constitution, how must laws and legal rulings of one state be treated by other states?

4) What are some rights granted to people accused of crimes?

5) According to Article V, what two methods can be used to ratify constitutional amendments?

6) What are the civil rights amendments?

Critical Thinking: Write Your Opinion

1) Why do you think Article V is so important to the Constitution?

2) Which amendment to the Constitution do you think is the most important to your life?

Test Taking Tip When studying for a test, review any tests or quizzes you took earlier that cover the same information.

"Though the President is Commander-in-Chief, Congress is his commander." This is *"a government of the people and Congress is the people."*

Thaddeus Stevens
Speech in House of
Representatives
January 3, 1867

Chapter

4

The Legislative Branch

The federal government of the United States is divided into three separate branches. Each part has special powers granted to it by the Constitution. One branch is the legislative branch, which is Congress. The executive branch includes the President, Vice President, and the President's cabinet. Another branch is the judicial branch, which is made up of federal courts and judges.

Most of the people who run the federal government meet and work in the capital city, Washington, D.C. The letters "D.C." stand for the words *District of Columbia.* Washington, D.C., is located between the states of Maryland and Virginia. Most of the work of the legislative branch is carried on in the United States Capitol Building. In Chapter 4, you will learn about the legislative branch.

Goals for Learning

★ To identify the powers given to Congress by the Constitution

★ To identify the legislative branch as one of the three main branches of the federal government

★ To describe the work of Congress and its organization into the Senate and House of Representatives

★ To explain how the members of the Senate and House of Representatives are chosen, their qualifications, and the length of their terms

★ To describe how a bill becomes a law

Words to Know

*Citizen
A person given certain rights, duties, and privileges because he or she was born in, or chooses to live in, a city, state, or country

Minority
A group that is a smaller part of something or that is different in some way

*Representative
A member of the House of Representatives; a person who is given the power to act for others

Resident
A person who lives in a place

Serve
To spend a period of time carrying out a duty

*Term
A period of time for carrying out a duty

The Congress of the United States is divided into two parts: the House of **Representatives** and the Senate. The writers of the Constitution did not want one group of officials to become too strong, so they made two parts to the Congress. The men and women who work in these two houses of the Congress are elected by the voters in each state. Every new law for our country must be passed by a majority of votes in both the Senate and the House of Representatives.

How Many Senators Represent Each State?

The writers of the Constitution wanted to be sure that every state would be represented equally in the Congress. Each of the fifty states elects two senators to **serve** in the Senate. Each state, no matter how large or how small its population, has the same number of votes in the Senate as any other state. There are one hundred senators serving in the Senate.

Who Can Be a Senator?

To run for the Senate, a candidate must be at least thirty years old. He or she must have been a United States **citizen** for at least nine years. A candidate for the senate must be a **resident** of the state he or she represents. A senator serves a six-year **term.** Only one-third of the Senate membership is elected at any one time.

How Many Representatives for Each State?

Four hundred and thirty-five elected officials serve in the House of Representatives. The House of Representatives is set up to reflect the size of each state's population. States that have more people living in them send more representatives to Congress than states that have fewer people. Each state is divided into districts. Each district elects its own representative.

Thomas P. (Tip) O'Neill, Jr., Democratic representative from Massachusetts, was Speaker of the House of Representatives from 1977-1987.

The leader of the House of Representatives is known as the Speaker of the House. The Speaker is one of the representatives who is elected by the majority party members to serve for two years. The Speaker runs the House's business.

Who Can Be a Representative?

A representative must be at least twenty-five years old. He or she must have been a citizen of the United States for at least seven years. A representative must also be a resident of the state he or she represents and live in the district he or she represents. A member of the House of Representatives serves a two-year term. All members of the House are elected in November of each even-numbered year.

SECTION 1 REVIEW Complete the sentences below by writing the missing words on a separate sheet of paper.

1) Each of the fifty states has ___ Senators who serve a ___ year term.

2) The total number of representatives who serve in the House of Representatives is ___. Each serves a ___ year term.

3) The number of representatives a state has reflects the state's ___.

In the next section, identify the part of Congress where the following people serve. Write your answer (*Senator* or *Representative*) on a separate sheet of paper.

a) Thomas Jacks is 28 and serves the district where he lives.

b) Chris Todd has been in Congress four years and has been re-elected once.

c) Patricia Lee has been in Congress for six years and is running for re-election for the first time.

What do you think

Why does each state have the same number of senators and a different number of representatives?

Citizens & Government

Four People Who Served

Margaret Chase Smith, Barbara Jordan, Benjamin Nighthorse Campbell, and Henry B. Gonzalez have represented **minority** groups in the U.S. Congress. Minority groups are a smaller part of the population. For many years, a number of these Americans were not represented in Congress.

Margaret Chase Smith was born in Maine in 1897. In 1940, Smith was elected to complete her husband's term when he died. Later she won re-election to the House of Representatives and was elected to the Senate. She was the first woman to be elected to both houses of Congress. Smith served in the Senate until 1973.

Barbara Jordan was born in Houston, Texas, in 1936. She became a lawyer and served as a state senator in Texas. In 1973, she became the first southern African-American woman elected to the U.S. House of Representatives.

Benjamin Nighthorse Campbell, a Northern Cheyenne Indian Chief, was elected to the United States Senate from Colorado in 1992. He is the first Native American to serve in the Senate. Campbell served in the U.S. Air Force, and was a member of the United States judo team in the 1964 Olympic Games in Tokyo.

Henry B. Gonzalez was born in 1916 in San Antonio, Texas. His parents were Mexican refugees. In 1961, he became the first Mexican-American from Texas to be elected to the House of Representatives. He served as a representative for over thirty years.

Review

1) Why is it difficult for people from minority groups to be elected to Congress?

2) Why is it important to have all groups of people represented in government?

Words to Know

Adjourn
To bring a meeting to an end

★**Bill**
A proposed new law

Economic depression
A time of low business activity and high unemployment

★**Joint committee**
A committee that includes members of both houses of Congress

Permanent
Lasting a long time or forever

★**Pocket veto**
When a bill is dropped because the President does not act on it

★**Regulate**
To control or direct

Reject
To refuse to accept

Resignation
An announcement that a person is leaving a job

Seniority system
Appointing people to jobs based on years of service

★**Session**
The period of time each year when Congress meets

The Senate and House of Representatives begin their **sessions** in Washington, D.C., early in January. Each term of Congress has two sessions. The first session begins in January of odd-numbered years. For example, the first session of the 105th Congress begins in January 1997. The second session begins in January 1998.

Each session usually lasts until the work is completed. Sometimes Congress does not **adjourn** until late fall. Near the end of the session, the senators and representatives vote on a day to adjourn. If a serious problem comes up after Congress has adjourned, the President may ask Congress to come back and hold a special session. Such a special session would last until the problem is solved. For example, in 1933, President Roosevelt called a special session. The country was in an **economic depression.** The President wanted Congress to pass laws that would help end the depression.

What Are the Duties of Congress?

The most important duty of Congress is to make laws. The Constitution also gives Congress the power or duty to collect taxes, maintain the armed forces, **regulate** trade, and punish certain crimes. Congress also may suggest amendments to the Constitution.

Congress can investigate, or check, on the other two branches of the federal government. In 1973, a committee was formed in the Senate to investigate activities of the executive branch. At this time, the White House staff was investigated because of a break-in of Democratic party offices in the Watergate apartments. The committee hearings were televised. The investigation led to the **resignation** of President Nixon.

In order for the Senate and House to do their work well, they must have good leaders. "Floor" leaders are chosen during the early part of the sessions. These floor leaders are very important because they tell other senators and representatives about the new **bills** that will be voted on. They also encourage the other members to take part in the voting. They work closely with the Speaker of the House and the President of the Senate to manage debates and committee business.

Where Do Ideas for Laws Begin?

A bill is an idea for a new law or a change in an old law. An idea for a bill can come from citizens who write their senators or representatives with a suggestion. Ideas for laws can also come from special groups, such as business people, veterans, or parents. The President of the United States, senators, and representatives also can suggest ideas for bills.

How Do Bills Become Laws?

A new bill can be introduced in either the Senate or the House. Thousands of bills are considered by Congress each year. It would not be possible for all of the members to look at all of these bills. The work of studying the bills is turned over to many smaller groups, or committees. After a bill is introduced in the House or the Senate, it is sent to a committee for study.

What Happens to Bills in Committees?

Committees decide which bills are important enough to send to the House or Senate for all members to consider. Many bills are **rejected** by committees and never given further consideration. An approved bill is sent to the House of Representatives or Senate for debate and voting. After a bill passes one house of Congress, it is sent to the other. If a bill is passed by both the House of Representatives and the Senate, it is sent to the President.

The President either signs the bill, vetoes the bill, or does nothing. If the President does nothing, the bill becomes a law after ten working days. If the President vetoes the bill, it

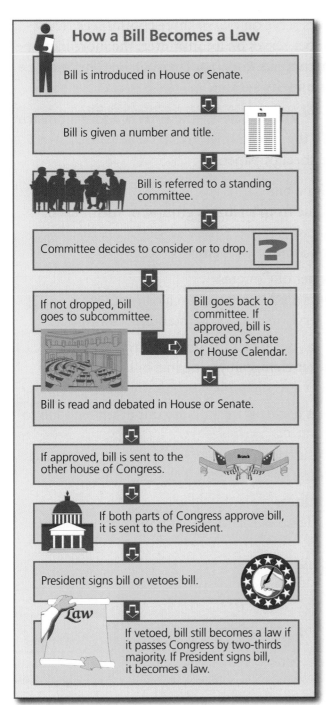

How a Bill Becomes a Law

Bill is introduced in House or Senate.

⬇

Bill is given a number and title.

⬇

Bill is referred to a standing committee.

⬇

Committee decides to consider or to drop.

⬇

If not dropped, bill goes to subcommittee.

Bill goes back to committee. If approved, bill is placed on Senate or House Calendar.

⬇

Bill is read and debated in House or Senate.

⬇

If approved, bill is sent to the other house of Congress.

⬇

If both parts of Congress approve bill, it is sent to the President.

⬇

President signs bill or vetoes bill.

⬇

If vetoed, bill still becomes a law if it passes Congress by two-thirds majority. If President signs bill, it becomes a law.

can still become a law if it passes Congress by a two-thirds majority. If the President does nothing and Congress adjourns before the ten-day period, the bill does not become law. This is called a **pocket veto.**

Each part of Congress has a number of **permanent** committees called *standing committees.* Each considers a specific topic, such as how the United States gets along with foreign governments. Another committee takes care of the needs of the armed services. Another decides how to raise money to run the federal government. This committee is called the Ways and Means Committee. A few committees are made up of members from both parts of Congress. These are called **joint committees.**

Who Serves on Congressional Committees?

Each senator and representative must serve on at least one standing committee. He or she is asked to serve on a committee by special groups from political parties. Members of Congress always hope to be put on important committees. The Foreign Affairs, Ways and Means, and Armed Services committees are important committees.

Some members serve on two or three committees. The longer a member serves on a committee, the more likely he or she is to become its leader, or chairperson. This practice is called the **seniority system.**

SECTION 2 REVIEW Choose the correct ending for each sentence from the two endings given. Write your answers on a separate sheet of paper.

1) The idea for a bill
   (a) can come from a citizen, groups, or members of Congress.
   (b) cannot come from members of Congress.

2) Each member of Congress
   (a) decides whether to serve on a committee.
   (b) must serve on at least one standing committee.

3) Congress has permanent committees that
   (a) can never change anything in a bill.
   (b) consider specific topics such as the armed services.

4) Committees decide if the bills are important enough to send to
   (a) the President.
   (b) the House of Representatives.

5) Joint committees
   (a) are made up of members from the Senate and the House.
   (b) make bills into law.

What do you think

Why doesn't Congress adjourn on the same date each year?

Media & Government

Government on Cable TV

called a gavel, on a table or desk. The television coverage also begins and ends when the gavel is used. When the Senate is not in session, C-SPAN 2 broadcasts other political news, including news about candidates. C-SPAN also has viewer call-in programs in which people can talk with policy makers.

C-SPAN stands for Cable Satellite Public Affairs Network. It is a television network that shows only political events and meetings. C-SPAN was started in 1979. It allows American citizens to see the actual, day-to-day work of the U.S. House of Representatives and the U.S. Senate.

C-SPAN has broadcast the sessions of the House of Representatives since 1979. C-SPAN 2, a second channel, began broadcasting the proceedings of the United States Senate in 1986. These channels provide what is called "gavel-to-gavel" television coverage. Meetings of the House and Senate begin and end with the knocking of a wooden hammer,

Thomas P. (Tip) O'Neill, Jr., Speaker of the House of Representatives from 1977-1987, agreed to allow C-SPAN to broadcast the House sessions. The cameras are controlled by employees of the House of Representatives. There are no reporters and no commercials.

Review
1) How would watching the Senate or House sessions be different from hearing a report of the meeting on a commercial television channel?

2) How can C-SPAN help viewers keep informed about government without using reporters to explain what is happening?

Words to Know

Admit
To allow or permit to enter

Defend
To protect from attack or harm

★Elastic clause
A part of the Constitution that gives Congress power to make laws as needed

Flexible
Capable of being bent or changed

Function
The act or operation expected of a person or group

★Military
Having to do with war or the armed forces

Power
Authority to take action; the right to decide

Requirement
A quality that is needed or required

Restrict
To limit

Standard
A rule or model that is set to control quality, size, or how something is done

Article 1, Sections 8 and 9, of the Constitution lists the powers Congress has and the powers it does not have.

What CAN Congress Do?

- Congress can raise and collect taxes to pay for the salaries of government employees and to maintain government **functions.** The government needs a great deal of money to carry on its work and to maintain programs that care for people who need special assistance.

- Congress watches over trade and business activities and passes laws to protect business and consumers. Congress runs the system of national highways. These roads help businesses move their products across the country.

- Congress **defends** the nation against enemies. It can declare war. Congress established the army, navy, and other **military** services.

- Congress may set **standards** of weights and measures.

- Congress decides on citizenship **requirements** for people from other countries to become United States citizens. Congress also **admits** new states to the United States.

What CAN'T Congress Do?

The writers of the Constitution **restricted** the **power** of Congress. For example, Congress might pass a bill that is signed into law. However, if the Supreme Court says that the law goes against the Constitution, the law is taken away.

Congress cannot make laws that take away the rights guaranteed by the Bill of Rights. The Bill of Rights is made

Congress listens to President Clinton's "State of the Union" address in 1996.

up of the first ten amendments to the Constitution. The Bill of Rights guarantees to citizens basic rights such as freedom of religion, freedom of speech, and freedom of the press.

Congress cannot make laws about such things as elections, education, or marriage. The Constitution gave the states the power to control those things. Congress cannot take money from the federal government without passing a law to do so.

What If New Problems Arise?

The writers of the Constitution knew that problems would come up that were not mentioned in the Constitution. The last part of Article I, Section 8, is called an **elastic clause.** It tells Congress that it can make all laws necessary for carrying out its duties. In other words, Congress is able to make changes, or be **flexible** when making decisions. For example, Congress was given the power to set up an army and navy to protect citizens. After a few years Congress saw that in order to have the best army and navy, military colleges were needed to train officers. Congress passed a law that gave money to set up and run military colleges. The U.S. Military Academy at West Point, New York, and the U.S.

Congress must approve the use of American military forces for peacekeeping missions. American soldiers were in Bosnia in 1995 as part of such a mission.

Naval Academy at Annapolis, Maryland, are the two oldest military colleges. This is an example of how Congress used the power granted it by this clause to provide better military defense for the United States.

SECTION 3 REVIEW Choose the best word to complete each sentence. Write your answers on a separate sheet of paper.

1) Congress can raise and collect (roads, taxes, programs) to operate the federal government.

2) The government has special (needs, crimes, programs) that care for people who need assistance.

3) Congress may set the standards for weights and (temperatures, measures, heights).

4) Through its power, Congress has set up military services to (collect, defend, declare) our country.

5) Congress set up a system of national highways through the (place, power, nation) given to it by the Constitution.

6) Congress has the power to (weigh, declare, raise) war.

7) Congress decides on (citizenship, weight, tax) requirements for people from other countries.

8) (Washington, D.C., Congress, Capital) admits new states to the United States.

9) Congress cannot make laws about (marriage, taxes, business).

10) The elastic clause allows Congress to make (laws, amendments, committees) it needs to carry out its duties.

What do you think **?**

Why do we have many more laws today than we did fifty years ago?

★ The three branches of the federal government are the legislative, executive, and judicial branches.

★ The Constitution has given the legislative branch the power to make laws that affect all of the states and the country as a whole. Each state can also make certain laws for itself.

★ The lawmaking body of the legislative branch is called the Congress. Congress is divided into two separate parts: the Senate and the House of Representatives. The citizens of each state elect their own senators and representatives, who represent them in Congress.

★ Every January all of the senators and representatives go to Washington, D.C. to begin their work. Leaders are chosen for each part of Congress. In order to carry out their tasks, the senators and representatives work in committees. The committees study all of the new bills that are given to them. After one part of the Congress passes a bill, it must be passed by the other part. Then the President must consider it. If the President signs the bill, it becomes a law.

★ The Constitution gives Congress the power to collect taxes, take care of trade, and provide for defense.

★ Congress cannot pass laws that take away individual rights given by the Bill of Rights, interfere with state laws, or take money from the government without passing a law.

★ The elastic clause gives Congress the power to take action as times change, even if this power is not written in the Constitution.

Comprehension: Identifying Facts

Complete the sentences below using words from the Word Bank. Write your answers on a separate sheet of paper.

WORD BANK

committee
considered
elected
introduced
majority
passed
population
reject
session
veto
vote

1) The number of representatives from each state is determined by the size of the state's ___.

2) Senators and representatives are ___ by voters in their own states.

3) Congress meets in January each year to begin a ___.

4) Each senator and representative must serve on at least one ___ during a session.

5) Thousands of new bills are ___ in Congress each year.

6) After a bill is ___ by a committee, two things may happen to it.

7) A committee can ___ a bill.

8) A committee can approve a bill and give it to the Senate or House to consider and ___ on.

9) If a ___ of the members vote in favor of a bill, the bill is sent to the other house of Congress to be considered.

10) A bill must be ___ by both houses of Congress before it can go to the President.

11) The President may accept or ___ a bill.

Comprehension: Understanding Main Ideas

On a separate sheet of paper, write the answers to the following questions using complete sentences.

1) What are the three main branches of the federal government? Which branch is Congress?

2) What is the most important work of Congress?

3) How are senators' and representatives' terms of office different?

4) What are the qualifications for senators and representatives?

5) Describe three steps a bill must take before it becomes a law.

6) What are two things that Congress does not have the power to do?

Critical Thinking: Write Your Opinion

1) Why is the elastic clause of the Constitution important?

2) What are some reasons a President might call for a special session after Congress has adjourned?

3) Why might the President use a pocket veto?

Test Taking Tip When you have to pick one answer from several choices, identify the ones you know are wrong first.

"One may choose to measure the success of a President not only by what the President accomplishes but also by what others accomplish under the President's leadership."

President Franklin Delano Roosevelt

Chapter

5

The Executive Branch

Franklin Delano Roosevelt was President of the United States from 1933 - 1945. He led the country during the Great Depression and World War II. Roosevelt greatly expanded the power of the presidency.

In Chapter 5, you will learn about the office of the President and how the President is in charge of the executive branch.

Goals for Learning

★ To describe the executive branch as the branch of the government that carries out laws made by Congress

★ To explain the process used to elect the President, the qualifications required to be a candidate, and what happens if the office of President becomes vacant

★ To identify the duties of the President as chief diplomat, chief legislator, party leader, and world leader

★ To name agencies and organizations that advise and assist the President

Words to Know

★**Adviser**
A person who gives information, advice, or help

★**Agency**
A division within the executive branch that serves a special purpose

Organization
A group that carries out certain activities

Staff
A group of people who advise or assist a chief executive officer

The executive branch is one of the three parts of the federal government. The executive branch carries out the laws made by the legislative branch.

Who Is in Charge of the Executive Branch?

The President of the United States is the leader of the executive branch.

Article II of the Constitution sets up the office of President:

Section 1. (1) *The executive power shall be vested in a President of the United States.*

The Constitution goes on to explain the duties and responsibilities of the President. Over the years, the power of the President has increased as government has grown larger.

The President is the nation's "chief executive." As chief executive, the President is responsible for everything that is done by the different groups who work in the executive branch.

Many assistants work in the executive branch to help the President carry out the laws. The Vice President is the President's main assistant. If the President cannot carry out the duties of the office, the Vice President becomes President. The President also has a **staff** of **advisers.** These advisers assist the President by gathering information, answering mail, and planning schedules. They also provide support in other ways.

How Is the Executive Branch Organized?

There are many departments and **agencies** within the executive branch. The men and women in these **organizations** carry out the day-to-day work. The President has to know what goes on in all these departments and agencies. Final responsibility for all that happens in the executive branch

This presidential seal is shown usually when the President makes speeches or holds press meetings.

rests with the President. You will learn more about the executive departments in Chapter 6. In Chapter 7, the independent agencies of the executive branch are discussed.

SECTION 1 REVIEW Use the words from the Word Bank to complete the sentences below. Write your answers on a separate sheet of paper.

WORD BANK

advisers

agencies

chief executive

departments

executive branch

Vice President

1) The part of the federal government that carries out the laws of the nation is the ___.

2) The President is sometimes called the ___.

3) The ___ becomes President if for any reason the President cannot carry out the duties of the office.

4) The President has a staff of ___.

5) There are many ___ and ___ to carry out the work of the executive branch.

What do you think

Why does the President need the help of so many departments and agencies?

Words to Know

★**Campaign**
To work on activities connected to getting elected to a political office

★**Electoral College**
A group of people chosen by political parties to vote for the President and Vice President

★**Polling place**
A place where people cast their votes

Qualification
A skill or quality a person must have to fill a job or position

★**Secret ballot**
A ballot that contains candidates' names and is marked in a private voting booth

Every four years on the Tuesday following the first Monday in November, the people of the United States vote for a President and Vice President. This day is called Election Day.

Who Can Be President?

The Constitution says that a candidate for President must have certain **qualifications.** A candidate for President must be:

• a native-born American citizen

• at least 35 years old

• a resident of the United States for at least 14 years.

How Do Candidates Campaign for President?

Before election day, candidates **campaign** or "run for office" for many months. The candidates tell people what they believe and how they will lead the country. They make speeches and political advertisements to persuade people to vote for them.

On election day, voters go to a **polling place** where each person is guaranteed the right to vote in secret. People vote in the privacy of a voting booth. This is called a **secret ballot.**

Votes are counted very quickly. Citizens usually know by the end of the election day which candidate has won. However, to make the election official, the **Electoral College** must meet in December.

What Is the Electoral College?

The Electoral College is a group of electors who vote for President and Vice President. The number of votes that citizens cast in a Presidential election is called the "popular vote." Although citizens vote for the President and Vice President by name, they are actually voting for an elector. The elector who wins the most popular votes will vote for that President and Vice President when the Electoral College meets about one month later.

Each state has the same number of electors as it has senators and representatives. If a state has two senators and eight representatives, that state will have ten electoral votes. There are a total of 538 electoral votes. A candidate

President Bill Clinton campaigned for re-election in 1996. His victory gave him his second term in the White House.

Bob Dole, former Senate Majority Leader, was the Republican candidate for President in 1996.

needs 270 electoral votes to win the election. All the votes for a state are given to the candidate who wins the state's popular vote.

The Electoral College system was set up by the Constitution. Today, many people think this system is confusing and no longer needed. They believe that the President and Vice President should be elected by popular vote without the electors.

How Many Times Can a President Be Elected?

A limit of two terms as President was set by the Twenty-Second Amendment to the Constitution in 1951. A limit was put on the number of terms a President could serve because people believed it was important to have a change of leaders. Franklin Roosevelt was the only President to serve more than two terms. He was elected President four times.

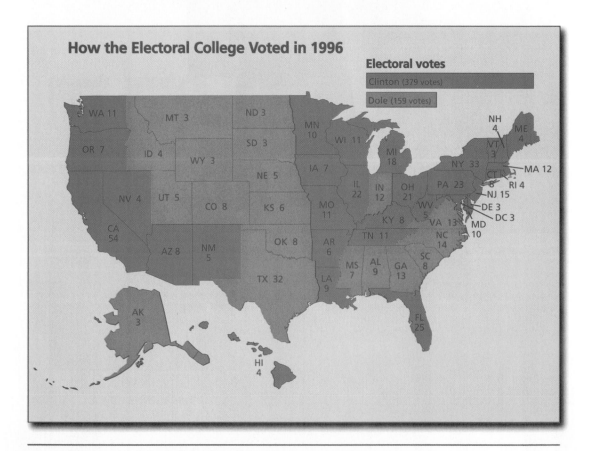

How the Electoral College Voted in 1996

Electoral votes
Clinton (379 votes)
Dole (159 votes)

Harry Truman's Surprise Victory

Vice President Harry S. Truman became President in 1945 when President Roosevelt died. Truman was known as a hard worker who had good common sense, and was dedicated to his public service. He also became known for his ability to make bold decisions under pressure.

After the war in Europe ended, things changed for Truman. The Truman Administration was blamed for the country's economic depression. Truman's popularity with voters was low at the beginning of the 1948 presidential election campaign.

The Republicans were sure they could defeat Truman. Thomas E. Dewey was nominated as the Republican candidate. The Democrats were divided. Many Democrats did not want Truman, but he won the Democratic party nomination. He began his campaign by severely criticizing the Republican Congress, which he referred to as "good for nothings."

Truman decided to take his personal message directly to the people, especially the farmers and workers of the country. He traveled by train on a six-week, "whistle-stop" tour of the country. He stopped at hundreds of small towns where large numbers of people came out to hear him.

On election day, many people were sure Truman would lose. Some newspapers even printed headlines announcing Dewey's victory the night before the election. However, when the votes were counted, Truman had defeated Dewey. It was one of the biggest political upsets in history. Truman captured 303 electoral votes, while Dewey had only 189.

Review

1) Who was the Republican candidate for President in 1948?

2) Why do you think the Republicans thought they could defeat Truman and the Democrats?

3) How did Truman campaign for President in 1948?

4) Do you think a whistle-stop train tour would work today? Why, or why not?

Inauguration Day

The President takes office January 20 at noon, which is about two months after the election. This date and time is set by the Twentieth Amendment of the Constitution. The day is called Inauguration Day. The new President takes a pledge with the United States chief justice to ". . . Faithfully execute the office of President of the United States . . ." This is usually held in front of the U.S. Capitol Building. As many as 100,000 people come to watch. People can also watch on television. Once the President makes the pledge, he or she gives a speech to the country for the first time as President.

SECTION 2 REVIEW Write the answers to these questions on a separate sheet of paper.

1) What qualifications must a candidate for President have?

2) How often do the voters in the United States elect a President and a Vice President?

3) What does it mean to vote by secret ballot?

4) How many electors does each state have?

5) Why can a President serve only two terms?

 What do you think ?

Why is it better to vote by secret ballot than to vote publicly, in front of others?

Media & Government

The First Presidential Debate

The presidential election of 1960 between John F. Kennedy and Richard M. Nixon was the first time that television played a major role in an election.

Kennedy and Nixon appeared in four televised debates in which they answered questions about campaign issues. Millions of people watched the debates. Kennedy introduced his plan for government, called the "New Frontier," in which he promised to work for health care for older Americans and stronger civil rights laws. Kennedy appeared very handsome and young. He also seemed to be less nervous than Nixon. In the election, Kennedy defeated Nixon by a slim margin, a little more than 100,000 votes of the 68 million votes cast. Many people feel Kennedy won the election as a result of the televised debates.

Since these first Kennedy-Nixon debates, every presidential campaign has included a televised debate.

Review

1) How does a debate help people decide which candidate to vote for?

2) What might candidates do during a debate that would lessen their chance of winning the election?

3) Why do candidates sometimes avoid stating their views strongly?

Words to Know

Assassinate
To kill a politically important person

Budget
A plan for how money will be taken in and spent

★Commander
A person who has full control of a group

★Diplomat
A person appointed to represent his or her country in another country

★Legislator
A person who makes or passes laws

★National debt
Money borrowed by the federal government on which interest must be paid

Resign
To give up an office or job; to leave one's office

As the leader of the executive branch of the government, the President is **commander** in chief of the armed forces. A President does not actually lead forces into battle but can send military forces anywhere in the world. The President is always in close touch with the country's military leaders.

What Are the President's Diplomatic Duties?

The President is the chief **diplomat** of the United States. In this role, the President is responsible for maintaining friendly relationships with other nations in the world. The President appoints ambassadors to represent the United States in foreign countries. When representatives of foreign countries visit the U. S., the President welcomes them. The President often travels around the world to speak to leaders of other countries.

President Bill Clinton met with Israeli and Palestinian leaders Itzhak Rabin and Yassar Arafat to talk about peace in the Middle East.

What Is the Federal Deficit, or the National Debt?

The federal government collects and spends trillions of dollars each year. When the money the government spends is more than it collects, it has to borrow money to run the country. The money the government borrows is called the **national debt,** or the federal deficit. When people or governments borrow money, they must pay the money back and pay a fee called *interest* on the loan.

Since 1951, the government has spent more than it has collected. The federal government pays a huge amount of interest on the national debt each year. Around 20 percent of government spending goes to pay interest on the national debt.

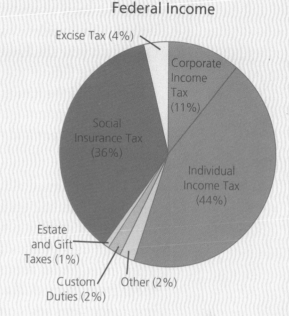

Federal Income

Excise Tax (4%)
Corporate Income Tax (11%)
Social Insurance Tax (36%)
Individual Income Tax (44%)
Estate and Gift Taxes (1%)
Custom Duties (2%)
Other (2%)

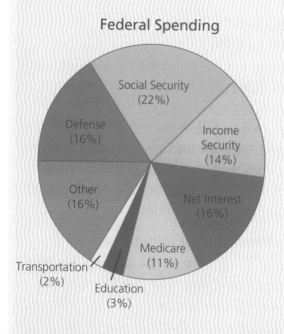

Federal Spending

Social Security (22%)
Defense (16%)
Income Security (14%)
Other (16%)
Net Interest (16%)
Transportation (2%)
Education (3%)
Medicare (11%)

Reducing the national debt and creating a balanced budget are important campaign issues. The national debt is so large that it can't be paid back all at once. If there were a balanced budget amendment to the Constitution, the government could not spend more than it collects. A balanced budget would keep the national debt from growing.

What Are the President's Legislative Duties?

The President is the chief **legislator.** All bills passed by Congress must be sent to the President to be signed or vetoed. The President can also suggest new laws to Congress. Once each year the President addresses Congress with a "State of the Union" message. In this talk, the President tells Congress and the nation about the condition of the country. The President points out what is important for the country in the coming year and tells what the government is planning to do.

The President must also prepare a **budget** for the nation each year. This budget is given to Congress. The members of Congress study it carefully. When it is approved, the President uses this budget for running the government. The United States receives money to operate the government from individual and business income taxes, social insurance taxes and contributions, estate and gift taxes, customs duties, and deposits of earnings in the Federal Reserve Banks.

What Is the President's Role as Political Party Leader?

When a candidate runs for President, he or she has already chosen a plan for running the government. This plan is made up by the candidate's political party. When elected, the President is expected to follow the party's plan and try to get Congress to put the plan into action. This is one way the President acts as political party leader. Another way is that the President appoints people from the political party to important jobs to help run the nation.

Why Is the U.S. President a World Leader?

Smaller nations of the world look to the leaders of powerful nations for help and guidance. The President of the United States is a world leader whose actions are followed and studied by people of other countries and by their leaders. In the role of world leader, the President works to promote peace.

What Happens If the President's Office Becomes Vacant?

Amendment Twenty-Five of the Constitution provides for filling a vacancy in the office of President or Vice President. If the President dies or **resigns** from office, the Vice President becomes President. If the office of Vice President is vacant, the President nominates a Vice President who must be approved by a majority of both houses of Congress.

The office of President may become vacant for several reasons. William Harrison, Zachary Taylor, Warren Harding, and Franklin D. Roosevelt all died in office. William McKinley, Abraham Lincoln, James Garfield, and John F. Kennedy were **assassinated.** Richard Nixon resigned.

SECTION 3 REVIEW Choose the best word for each sentence. Write your answers on a separate sheet of paper.

1) The President is (commander in chief, chief legislator, diplomatic leader) of the armed forces.

2) In the "State of the Union" message, the President tells the whole nation about the (Congress, budget, condition) of the country.

3) The President is the leader of his or her (political, constitutional, annual) party.

4) The President can (elect, appoint, force) people in his political party to jobs.

5) The President is a (limited, weak, world) leader.

What do you think ?

What actions of the President do you think change the President's popularity with citizens?

The duties of the executive branch have grown. The early Presidents had a few assistants. Now thousands of people help the President in some way. One set of advisers is called the cabinet. The President has many assistants within the executive branch.

What Is the President's Cabinet?

The President's cabinet is made up of the heads of the fourteen executive departments. The President appoints cabinet members, but they must be approved by the Senate. The cabinet usually meets with the President once a week. Cabinet members report on what is happening in their departments. The Vice President and the heads of some of the agencies of the Executive Office attend these meetings. You will learn more about the President's cabinet and the independent agencies of the executive branch in Chapters 6 and 7.

What Is the Executive Office?

The Executive Office is made up of many advisers and aides. There are also many agencies in the Executive Office. These individuals and agencies help the President carry out the duties of office. They manage the day-to-day work and advise the President. Most of the people in the Executive Office work in the White House or in nearby buildings. Some of the agencies in the Executive Office are described here.

The White House Office

The people closest to the President are in the White House Office. These people often are longtime supporters of the President. The press secretary supplies White House news to the press. Another assistant helps write the President's speeches. The President also has a personal doctor. The White House counsel gives the President legal advice about policy decisions. The White House Office is led by the President's chief of staff.

The National Security Council

The National Security Council (NSC) advises the President about **security,** or safety, of the country. It is concerned with military and foreign policy. The Central Intelligence Agency (CIA) works under this council. The CIA's job is to gather information about the country's security. Agents of the CIA work in all parts of the world and report their findings to the NSC. The President, Vice President, the secretaries of state and defense, and the head of the CIA are on the National Security Council.

The Office of Management and Budget

The Office of Management and Budget (OMB) is in charge of preparing the federal budget. This budget is prepared yearly and lists all the money (income) that is expected and the ways it will be spent by the government. When the budget is ready, the President presents it to Congress. In addition to writing the budget, the OMB studies how the executive branch is run. It makes suggestions to the President for improvements and changes.

A Government Shutdown

The federal budget is the responsibility of the President and Congress. Congress approves the federal budget once a year by passing a set of **appropriations bills.** These bills give each government agency the money it needs for the year. The government's business year goes from October 1 to September 30 of the next year.

In 1995, Congress failed to pass many of the appropriations bills by October 1. There were many disagreements between the Congress and the President over cuts the Congress proposed in welfare, education, and medical programs.

The President vetoed many of the appropriations bills that Congress passed.

Because Congress and the President did not agree on the appropriations, parts of the government were shut down. Agencies and government offices that were considered "non-essential" were closed. This shutdown meant that over 250,000 government employees could not go to work and were not paid. Most national parks and monuments were closed. People who wanted to travel outside the United States could not get passports and had to cancel their plans. After several months, Congress passed temporary legislation to reopen many government offices until September 30 of 1996.

Council of Economic Advisers

The President gets information about the nation's **economy** from the Council of Economic Advisers. This small group reports to the President about money matters and also suggests needed programs. The President uses this information to report to Congress and to the American people about our economy.

Council on Environmental Quality

The condition of the **environment** is one of the President's responsibilities. Clean water, clean air, and careful use of **natural resources** are controlled by the government. This is done, in part, by the Council on Environmental Quality.

Other Councils

Several other councils inform the President about foreign trade and **labor** matters. The President is also kept informed about the latest research in science.

SECTION 4 REVIEW Choose the best word to complete each sentence. Write your answers on a separate sheet of paper.

1) The heads of the executive departments make up the President's (cabinet, council, agency).

2) The (cabinet, White House Office, Supreme Court) is part of the Executive Office.

3) The President's press secretary works in the (Senate, cabinet, White House Office).

4) The National Security Council gathers information about the (pollution, security, press) of the nation.

5) The budget for the nation is prepared by the (Office of Management and Budget, White House Office).

What do you think Why is it important for the President's press secretary to give reporters accurate information?

★ The President of the United States serves as leader of the executive branch, commands the armed forces, and acts as chief diplomat and chief legislator.

★ Every four years the citizens of the United States elect a President. A candidate for President must be at least thirty-five years of age, a native-born American citizen, and a resident of the United States for fourteen years.

★ The Vice President is next in line if the President dies or resigns.

★ The executive branch carries out the laws made by Congress.

★ As head of a political party, the President tries to put the party's plans into action and appoints people from the party to fill important government jobs.

★ The President's cabinet is made up of the heads of the fourteen executive departments. The President appoints cabinet members, but they must be approved by the Senate.

★ The Executive Office includes people and agencies that manage the President's day-to-day work and advise the President.

U.S. Presidents Since World War II

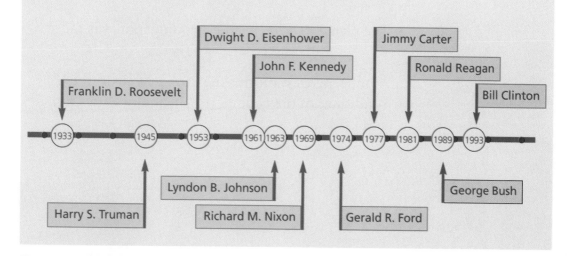

Comprehension: Identifying Facts

Use words from the Word Bank to complete the paragraphs below. Write your answers on a separate sheet of paper.

WORD BANK

advisers
appointed
budget
cabinet
electors
environment
Office
responsible
security
Vice President

1) The President is ____ for everything that happens in the executive branch of government.

2) If the office of President becomes vacant, the ____ takes over.

3) The President is really elected by ____ who are chosen from each state.

4) The President has many ____ who assist in carrying out the duties of the President.

5) The heads of the executive departments are known as the President's ____.

6) The cabinet members are ____ by the President.

7) The closest advisers to the President are the members of the Executive ____.

8) Some of the matters taken care of by the National Security Council have to do with the nation's safety, or ____.

9) The plan for taking in and spending money is called a ____.

10) Another agency informs the President about the conditions of the nation's ____, including water, air, and land.

Comprehension: Understanding Main Ideas

On a separate sheet of paper, write the answers to the following questions using complete sentences.

1) During presidential elections, how are state electors chosen?

2) As a world leader, what are at least two duties of the President?

3) How does the President report on the condition of the country to the Congress and nation?

4) Who makes up the President's cabinet and what do they do?

Critical Thinking: Write Your Opinion

Some people think that a President should serve one six-year term rather than be allowed to serve two four-year terms. Do you think this would be a good idea? Why, or why not?

Test Taking Tip If you do not know the meaning of a word in a question, read the question to yourself, leaving out the word. See if you can figure out the meaning of the word from its use in the sentence.

"A Council would not only be a check on a bad president but a relief to a good one."

Benjamin Franklin
Constitutional Convention, 1787, during a debate over creating a cabinet

Chapter

6

The President's Cabinet

George Washington, the first President of the United States, had four main advisers. Congress created a Department of State, Department of War, and a Department of the Treasury. The heads of the departments were called secretaries. Congress also created an attorney general's office to help the President with legal matters. The secretaries and the attorney general met with President Washington often. They became known as the President's cabinet. Today the President's cabinet is made up of the heads of fourteen executive departments. Cabinet members are appointed by the President and approved by Congress. In Chapter 6, you will learn about the fourteen executive departments and what each department does.

Goals for Learning

★ To identify the names of the executive departments

★ To give reasons why the number of executive departments has increased

★ To describe the responsibilities of the Departments of State, Treasury, and Justice

★ To identify the responsibilities of each of the executive departments

The President has a group of advisers called the **cabinet.** The cabinet is made up of the heads of fourteen executive departments. Cabinet members are appointed by the President, but they must be approved by Congress before they can serve. They are all called secretaries except for the head of the Justice Department, who is called the attorney general.

Each cabinet member is responsible for running her or his executive department and for advising the President. A secretary must have knowledge and experience in the area of the department she or he leads. The secretary of agriculture, for example, may be a farmer or have a background in agriculture. The secretary of the treasury should have financial experience.

Cabinet members meet with the President as a group to discuss important issues. The cabinet helps the President make decisions.

How Are the Executive Departments Organized?

Many people work with the secretaries of the executive departments as they carry out their duties. Each department is made up of smaller units called bureaus, offices, services, or divisions. These offices are not all in Washington, D.C. They are scattered throughout the country wherever they are needed to serve the people. The Department of Agriculture, for instance, has offices in every state so that it can help farmers and **consumers** through its many food services. Its Food and Nutrition Service provides food stamps and maintains the school lunch program. These programs make food available to those in need.

Executive Departments

Department of Agriculture
Oversees farmers to make sure food production meets demand. Inspects meat, poultry, and dairy products.

Department of the Interior
Oversees the country's natural resources.

Department of Commerce
Oversees business and trade within the United States and in foreign countries.

Department of Justice
Enforces federal laws.

Department of Defense
Maintains the country's defense and provides military training for the Army, Navy, and Air Force.

Department of Labor
Provides services for American workers and establishes safety standards for workplaces.

Department of Education
Oversees the country's schools.

Department of State
Maintains relationships with other countries and protects American citizens while they are in other countries.

Department of Energy
Finds and protects sources of energy.

Department of Transportation
Oversees the nation's system of highways, railroads, air travel, and waterways.

Department of Health and Human Services
Handles programs to promote the social and physical well-being of American citizens.

Department of the Treasury
Collects taxes, borrows money, pays bills, and prints money.

Department of Housing and Urban Development
Deals with problems of cities related to housing, conservation, and air pollution.

Department of Veterans Affairs
Provides services to veterans of American wars and maintains national cemeteries and veterans hospitals.

Why Has the Number of Departments Grown?

Through the years more departments were added as they were needed. These departments were set up by Congress, with Senate approval, to take care of certain areas of the government. Some departments have been closed and others have been combined as the country's needs have changed.

SECTION 1 REVIEW On a separate sheet of paper, answer each of the questions using complete sentences.

1) What is the purpose of the President's cabinet?

2) Why has the number of departments increased over time?

3) Except for the Justice Department, what are the heads of departments called?

4) What is the head of the Justice Department called?

5) Why does the Department of Agriculture have offices in most states?

What do you think

If there were a serious outbreak of flu in the United States, what are some things that the secretary of health and human services might report to the President at a cabinet meeting?

Words to Know

★**Consul**
A person who is appointed to represent the commercial interests of United States citizens in a foreign country

★**Consulate**
The building where a consul works

Counterfeit
Imitation or fake

★**Foreign policy**
The plan a country follows in dealing with other countries

★**Illegal**
Against the law

★**Minister**
A person who is appointed to help an ambassador

The Departments of State, Treasury, and Justice make policy and advise the President on important areas of our national life, such as **foreign policy,** the economy, and legal matters.

What Are the State Department's Responsibilities?

The Department of State helps to create foreign policy and to maintain cooperative relationships with other countries.

The State Department sends people all over the world to represent the United States. Ambassador is the title given to a person who works for the State Department in a large foreign country. In a smaller country the title is **minister.** A **consul** is a representative sent to a foreign city. His or her office is called a **consulate.** A consulate can be found in almost every large foreign city in the world. Consuls and their staffs try to build up foreign trade and commerce for the United States. They also protect American citizens who travel, work, or own property in foreign countries.

The State Department is in charge of passports, which Americans need when they travel to foreign countries.

What Are the Treasury Department's Responsibilities?

The Department of the Treasury collects taxes, borrows money when it is needed, and pays back the money. It supervises the making of paper money and coins. It is responsible for letting the President know about the financial standing of the United States. The Treasury Department makes sure that government money is spent as Congress has decided it should be spent.

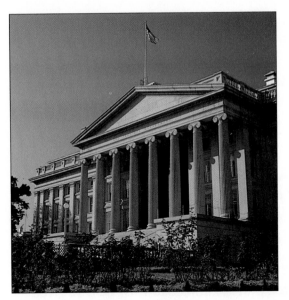

United States coins and paper money are produced at the Denver Mint. The U.S. Treasury Department has mints in Denver, San Francisco, Philadelphia, and West Point, New York. The Treasury Department's main office (pictured above) is in Washington, D.C.

These important duties are taken care of by smaller units of the Department of Treasury:

The *Internal Revenue Service (IRS)* collects taxes from individuals and from businesses.

The *Customs Service* collects import taxes on goods that are brought in from foreign countries. To do this, Customs examines, samples, and inspects the foreign goods. Customs agents also patrol airports, seaports, and borders to stop people or groups from bringing things into the country that are not wanted. Agents use specially trained dogs to sniff out drugs or food being brought in **illegally** from other countries.

The *Secret Service* protects the President, the first family, and certain other people. It also enforces laws against making of **counterfeit** money—money that looks like real money. It is a federal crime to make or use counterfeit money.

What Are the Justice Department's Responsibilities?

The Department of Justice enforces federal laws. The head of the department is the attorney general. All lawsuits in the Supreme Court that involve the United States government are handled by the Justice Department.

The Justice Department is made up of many agencies:

The *Federal Bureau of Investigation (FBI)* carries out investigations when a federal law is violated, or broken. The FBI can arrest anyone who is accused of committing a crime against the federal government.

The *Immigration and Naturalization Service (INS)* patrols the nation's borders to keep people from coming into the country illegally.

The *Bureau of Prisons* is responsible for all persons convicted of federal crimes and sent to prison. It runs all of the federal prisons and other institutions that house federal prisoners.

SECTION 2 REVIEW On a separate sheet of paper, write the name of the department that does each of these activities.

1) Prints money

2) Guards the nation's borders to prevent people from entering the country illegally

3) Is concerned with how the United States deals with other countries

4) Advises the President about the financial standing of the country

5) Helps protect Americans overseas

What do you think

Why do you think the Departments of State and Treasury were two of the first departments Congress created?

Janet Reno, Attorney General

Janet Reno is the first woman to serve as United States attorney general. President Bill Clinton appointed Reno to this position in 1993.

Reno practiced law in Miami and was Florida state attorney general before becoming United States attorney general. As head of the Justice Department, Reno's duties include presenting cases in court for the government. She also advises the President and other members of the executive department in legal matters. Reno sometimes speaks to the press. When President Clinton announced a plan to stop illegal immigration into the United States from Mexico, Reno held a news conference to tell how the plan would work. Her role was to support the President's plan and to explain it.

One of Reno's most well-known actions involved a religious group called the Branch Davidians. The Branch Davidians killed four FBI agents during a raid in 1993. Shortly after, Reno ordered the FBI to launch tear gas into the Daviidians' building. A fire broke out and killed 80 of the Davidians.

Reno grew up in Florida in a house her mother built on the edge of the Florida Everglades. She lived in this house until she moved to Washington, D.C., to become attorney general. In high school, Reno was on the debating team. After graduating from Harvard Law School, Reno had trouble finding work as a lawyer because she was a woman. She did get a position in the Dade County States Attorney Office and later became a partner in a Miami law firm. As Florida attorney general, she was tough on crime. People who were prosecuted by her office and were convicted received long prison sentences.

As United States attorney general, Reno pledged to:

- Reduce crime and violence by keeping people convicted of serious crimes in jail.

- Keep children away from gangs, drugs, and violence through prevention and intervention programs.

Review

1) What are Reno's duties as United States attorney general?

2) How can prevention programs keep children away from drugs? from violence?

Words to Know

Conservation
The care and protection of natural resources

Discrimination
Treating people unfairly because of their race, sex, or age

★**Insurance**
To buy protection from an unplanned loss of property

Minimum
The smallest number or quantity possible

★**Patent**
An official document granting the right to make and sell an invention

Surplus
Amount over what is needed

Land and business issues in the United States are taken care of by the Departments of Agriculture, Commerce, Interior, and Labor. Sometimes these departments develop laws or regulations to protect the land or to help farmers. They may also develop laws or regulations that protect workers or trade.

What Does the Department of Agriculture Do?

The well-being of the United States and its people depends on farmers. Farmers have the important job of producing food for the people of our country. The government helps by buying **surplus** food and assisting farmers in selling crops to foreign countries. The department also helps farmers organize into cooperative groups for selling crops. The "co-ops," as they are called, can help farmers buy supplies and equipment at lower prices.

Many agencies within the Agriculture Department help farmers in planning and using the best farming methods. These agencies keep farmers informed about the market for livestock and crops. Such agencies also try to help farmers get the money they need to do their work. Two agencies that tend to these farm concerns are the *Soil **Conservation** Service* and the *Farmers Home Administration,* which lends money to farmers.

The Department of Agriculture provides states with funds for the school lunch program that provides healthy, low-cost lunches to students. Food stamps are available to help low-income families or individuals buy food. The Department of Agriculture is responsible for inspecting and grading meat, poultry, and dairy products.

American Farmers

Many American farms are small family businesses. The cost of running a farm is high, and farming has many risks. Crops are sometimes lost because there is either too much rain, or not enough rain. To help farmers, the federal government provides crop **insurance** and low-cost loans.

Many American farmers sell their crops to other countries. In recent years, the demand for American crops has decreased. Some countries that used to buy American crops, are now producing all the crops they need. The government sometimes limits import of certain crops so that American farmers will be able to sell more crops in the United States.

Because it is difficult to run a farm, many of the small, family farms have been sold. Sometimes smaller farms are combined to make large farms that are run as businesses.

What Does the Department of Commerce Do?

Business and trade are important to the United States' economy. The Department of Commerce is concerned with business and trade in this country and in foreign countries. The department is made up of several agencies.

The *Census Bureau* counts the number of United States' citizens every ten years and prepares a report on the population. It also gathers and publishes information about the state of the economy, population growth, and employment and housing opportunities. This information helps businesses choose locations for factories.

The *U.S. Patent Office* issues **patents** to people who invent new products or ideas. A patent protects the idea so that someone else cannot make and sell the product while the patent is in effect.

The *U.S. Weather Bureau* gathers information about storms, frosts, floods, and earthquakes. This information is broadcast to help protect farmers, pilots, and others from loss or danger caused by severe weather.

The *National Bureau of Standards* sets standards for the quality of manufactured goods and for methods of measurement to see that goods are the right size or weight for all countries.

What Does the Department of the Interior Do?

The Department of the Interior makes sure that the country's natural resources are used wisely. These resources include land, water, and minerals, as well as fish and wildlife. The Interior Department also looks after national parks and dams built by the federal government.

The Department of Interior's Fish and Wildlife Service helps to protect endangered species like this spotted owl.

The Interior Department has many divisions. The National Park Service, the Bureau of Indian Affairs, and the Fish and Wildlife Service are part of the Interior Department.

What Does the Department of Labor Do?

The Department of Labor offers many services to American workers. It sees that federal laws concerning labor are carried out, such as those on child labor and **minimum** wages. Child labor laws protect children under 16 from working during school hours, or from working in dangerous jobs.

There are many agencies or divisions of the Labor Department. The *Employment Standards Administration* makes sure rules about minimum wages are followed by businesses. It also enforces fair hiring practices that protect minorities, women, veterans, and disabled people from **discrimination.**

Minimum Wage Increases

The minimum wage businesses can pay workers changes from time to time. In 1991, the minimum wage was $4.25 per hour. In 1996, President Clinton signed into law some minimum wage increases. The law set the minimum wage at $4.75 per hour from October 1, 1996, to September 1, 1997. The law set the minimum wage to $5.15 per hour after September 1, 1997.

The *Occupational Safety and Health Administration (OSHA)* sets safety standards and inspects businesses to make sure work places are safe. Employers who do not meet safety standards may be fined or closed down.

The *Employment and Training Administration* helps people find jobs. It also manages unemployment insurance, which provides income for a period of time to people who have lost their jobs.

SECTION 3 REVIEW Match the department or office in Part 1 to the correct description in Part 2. Write your answers on a separate sheet of paper.

Part 1, Department

1) Farmers Home Administration
2) Census Bureau
3) U.S. Patent Office
4) U.S. Weather Bureau
5) Department of Commerce
6) Department of the Interior
7) Department of Agriculture
8) Occupational Safety and Health Administration (OSHA)

Part 2, Description

a) Protects inventors
b) Lends money to farmers
c) Gathers information about storms, earthquakes, and floods
d) Manages business and trade
e) Oversees the use of natural resources
f) Reports population count
g) Helps farmers in raising and selling crops
h) Sets standards for safe work places

Words to Know

Words to Know

★Civilian
A person not in the military or naval service

Cosmetics
Materials containing chemicals people use to improve their appearance

Disabled
To be physically or mentally handicapped

Economical
Operating with little waste of money

Efficient
Well-run or operating smoothly

Pollution
A state of being unclean

Prosper
To succeed, thrive, or gain wealth

Statistics
Numerical data gathered in order to present information

Several executive departments were created after World War II. Some of the newer departments were changed or combined with other departments. The departments that were added or changed helped manage the country's changing needs and provided services for citizens.

What Are the Responsibilities of the Department of Defense?

The Department of Defense was established in 1947. Congress decided to combine the earlier Departments of War and Navy. All of the country's armed forces are under the control of this department. The secretary of defense is a **civilian.** Each branch of the armed forces has a secretary who is also a civilian. The Department of Defense headquarters is in the Pentagon in Washington, D.C.

In peacetime, the Defense Department participates in many activities that are important to the country's defense. One branch of the Defense Department, the *Army Corps of Engineers,* helps to see that rivers and harbors are maintained and improved to promote flood control.

The Defense Department is responsible for the *military academies,* the schools that train officers for military service. They are the Naval Academy at Annapolis, Maryland; the Army's Military Academy at West Point, New York; and the Air Force Academy at Colorado Springs, Colorado.

How Does the Department of Housing and Urban Development Help Cities?

The Department of Housing and Urban Development (HUD) was established in 1965 to help the cities. HUD helps provide homes, repair buildings, and protects consumers. It deals with all types of problems, including aid in financing housing, promoting water conservation, protecting cities from air **pollution,** and developing communities.

 Why Is the Department of Transportation Needed?

For a nation to **prosper,** it is important to be able to move goods and services from place to place quickly. The citizens of a country also need to be able to travel from place to place. The Transportation Department was created in 1966 to make all methods of travel more **economical** and **efficient.** This department sets safety standards for vehicles.

The *Coast Guard* is operated by the Department of Transportation in peacetime. The Coast Guard protects life and property at sea. It also enforces federal shipping laws. During wartime, the Coast Guard is operated as a division of the Navy.

Why Is the Department of Energy Needed?

The United States depends on other countries for most of its petroleum. The country needs to protect its decreasing supplies of oil. The Department of Energy was created in 1977 to find and protect sources of energy such as water power, oil, and natural gas. It also regulates the sale of fuel and electricity.

The Energy Department sets up programs to find new ways to produce energy. For example, the *assistant secretary for energy efficiency and renewable energy* directs programs to develop the use of solar energy, or energy from the sun. It helps industry and private citizens find ways to use solar energy. Using energy from the sun helps conserve our supplies of oil and natural gas. This office also does research on the use of nuclear power as another energy source.

What Does the Health and Human Services Department Do?

The Department of Health and Human Services (HHS) was created in 1979. It handles the country's health and social service programs. One agency within HHS, the *Food and Drug Administration (FDA),* is responsible for research into the treatments and cures for diseases, and the enforcement of laws concerning food, drugs, and **cosmetics.** This department is also responsible for providing aid to people who are **disabled.**

How Does the Department of Education Help Schools?

The Department of Education was created in 1979. It oversees the country's educational systems and provides financial help for all levels and types of education. Elementary schools, high schools, colleges, and educational programs for people who have specials needs may receive aid from this department. The department gathers and reports **statistics** about schools. It also encourages programs to improve education.

Why Was the Department of Veterans Affairs (VA) Established?

The Veterans Administration was created in 1930. In 1989, it became an executive department and was renamed the Department of Veterans Affairs. It provides services to ex-military people and their families. Its services include health care and educational assistance programs. This department operates about 170 veterans' hospitals and is responsible for more than 100 national cemeteries.

SECTION 4 REVIEW   On a separate sheet of paper, write the word from the Word Bank that completes each sentence below.

WORD BANK
agencies
cities
Defense
Medicare
Transportation

1) The military is the main concern of the Department of ___.

2) The Social Security Administration is one of the ___ within the Department of Health and Human Services.

3) Housing and Urban Development deals with problems of ___.

4) The Department of ___ sets standards for vehicle safety.

5) The Department of Health and Human Services provides health care to the elderly through ___.

Media & Government

Government on the Internet

The Internet is a large computer network. Private groups started it in the 1960s. It became more popular in the 1990s when government legislation made it available to education.

It is used daily by many people to send and receive "e-mail" messages. Information about the executive departments can be found on the Internet through the World Wide Web. Each department has a "home page" on the World Wide Web. The home page lists things you might want to know about the department. Internet users can click on a topic to find additional information. These pages contain current department news, programs offered by the department, and publications and services available to citizens, as well as addresses and phone numbers.

The White House also has a World Wide Web site. People who are on the Internet can learn more about the federal government from the White House site. People can look at government documents and connect to other government departments and agencies.

To use the Internet a person needs a computer, certain software, and a modem. A modem connects the computer to a telephone line that goes to the Internet.

Review

1) What are some things you would like to learn about the White House?

2) What are some things you might learn about the Department of State from the Internet?

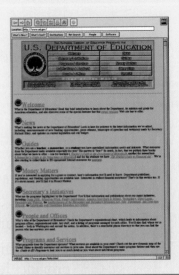

★ There are fourteen executive departments in the executive branch.

★ Cabinet members are the secretaries, or heads, of the executive departments.

★ The Departments of State, Treasury, Justice, and Defense are responsible for our relations with other countries, for the country's economy, for enforcing federal laws, and for providing a strong military force.

★ The Departments of Interior and Agriculture are responsible for protecting the United States' natural resources and overseeing agricultural and farming activities.

★ The Department of Commerce oversees business and trade within the United States and between the United States and foreign countries. The Department of Labor sees that federal labor laws are enforced to protect American workers.

★ The Department of Health and Human Services handles the Social Security Administration and Medicare, and enforces food and drug laws.

★ The Department of Education is concerned with helping the nation's schools.

★ The Department of Housing and Urban Development was set up to help with housing and other problems of big cities.

★ The Department of Transportation was created to plan and maintain highways, railroads, airports, and waterways.

★ The Department of Energy works to protect our sources of energy and to find new sources.

★ The Department of Veterans Affairs provides services to veterans and their families.

Comprehension: Identifying Facts

Write the answers to the following questions on a separate sheet of paper.

1) What are the names of the fourteen executive departments?

2) What departments did George Washington have?

3) Which department collects taxes?

4) Which department is concerned with the quality of schools?

5) Which department looks after community development projects?

6) Which department is in charge of the military?

7) Which department includes the FBI?

8) Which department helps farmers grow and sell crops?

9) Which department oversees business and trade?

10) Which department finds sources of oil?

11) Which department promotes social and physicial well-being?

12) Which department protects natural resources?

13) Which department has ambassadors?

14) Which department sets minimum wage laws?

15) Which department oversees railroads?

16) Which department provides services to veterans?

17) Which department protects the President?

18) Which department has consuls?

Comprehension: Understanding Main Ideas

On a separate sheet of paper, write the answers to the following questions using complete sentences.

1) Today there are fourteen executive departments to aid the President. What important group is made up of the heads of these departments?

2) The Department of State sends people worldwide to represent our government. Name three different types of representatives and their purpose.

3) What are three natural resources that are the responsibility of the Department of the Interior?

4) Name three services provided by the Department of Labor.

5) Why has the number of executive departments increased?

Critical Thinking: Write Your Opinion

1) Which of the executive departments do you think is most important? Which one is least important? Give reasons for your answer.

2) Write some ways that you have benefited from the work of the departments or agencies described in this chapter.

| Test Taking Tip | When studying for a test, review the topics in the chapter, then make up a practice test for yourself.

U.S. MAIL

Chapter

Independent Agencies

7

Independent agencies are created by Congress to deal with certain matters that no other department of government handles. These agencies are a part of the executive branch. The President appoints the heads of the agencies. Even though these agencies are independent, the other branches of government have some say in how the agencies are run. In the legislative branch, the Senate must approve the President's appointments and Congress must approve the budgets of the agencies. Also, the agencies must file reports with Congress once or twice a year.

Sometimes the judicial branch reviews the decisions the other branches make about the independent agencies. Congress may decide that an agency is costing too much money and give the agency less money. Congress sometimes decides that an agency is no longer needed and closes the agency. In Chapter 7, you will learn more about government agencies.

Goals for Learning

★ To identify the independent agencies and their purpose within the executive branch

★ To explain the difference between regulatory commissions and executive agencies

★ To identify and describe the activities of several regulatory commissions

★ To identify and describe the activities of several executive agencies

The Executive Office of the President, the executive departments, and the independent agencies make up what is known as the federal **bureaucracy.** A bureaucracy is an organization that has several levels. Each level reports to the level above it in rank or authority.

In a bureaucracy, there is a line of authority. It is like a **pyramid.** Officials or units at the top have control over, or direct, the units in the middle, and officials at the middle levels direct those at the bottom. Each person working in the bureaucracy has **specific** job duties.

At the top of the pyramid is the President of the United States, who has the highest position in the country. It is the President's responsibility to see that all parts of the executive branch function as they should.

At the next level is the small group that makes up the Executive Office of the President. These individuals and agencies directly assist the President.

Next come the executive departments, or cabinet. The attorney general and department heads make up the President's cabinet.

The bottom part, or foundation, is made up of many agencies that are the largest part of the federal government.

In this chapter, you will learn about some of the groups in the lower part of the pyramid. There are about 75 of these groups. We talk about them as independent agencies. However, they have many different titles. Some of them are called agencies, but others are called *commissions, boards,* or *administrations.* Each one has some part in **administrating** the federal government.

The Executive Branch

President of the United States

Executive Office of the President

White House Office

Office of Management and Budget

Council of Economic Advisers

National Security Council

Office of National Drug Control Policy

Office of the United States Trade Representative

Council on Environmental Quality

Office of Science and Technology Policy

Office of Administration

Executive Departments

Department of State

Department of the Treasury

Department of Defense

Department of Justice

Department of the Interior

Department of Agriculture

Department of Commerce

Department of Health and Human Services

Department of Housing and Urban Development

Department of Transportation

Department of Energy

Department of Education

Department of Veterans Affairs

Some Independent Agencies

Federal Reserve System

Federal Trade Commission

Securities and Exchange Commission

Federal Communications Commission

National Labor Relations Board

Federal Maritime Commission

Consumer Product Safety Commission

Nuclear Regulatory Commission

Commodity Futures Trading Commission

Federal Energy Regulatory Commission

Environmental Protection Agency

Equal Employment Opportunity Commission

Farm Credit Administration

Federal Deposit Insurance Corporation

Federal Housing Finance Board

General Services Administration

National Aeronautics and Space Administration

Office of Personnel Management

Selective Service System

Small Business Administration

Social Security Administration

U.S. Postal Service

The Farm Credit Administration (FCA) is an independent agency that lends money to farmers.

SECTION 1 REVIEW On a separate sheet of paper, write the answers to the following questions using complete sentences.

1) What are the three major parts of the federal bureaucracy?

2) What makes up the bottom of the pyramid illustrating the federal bureaucracy?

3) Who represents each executive department?

4) What office directly assists the President?

5) Whose responsibility is it to see that the executive branch functions as it should?

What do you think

Why are so many different departments and organizations needed to make the government work?

Words to Know

Communication satellites
Manufactured objects that travel around the earth in outer space; they are used to send information

★Free enterprise
Freedom of private businesses to operate without government interference

Frequency
The location on the airwaves that a radio or television station uses

★Interstate
Between or connecting two or more states

Nuclear
Having to do with energy produced from atoms

Radioactive material
Substances that release harmful radiation

★Regulatory commission
An agency that enforces rules and regulations

About twelve of the independent agencies are **regulatory commissions.** They make rules for activities that are important to the country's economy. They also enforce their rules and regulations. Each of these agencies is led by a board or commission of five to seven members. The members are appointed by the President and must be approved by the Senate.

What Are Some of the Regulatory Commissions?

The *Federal Trade Commission (FTC)* was set up in 1914 to prevent unfair trade practices that would harm the **free enterprise** system in our country. The FTC enforces laws that protect the public from such things as price fixing, false labeling, and advertising that makes untrue claims. The FTC also sees that products put on the market are safe. For example, the commission makes sure that fabric that burns easily is not used in children's clothing. This agency also assures that labels on products are truthful so that a buyer knows what he or she is getting.

The *Federal Communications Commission (FCC)* controls who can have a license to broadcast information over the airwaves and what **frequencies** may be used. The FCC was set up in 1934. It requires radio and television stations to make some public service broadcasts. It decides how much use can be made of **communication satellites.** The commission sees to it that the nation's communication system can take care of emergencies. In case of a natural disaster, such as an earthquake or flood, communication is very important. This agency sees that good communication is available to the public.

The *Nuclear Regulatory Commission (NRC)* was established in 1974 to see that nuclear power plants operate safely. After World War II, the United States became interested in the development of **nuclear** power for peaceful

The First Independent Agency

President Grover Cleveland created the **Interstate** Commerce Commission (ICC) in 1887. The ICC was established to regulate the railroads. The railroads did not always treat the public fairly. Congress felt that the railroads had taken too much land and were charging too much to carry freight. The creation of the ICC gave the government the right to reclaim land and to regulate the fares and schedules.

The agency regulated all commercial transportation between states. It regulated trains, buses, trucks, and boats. In 1995, Congress felt the ICC was no longer needed. It was closed in 1996.

uses. The NRC gives permission for **radioactive material** to be stored or transported for civilian use. The commission studies ways to make working with nuclear material safer. It may shut down any nuclear plant that is a danger to public health.

 The *National Labor Relations Board (NLRB)* was set up in 1935 and has two main purposes:

- To see that employees are treated fairly by their employers and by labor organizations

- To hold secret ballot elections when employees vote on whether they wish to be represented by a labor organization. Employees may file complaints and lawsuits against employers or unions through this agency.

SECTION 2 REVIEW Decide which agency each description fits. Write the name of that agency on a separate sheet of paper.

1) Gives licenses to radio and television stations.

2) Is responsible for safety at nuclear power plants.

3) Holds elections when employees vote on being represented by a labor organization.

4) Protects the consumer from untruthful advertising claims.

5) Gives permission for radioactive materials to be transported.

What do you think **?**

What could happen in the areas of trade, broadcasting, or nuclear power if there were no federal regulations?

Alerting Citizens to Emergencies

The Federal Communications Commission (FCC) is in charge of letting the country know when there is an emergency that involves the whole nation. Emergencies such as bad weather or a war could put many people in danger. Following World War II, the FCC established a federal alert system. This first system was called "Conelrad" for CONtrol ELectromagnetic RADiation. Its purpose was to give the President a way of letting the people know when there was a national emergency. Later Conelrad was replaced by the Emergency Broadcasting System (EBS).

To make sure that the EBS alert system was working, it was to be tested during radio broadcasts. An announcer would say that the program was being interrupted. After a minute of silence, the radio station would return to regular programming. If there were an emergency, programming would be interrupted and listeners would be told what to do.

In January, 1997, an improved national alert system, called the Emergency Alert System (EAS) was begun. All participating radio and television stations were required to install and operate special new emergency alert equipment. The new EAS equipment makes it possible for state and local emergency communication committees to broadcast information about floods, fires, storms, or accidents that could affect people's safety. In some cases, the new EAS equipment will automatically broadcast tests of emergency information without the help of station personnel.

Review

1) What is the name of the new national alert system?

2) How can broadcasting emergency information help when the weather is severe?

3) How might an alert help in the event of a military attack?

4) For what other kinds of emergencies might such a system be used?

Words to Know

Aeronautics
The science of designing, building, and flying aircraft

Bankrupt
Without money; declared legally unable to pay one's bills

Controversy
Discussion between people who hold opposite views

★**Endowment**
A gift given to a person or organization to provide income

Gamble
To play a game for money or property

★**Grant**
A gift of money to be used for a certain purpose

Humanities
Study of human thought and experience in literature, history, music, and art

Lottery ticket
A ticket that gives someone a chance to win money

★**Medicare**
Government medical insurance for people over 65

Other independent agencies within the executive branch are organized like the executive departments. Each of these agencies is headed by one person. Some of the agencies have many employees and are run like large businesses. Others have only a few employees and small budgets. Some of the agencies provide service to the public and do not have power to enforce rules or regulations.

The *National **Aeronautics** and Space Administration (NASA)* was established in 1958 to help develop peaceful uses for outer space. This government agency is well known to most people. NASA has put satellites and astronauts into space and made it possible to walk on the moon. It did research for the creation of Spacelab, which scientists use for experiments as it orbits high above the earth. NASA's space shuttle program has allowed people to go into space several times in the same vehicle. The shuttle missions are used to explore outer space, to repair damaged satellites, and to perform experiments for industry and medicine. NASA has also led efforts to build a permanent space station with Canada, Japan, Italy, Russia, and nine European countries.

The *Environmental Protection Agency (EPA)* protects the country's environment. The United States has become more crowded with people and industry. When the country was younger, few people worried about over-used land or cities becoming too crowded. Now these are important concerns. People and industry can pollute air and water and harm the land. The EPA was set up in 1970. It enforces laws that Congress passes to keep air and water clean and to prevent pollution.

The *Social Security Administration (SSA)* became an independent agency in 1994. Before that it was a part of the Department of Health and Human Services. The SSA spends more money than any of the other independent agencies and employs more than 65,000 people. Most of the money is paid to retired or disabled workers and dependent survivors of workers. Health care for people over 65 is handled by this agency. The program that provides medical service is called **Medicare.**

The *National Foundation on the Arts and the Humanities* encourages the development of arts and literature of the country. Congress set up this foundation in 1965 because of the importance of supporting the arts. Two groups, the National **Endowment** for the Arts, and the National Endowment for the Humanities, do the work of the agency. They make **grants** available to theaters, museums, music groups, individuals, and groups to promote the arts and humanities in our country. There

The Environmental Protection Agency enforces laws to prevent air and water pollution.

is **controversy** about this agency. Some lawmakers don't want to use government dollars to support the arts. They feel that support for the arts and humanities should come from private groups.

FDIC The *Federal Deposit Insurance Corporation (FDIC)* insures money deposited in banks. During the Great Depression of the 1930s, many businesses and factories closed down. People lost their jobs, and many banks failed. Congress saw the need to protect people's money and to protect the banks from **bankruptcy,** so it set up the FDIC in 1933. This agency will repay a person's money, up to $100,000, if a bank fails.

The *United States Postal Service* is run like a private business. It was originally part of the President's cabinet. In 1971, it became an independent agency. The Postal Service operates and protects the nation's mail service. It has a board headed by a postmaster general. Postal workers have a union just as workers have in many other industries. The Postal Service has certain powers to enforce laws concerning the mails. These laws make it illegal to send items such as firearms or liquor through the mail. There is also a law against mailing **lottery tickets,** which are a form of **gambling.** If any such offense is found, the case is turned over to the Justice Department.

The *Peace Corps* is an independent agency that was originally part of the State Department. The Peace Corps was set up in 1961. The goal of the Peace Corps is to bring about peace and friendship between the United States and other countries. American citizens who volunteer as teachers, farmers, engineers, or for other jobs are carefully chosen, trained, and sent to foreign countries where their skills are needed. Another program is the Peace Corps World Wide Schools Program. In this program, students exchange letters and information with young people in other countries.

SECTION 3 REVIEW On a separate sheet of paper, write the complete sentences by matching the sentence beginning in Part 1 with the correct sentence ending in Part 2.

Part 1, Beginning of Sentences

1) NASA was established . . .

2) The Postal Service is run like a private business and is . . .

3) Spacelab is used by scientists . . .

4) The goal of the Peace Corps is . . .

5) Endowments make grants available . . .

6) The FDIC was set up to protect . . .

Part 2, Ending of Sentences

a) . . . for experiments as it orbits above the Earth.

b) . . . to theaters, museums, music groups, and talented individuals.

c) . . . people's money and the banks from bankruptcy.

d) . . . headed by the postmaster general.

e) . . . to bring about peace and friendship between the U. S. and other countries.

f) . . . to help establish peaceful uses of space.

What do you think

Why is or isn't it a good idea to use government funds to support the arts and humanities?

The Civil Service System

In the early years of the United States government, Presidents often chose people from their own party for government jobs. Sometimes Presidents let federal employees go and gave their jobs to people from their own party. Many government jobs were filled by people who were not trained for their job.

In 1883 Congress passed the Pendleton Act. It said that hiring of government employees must be based on a person's skill. Today people applying for government jobs are given tests before they can be hired. The Civil Service Reform Act of 1978 set up two independent agencies, the *Office of Personnel Management (OPM)* and the *Merit Systems Protection Board*. These agencies test and hire federal employees and set standards for job performance.

To get a government job, people follow these steps:

1. Find out what jobs are available. They can call the Job Information Center for the United States government in Washington, D.C., at (202) 606-2700. Post offices and libraries also have information about government jobs.

2. Find out if they have the skills required for a particular job. Specific skills are needed for most civil service jobs. In addition, a high school diploma is usually needed.

3. Fill out an application form for the job they want.

4. Take the civil service test for the job. Names of people who pass these tests are put on a list of qualified applicants.

5. Wait for an interview. When a job is open, the first three applicants for that job will be interviewed. These applicants are sent a letter to inform them of the interview. If an applicant is not hired, she or he will be kept on the list and called when there is another opening for that job.

Review

1) Why is it important to have capable workers at all levels of government?

2) Which of the independent agencies would you like to work for? Why?

★ An independent agency's purpose is to deal with some matter that is not handled by any other part of the government.

★ Agencies include regulatory commissions and executive agencies.

★ Regulatory commissions make rules and regulate the activities they supervise.

★ The Federal Trade Commission (FTC) regulates trade practices and competition.

★ The Federal Communications Commission (FCC) supervises the nation's radio and television communication systems.

★ The Environmental Protection Agency (EPA) promotes and enforces laws to protect the environment.

★ The Nuclear Regulatory Commission (NRC) supervises nuclear power plants and storage of radioactive material, and studies ways to make nuclear power safe.

★ The National Labor Relations Board (NLRB) sees that employees are treated fairly by employers and by labor unions.

★ Executive agencies help the executive branch. They don't have power to enforce rules or regulations.

★ The National Aeronautics and Space Agency (NASA) explores peaceful uses of space.

★ The National Foundation on the Arts and the Humanities supports music, dance, theater, and museums.

★ The Federal Deposit Insurance Corporation (FDIC) insures money people deposit in banks.

★ The Postal Service is run like a private, self-supporting business.

★ The Peace Corps sends volunteers to teach skills that will help people in foreign countries.

★ Social Security Administration (SSA) programs assist retired and disabled workers.

Comprehension: Identifying Facts

Decide which agency each statement describes. On a separate sheet of paper, write the name of the agency.

1) Enforces laws intended to protect the environment.

2) Works to develop peaceful uses of space.

3) Supports the arts, including music, dance, and theater.

4) Sees that employers treat workers fairly.

5) Insures the money that people put in banks.

6) Gives permission for a radio station to broadcast.

7) Sees that nuclear power plants are operated safely.

8) Delivers mail.

9) Enforces rules about the labels that are put on consumer goods.

10) Enforces untrue claims in advertising.

11) Gives permission to store radioactive materials.

12) Enforces laws that protect against price fixing.

13) Holds ballots for labor organizations.

14) Pays money to retired or disabled workers.

15) Gives grants to the arts.

16) Will repay a person's money if a bank fails.

17) Enforces certain laws concerning the mail.

18) Sends U.S. citizens to other countries where their skills are needed.

19) Sends the space shuttle into outer space.

Comprehension: Understanding Main Ideas

On a separate sheet of paper, write the answers to the following questions using complete sentences.

1) How are the functions of a regulatory agency different from those of service agencies?

2) How does the National Labor Relations Board protect workers?

3) What information does the Federal Trade Commission require of labels on products?

4) What is the purpose of the National Foundation on the Arts and the Humanities?

5) What is the purpose of the Peace Corps?

Critical Thinking: Write Your Opinion

The space shuttle program is very expensive. Do you think it is worthwhile to spend so much money to learn more about outer space? Why, or why not?

Test Taking Tip Studying together in small groups and asking questions of one another is one way to review material for a test.

"*Laws are a dead letter without courts to expound and define their true meaning and operation.*"

Alexander Hamilton
The Federalist, 1788

Chapter

8

The Judicial Branch

One of the reasons the Articles of Confederation didn't work was that they did not set up a system of justice. Article III of the Constitution set up the third branch of the United States' government, the judicial branch. The judicial branch includes all of the federal courts. The most important court is the Supreme Court. It has the power to decide if Congress or the President have acted according to the Constitution.

In Chapter 8, you will learn how the judicial branch of the United States government sees that the Constitution is followed. The judicial branch includes the federal court system, courts of appeals, and the U.S. Supreme Court.

Goals for Learning

★ To identify the judicial branch as the branch of government that decides if the Constitution is being followed

★ To explain the types of cases heard by federal courts

★ To describe the difference between a district court and the United States court of appeals

★ To explain the types of cases reviewed by the United States Supreme Court

★ To describe the importance of the decisions made by the Supreme Court

★ To explain how the Supreme Court can bring changes to the Constitution

135

Words to Know

★**Defendant**
A person accused of doing something that is not legal

Disagreement
A quarrel; a difference of opinion

Disobey
To do something that is against the rules

Kidnap
To seize and hold someone for ransom

★**Tax Evasion**
Not paying taxes

★**Territory**
A part of the United States not included in any state but organized with a separate legislature

Violation
Breaking of a law or rule

Federal courts are set up to interpret the United States Constitution. Cases that involve **violation** of a federal law are heard in federal courts. The federal court system includes district courts, courts of appeals, and the Supreme Court.

Federal District Courts

A district court is the place where federal cases are heard. Each state has at least one district court. Some larger states are divided into two or more districts. In that case, each district has its own court. Several judges are assigned to each district court. District courts are the only federal courts that use juries. In most other federal courts, the judges make decisions without juries.

There is a chief judge for each district and one or more other judges. District court judges hear a wide variety of cases that may include bank robbery, **kidnapping,** counterfeiting money, or **tax evasion.** When a case comes to the district court, the judge explains to the jury the law that the **defendant** is accused of breaking. The jury decides if the defendant is guilty. If the defendant is found guilty, the judge decides on a sentence, or punishment.

Cases Heard in Federal District Courts

The Constitution gives federal courts the authority to hear cases that involve:

- A person, group, or company who **disobeys** any part of the Constitution, including the amendments.

- A person, group, or company who breaks federal laws passed by Congress, such as tax laws, postal laws, banking laws, or military laws.

- A foreign nation that sues the United States or a citizen of the United States.

- An ambassador who is accused of breaking the law of the country where she or he is serving.

- A crime that occurs on an American ship at sea.
- A crime that occurs on federal property.
- **Disagreements** between states.
- Lawsuits between citizens of different states.

Other Federal Courts

Congress has set up a number of other federal courts to handle special cases. Some of these are:

- The *Federal Claims Court* hears cases involving money claims against the federal government. A decision in favor of the person bringing the suit usually results in a sum of money being given to that person.

- The *Court of International Trade* hears cases from individuals and businesses about taxes collected by customs officials on imported goods.

- The *Court of Customs and Patent Appeals* hears cases appealed from the Court of International Trade, from people applying for patents, and from people whose patent rights have been violated.

- The *Territorial Courts* hear cases from people who live in **territories** of the United States overseas (Guam, Puerto Rico, the Virgin Islands, and the Northern Mariana Islands). These courts are the same as the federal district courts.

- The *Tax Court* hears appeals concerning payment of federal taxes. This court does not hear criminal cases, but settles disagreements about the amount or type of tax.

Other courts include: *Courts of the District of Columbia, Military Courts,* and the *Court of Veterans Appeals.*

SECTION 1 REVIEW On a separate sheet of paper, write the letter of the correct ending for each sentence.

1) A district court is the only federal court
   (a) in which a jury trial is held.
   (b) that is in the federal court system.

2) District courts are found
   (a) in every state.
   (b) only in the larger states.

3) An accused person is guaranteed a speedy public trial
   (a) in the state where the crime took place.
   (b) in Washington, D.C.

4) The trial jury is made up of
   (a) twelve persons who live in the community.
   (b) people chosen by the accused.

5) A district court judge explains to the jury
   (a) the law the defendant is accused of violating.
   (b) why the accused person is guilty or not guilty.

6) District courts hear cases in which a person is accused of breaking
   (a) federal laws passed by Congress.
   (b) state or local laws.

What do you think

Federal district courts may hear cases about disagreements between states. What are some things two states might disagree about?

Words to Know

*Circuit
An assigned district or territory

Interpret
To explain or tell the meaning of something

Procedure
A series of steps followed in a regular order

Reverse
To overturn or set aside

Vary
To change

*Verdict
The finding or judgment of a court

Accused people who feel that their trial was unfair in a district court may appeal, or ask a higher court to review the case. This review takes place in a court of appeals.

Congress set up the United States courts of appeals in 1891. These courts handle appeals from the district courts. The nation is divided into eleven large judicial areas known as **circuits.** There is also a circuit in the District of Columbia. Each circuit has a United States court of appeals. The number of judges **varies** from circuit to circuit.

How Does a Court of Appeals Work?

When a court of appeals gets a case to review, the judges study the history of the case. At least three judges take part in the review. The judges review the legal **procedures** involved in the case. They also **interpret** the laws. The judges listen to the lawyers from each side. They carefully check written records from the district court. When all the

United States Judicial Circuits

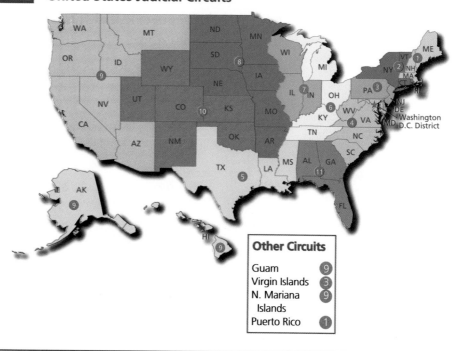

Other Circuits

Guam	9
Virgin Islands	3
N. Mariana Islands	9
Puerto Rico	1

facts are presented, the three judges vote. If the judges decide that justice was not done and the trial was not fair, the judges **reverse** the district court's decision or send the case back to the district court for a new trial. If the judges decide that the trial was fair, the district court **verdict** will stand. A decision made by the court of appeals is usually final. Sometimes the U.S. Supreme Court will hear appeals of decisions made by the courts of appeals.

SECTION 2 REVIEW Choose the best word to complete each sentence. Write your answers on a separate sheet of paper.

1) The (Constitution, Congress, Senate) set up the United States courts of appeals in 1891.

2) Every circuit has a United States court of appeals that reviews decisions made in (higher courts, state courts, district courts).

3) The judges in the court of appeals listen to arguments presented by the (accused, judges, lawyers) from each side.

4) A case may be sent back to a district court for a new trial if the judges decide that (justice, the procedure, the jury) was not done.

5) If the court of appeals decides the verdict was fair, the (judge, argument, decision) of the district court will stand.

What do you think ?

Why are judges in a court of appeals more concerned with the law and the Constitution than they are about a person's guilt or innocence?

Words to Know

Apportion
*To divide and
assign something
according to a plan*

★Brief
*A document that
describes the main
arguments with
supporting state-
ments and evidence*

Challenge
*To question the
truth or accuracy
of something*

★Impeach
*To accuse or charge
a public official of
misconduct*

Segregate
*To separate or set
apart from others*

The Supreme Court of the United States is the highest
court in the nation. Its decisions are final and cannot be
appealed. In most instances the Supreme Court receives
cases after they have passed through a district court and
the court of appeals. Someone has to **challenge** the law
involved in the case before the case can come to the
Supreme Court.

How Does the Supreme Court Work?

When a case is received, the Supreme Court decides
whether it will review the case. When the Supreme Court
decides to hear a case, the Court then makes a decision
about the law involved. It rules whether the law is unconstitutional. If the law is ruled unconstitutional, it is no
longer used.

There are nine justices, or judges, on the Supreme Court,
including a chief justice and eight associate justices. The
Supreme Court justices are appointed by the President.
These appointments must be approved by the Senate.
The Senate Judiciary Committee is in charge of approving
a justice. The committee holds hearings to see whether the
person who is appointed would be a good justice. A justice
may serve as long as he or she feels able to do so. Justices
may resign at any time. If they are accused of wrongdoing,
they may be **impeached,** or brought to trial by Congress.
Congress has the power to change the number of justices on
the Supreme Court. It has done so several times in history.

Supreme Court Sessions

The Supreme Court works in Washington, D.C. Its term,
or period of work, begins the first Monday in October each
year and continues until late June. For the first two weeks,
the justices hold public sessions, or sittings. All justices are
present and listen to the facts of each case. The chief justice
sits in the middle of the group. Lawyers from both sides are

The U.S. Supreme Court is the highest court in the country.

given a limited amount of time to explain their case. The justices may question the lawyers.

For the next two weeks, the justices study the facts of the case presented, and the lawyers provide them with **briefs** about the case. This period of study is called a recess. Throughout the rest of the term, the justices follow this pattern of sitting and recesses.

The decisions made in the Supreme Court are reached by a majority vote of the nine justices. Six justices must be present to call for a vote. After the court has voted, it writes an opinion. This is a carefully worded statement that explains why the decision was made. The writing of an opinion takes a long time. The reasons for and against the decision are written down. These opinions are then published in a series of books titled *United States Reports.*

Is the Supreme Court Too Powerful?

The decisions of the Supreme Court are final. Early in the history of our country, Thomas Jefferson and some other Americans did not agree with all the decisions the Supreme Court made. They thought the Supreme Court had become too powerful, because it could decide that a law was unconstitutional. However, not all Americans agreed. Many people thought that these rulings were good because laws were improved and rights were protected. These people thought that the changes kept laws up to date. Even though people sometimes question the power of the Supreme Court, it continues to use its power to change laws.

Can Supreme Court Decisions Change the Constitution?

In the past some Supreme Court decisions have even brought about changes in the Constitution. For example, the Constitution states in Article I, Section 9, that direct taxes must be **apportioned** according to the population of each state. This means that taxes must come equally from every state. In 1895 the Supreme Court ruled that income taxes were unconstitutional because they did not come evenly from each state. As a result of this decision, the Sixteenth Amendment was written, passed by all the states, and added to the Constitution. It stated that Congress was allowed to tax incomes without apportionment among the states.

Are Supreme Court Decisions Ever Changed?

The Supreme Court can make a decision that is the opposite of an earlier decision. This happened with the issue of **segregated** schools. Segregated schools were schools that separate African-American children from white children. In the 1880s many southern states set up these separate schools. Some Americans declared that the segregated schools were a violation of the Fourteenth Amendment. The Fourteenth Amendment states in part:

"...Nor shall any state deprive any person of life, liberty, or property, without due process of law; nor deny to any person within its jurisdiction the equal protection of the laws."

In 1896 a case called for the end of segregated schools because some people said these schools did not give equal education to all students. The Supreme Court was asked to decide whether these schools violated the Constitution. The

Court ruled in favor of segregated schools. The Court said that the schools were equal even though they were separate.

In 1954 another case concerning segregated schools came before the Supreme Court. The National Association for the Advancement of Colored People (NAACP) sued the Board of Education of Topeka, Kansas. The NAACP argued that the separate schools operating in Topeka were illegal. They claimed that the schools for white students were better equipped and not equal to the schools for African-American students. The NAACP said that this went against the Fourteenth Amendment. This time the Supreme Court ruled that the segregated schools were illegal because they went against the idea of equality stated in the Fourteenth Amendment. The Court said the schools should be changed immediately. This meant that it was no longer legal to keep the schools segregated. In this case, the Supreme Court had changed its mind and reversed the earlier ruling.

SECTION 3 REVIEW Select the correct word from the Work Bank to complete each sentence. Write your answers on a separate sheet of paper.

WORD BANK
eight
highest
life
opinion
opposite
review
Senate
unconstitutional

1) The Supreme Court is the ____ court in the nation.
2) The Supreme Court may decide whether or not to ____ a case.
3) The Supreme Court may decide that a law is ____.
4) There are ____ associate justices on the Supreme Court.
5) The justices are appointed for a ____ term.
6) An appointment of a Supreme Court justice must be approved by the ____.
7) An ____ is a carefully worded statement that explains why a decision was made.
8) Sometimes the Supreme Court can make a decision that is the ____ of an earlier decision.

Justice Sandra Day O'Connor

Sandra Day O'Connor was the first woman to be appointed as a Supreme Court justice. President Ronald Reagan appointed O'Connor to the Supreme Court in 1981.

O'Connor received her law degree in 1952 from Stanford University in Stanford, California. She held several jobs in the field of law, though she had some difficulty being hired as a lawyer. She recalls that most law firms didn't hire women at the time. However, she did work as an attorney for the U.S. Army in Germany. She was also an assistant attorney general for the state of Arizona.

When she was appointed to the Supreme Court, O'Connor was a state judge in

Arizona. She had also served as a state senator in Arizona. In 1973, she was voted senate majority leader for the Arizona senate. She was the first woman to hold such a position.

In her early years on the Supreme Court, O'Connor was considered a conservative. She believed the Supreme Court should interfere with laws only when necessary. This is called *judicial restraint*. In recent years, O'Connor has supported more liberal policies. Liberal policies favor change and support individual rights. She has voted in favor of policies that promote equality for women and minorities in the workplace. O'Connor is considered to be an independent thinker.

Review

1) How did O'Connor's work as a state judge in Arizona and in the Arizona senate help to prepare her to be on the Supreme Court?

2) Why should the Supreme Court interfere with laws only when necessary?

3) Why is it important for the Supreme Court to have justices who support the rights of women and minorities as O'Connor does?

Media & Government

The Media's Role in Presidential Appointments

The President appoints many of the people who have important positions in the federal government. For example, Supreme Court justices are appointed for life by the President. The legal background and beliefs of a Supreme Court justice affect the kinds of decisions the Supreme Court makes.

When the President appoints someone to the Supreme Court, the Senate Judiciary Committee is in charge of approving the new justice. The committee holds hearings to investigate the person appointed. Following the hearings, the committee votes on the appointment. The media's coverage of these hearings can influence whether the appointment is approved.

In 1991, President George Bush appointed Clarence Thomas as a Supreme Court Justice. There was some debate about whether Thomas had enough experience to be a justice. During the Senate Judiciary Committee hearings, a newspaper story accused Thomas of sexually harrassing Anita Hill, a woman who had worked for him. Sexual harrassment is when a person makes unwanted sexual comments or advances towards someone. The disagreements over Thomas's qualifications and the sexual harrassment charges turned the hearings into a very publicized event.

Many people watched the hearings on television. The hearings were conducted much like a trial. A team of lawyers presented Hill's story, and Thomas denied the harassment charges. The story was covered on daily news shows, on the front pages of most newspapers, and as the feature story in news magazines.

In the end, the committee voted 52-48 to approve Thomas as a justice. It was the closest vote for approving a justice in the committee's history. These hearings are an example of the power of the media to create and influence government.

Review
1) Why is it important for the Senate to approve a President's appointment to the Supreme Court?

2) Why would a newspaper reporter want to expose a public official's wrongdoing?

3) How do you think the media coverage of the Clarence Thomas hearings might have influenced the committee to vote against approving Thomas? to approve the appointment?

CHAPTER SUMMARY

★ The judicial branch includes all the federal courts and judges.

★ There are three main courts in the federal court system: district courts, the courts of appeals, and the Supreme Court.

★ All federal court judges are appointed by the government.

★ Cases that involve federal laws are tried within the federal court system.

★ District courts are located in every state and hold jury trials.

★ Congress has set up a number of other special courts: The Federal Claims Court hears money claims cases. The Tax Court hears appeals about taxes. The Court of International Trade hears cases about tariffs and taxes collected by customs officials.

★ The courts of appeals review cases from district courts.

★ The Supreme Court is the only court in the country that can decide which cases it will hear. The decision of the Supreme Court is final. The Supreme Court has the power to decide if the law involved in a case is constitutional. If the justices decide a law is unconstitutional, the law must be changed.

★ Sometimes the Supreme Court changes its mind and reverses an earlier decision.

★ Supreme Court justices are appointed by the President. One justice is named chief justice. The other eight justices are associate justices.

Comprehension: Identifying Facts

Choose the words from the Word Bank to complete the sentences. Write your answers on a separate sheet of paper.

WORD BANK

appealed
chooses
Constitution
court
district
innocent
judges
judicial
nine
reversed
Supreme
three

1) The ___ branch decides whether the Constitution is being followed.

2) There are ___ levels of federal courts.

3) A person in our country is ___ until proven guilty in a court of law.

4) The only federal courts that hold jury trials are ___ courts.

5) Tax Court is part of the district ___ system.

6) A decision from a district court may be ___.

7) At least three ___ review a case brought to a court of appeals.

8) There are ___ justices serving on the Supreme Court, and they are all appointed by the President.

9) After a trial has passed through the district court and the court of appeals, it may then go on to the ___ Court.

10) The Supreme Court ___ which cases it will hear.

11) The Supreme Court has ___, or changed, its decisions from time to time.

12) Supreme Court decisions have sometimes brought about changes in the ___ .

Comprehension: Understanding Main Ideas

On a separate sheet of paper, write the answers to the following questions using complete sentences.

1) Federal district courts hear cases of persons accused of breaking laws passed by Congress. What are these laws?

2) Why would a person go to an appeals court?

3) If the judges in a court of appeals decide a case was not tried fairly, what happens to the case?

4) What is included in a written opinion of the Supreme Court?

5) When does the Supreme Court hear cases?

Critical Thinking: Write Your Opinion

1) Do you think the Supreme Court should be allowed to change its mind and reverse an earlier decision? Give reasons for your answer.

2) If you were asked to serve on a jury, would you look forward to the experience or try to be excused from the responsibility? Why?

3) Do you think that the Supreme Court is too powerful? Why or why not?

Test Taking Tip   Do not wait until the night before a test to study. Plan your study time so that you can get a good night's sleep the night before the test.

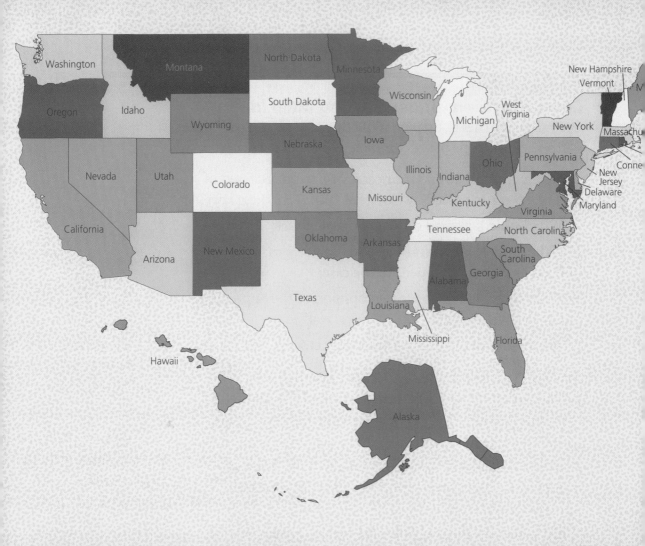

States in Order of Admission

1) **Delaware**
   "Diamond State"

2) **Pennsylvania**
   "Keystone State"

3) **New Jersey**
   "Garden State"

4) **Georgia**
   "Peach State"

5) **Connecticut**
   "Nutmeg State"

6) **Massachusetts**
   "Bay State"

7) **Maryland**
   "Free State"

8) **South Carolina**
   "Palmetto State"

9) **New Hampshire**
   "Granite State"

10) **Virginia**
    "The Old Dominion"

11) **New York**
    "Empire State"

12) **North Carolina**
    "Tar Heel State"

13) **Rhode Island**
    "The Ocean State"

14) **Vermont**
    "Green Mountain State"

15) **Kentucky**
    "Bluegrass State"

16) **Tennessee**
    "Volunteer State"

17) **Ohio**
    "Buckeye State"

18) **Louisiana**
    "Pelican State"

19) **Indiana**
    "Hoosier State"

20) **Mississippi**
    "Magnolia State"

21) **Illinois**
    "Prairie State"

22) **Alabama**
    "Yellowhammer State"

23) **Maine**
    "Pine Tree State"

24) **Missouri**
    "Show-me State"

25) **Arkansas**
    "The Natural State"

26) **Michigan**
    "Wolverine State"

27) **Florida**
    "Sunshine State"

28) **Texas**
    "Lone Star State"

29) **Iowa**
    "Hawkeye State"

30) **Wisconsin**
    "Badger State"

31) **California**
    "Golden State"

32) **Minnesota**
    "North Star State"

33) **Oregon**
    "Beaver State"

34) **Kansas**
    "Sunflower S

35) **West Virg**
    "Mountain S

36) **Nevada**
    "Sagebrush S

37) **Nebraska**
    "Cornhusker

38) **Colorado**
    "Centennial

39) **North Da**
    "Sioux State

40) **South Da**
    "Sunshine S

Chapter 9

The Fifty States

"...iberty and Independence"
Delaware state motto

In 1787, Delaware became the first state to approve the Constitution. Its motto, "Liberty and Independence," names the rights the states wished to keep when they became part of the nation. The name, "United States of America," means a group of states joined by the rule of the federal government in Washington, D.C. The individual states share the same goals and ideals. Although the fifty state governments are alike in many ways, each state has some rules that are different. Each state also gives smaller areas in the state, such as cities and counties, the power to rule themselves.

In Chapter 9, you will learn about how states are governed.

Goals for Learning

★ To explain the process Congress uses for admitting new states

★ To describe ways territories and states are different

★ To identify ways state governments are similar to the federal government

★ To explain how states obtain and spend money

★ To identify branches of state government and describe their responsibilities

Words to Know

*Statehood
*The condition of
being a state;
having all the
rights and benefits
of belonging to the
United States of
America*

In 1788, when the Constitution went into effect, the country was made up of thirteen states. When Alaska and Hawaii became states in 1959, the country had grown to fifty states. Most states entered the country before 1900. Only five states have been admitted since 1900.

How Are States Admitted to the United States?

The United States Constitution gives Congress the power to admit new states. Over the years Congress has acted thirty-seven times to admit new states to the country. Some states were formed by dividing old states. Maine was once a part of Massachusetts. Texas was an independent republic before it joined the country in 1845. Other states were formed from territory the United States bought or gained by wars and treaties with other countries.

What Is a Territory?

A territory is a region controlled by the United States government. The people living in U.S. territories are citizens of the United States, but they do not pay federal income taxes or have equal rights with other American citizens. Today, Puerto Rico, the Virgin Islands, Guam, American Samoa, and the Northern Mariana Islands are territories. All but the Northern Mariana Islands send an elected representative to the House of Representatives. The territories are not represented in the Senate. Territorial citizens do not vote in presidential elections.

How Does a Territory Become a State?

Most states began as territories. When the people of a territory want to become a state, the territory applies to Congress for admission to the United States. If Congress agrees that a territory is ready to become a state, it passes a special act. This act, called an Enabling Act, asks the people

Hawaii's capitol building is located in Honolulu.

of the territory to write a state constitution. When the new state constitution is approved by the people of the territory and Congress, the new state is admitted to the United States.

Many people in Puerto Rico are interested in **statehood.** If these territories were states, their citizens would have equal rights with other United States citizens. Some people in Puerto Rico are against statehood because they believe that Congress would make English the official language instead of Spanish. If Puerto Rico became a state, businesses would have to pay more taxes, its people would pay federal income taxes, and the island would lose financial aid it now receives from the United States.

SECTION 1 REVIEW Choose the word that completes each sentence correctly. Write your answers on a separate sheet of paper.

1) Alaska and Hawaii became states in (1900, 1959).

2) Most states in the United States began as (republics, territories).

3) A state (constitution, Congress) has to be written and approved before statehood is granted.

4) The United States (has, does not have) territories today.

5) People living in U.S. territories (are, are not) citizens and (do, do not) pay federal income taxes.

What do you think

Why do you think a territory might want to become a state? might not want to become a state?

Words to Know

★Borough
Name for local government in Alaska

★Charter
A document that states a group's purpose and plan

★Parish
Name for local government in Louisiana

★Reserved
Held aside for a special reason; for example, the states reserved some power for themselves

When the original thirteen colonies were under English rule, they were ruled by **charters.** Charters were documents given by England. They allowed each colony to govern itself. After the Declaration of Independence was written, each colony wrote its own constitution. Later, each new state wrote its own constitution.

Are All State Constitutions the Same?

All state constitutions are similar in certain ways. Each state constitution explains how the state government is to be set up and run. Most state constitutions contain the following parts:

- *Preamble*—States goals and purposes.
- *Bill of Rights*—Lists freedoms and rights given to each citizen.
- *Organization of the Government*—Lists the duties of the three branches of government.
- *Election Rules*—Explain how to handle elections and how to qualify for each office.
- *Other Regulations*—Give guidelines for providing state education, keeping order, building and caring for highways and roads, operating businesses, and collecting taxes.
- *Process for Making Amendments*—Explains ways to change or amend the laws and regulations that rule the state.
- *Amendments*—The actual changes that have been made to the state constitution.

Though state constitutions are similar, they are also different. Many laws and regulations differ from state to state.

Unusual Amendments

Amendments to state constitutions sometimes included laws and regulations that don't apply today. But at the time they were written, these laws and regulations seemed important. Some of these laws stayed in effect for many years, even though no one enforced them. For example:

- In Kentucky, it was illegal to throw eggs at a public speaker.

- In Oregon, to claim ownership of a wild animal, the owner had to tattoo his or her name on the animal.

- In North Carolina, it was unlawful to use an elephant to plow a cotton field.

How Are State Constitutions Like the U.S. Constitution?

The state constitutions use the United States Constitution as a model. They follow these same basic principles.

- **Popular sovereignty**
  People control their government because they elect the leaders.

- **Separation of powers**
  Each of the three branches of state government has separate and definite powers. This keeps any one branch from becoming too powerful.

- **Checks and balances**

  Each branch can check on the work of another branch. Certain actions and decisions must sometimes be approved by other branches. For example, judges appointed by the executive branch must be approved by the legislature.

- **Limited government**

  State and federal officials must obey the law. They must obey the Constitution. The government must never do anything that takes away an individual's basic freedoms as explained in the Bill of Rights.

Shared and Reserved Powers

Powers Reserved by States

- To establish local governments.
- To regulate trade within the state.
- To run elections.
- To establish schools.
- To license professional workers, such as doctors and lawyers.
- To protect the lives and property of the people.

Powers Shared by States and the Federal Government

- To make laws.
- To enforce laws.
- To establish courts.
- To collect taxes.
- To borrow money.
- To spend money for the health and welfare of people.
- To establish banks.

What Are "Shared" and "Reserved" Powers?

States share responsibilities with the federal government. These shared powers mean that both the state and federal government can do some things at their own levels. For example, both groups collect taxes. People are usually required to pay taxes to both the state and federal governments.

The states have certain powers that the federal government does not have. These are called **reserved** powers. The states reserved, or kept, these powers for themselves when they wrote and approved the United States Constitution.

How Do State Laws Affect People's Daily Lives?

Most laws and rules that affect the daily lives of people are made by state governments. Many of the laws that tell which actions are crimes are decided by the state. State laws also control guidelines for education, driving an automobile, and marriage.

State laws also explain how local governments are set up and operated. Local governments can be divided among county, city, township, village, **parish,** or **borough.** Boroughs are local governments in Alaska. Parishes are local governments in Louisiana. State law even decides how large school districts will be, although each district has its own officials.

SECTION 2 REVIEW On a separate sheet of paper, write the letter of the correct ending for each sentence.

1) The United States Constitution and the state constitutions were written
   (a) using the same basic principles as guidelines.
   (b) with different ideals or principles.

2) Separation of powers means that
   (a) all power is given to one branch of government.
   (b) power is divided among three branches of government.

3) The power to set guidelines for education, driving an automobile, and marriages is
   (a) shared with the federal government.
   (b) controlled by each state.

4) All state constitutions contain election rules which tell how
   (a) education is to be managed.
   (b) elections should be run, and lists the qualifications of candidates.

5) All state governments have
   (a) three branches — legislative, executive, and judicial.
   (b) only two branches to carry out the duties.

What do you think

Why might the speed limit be different in different states?

Words to Know

Fee
A sum paid or charged for a service

Funds
Sums of money set aside for a particular purpose

Percent
A part of the whole assigned to profit, taxes, commission, or other division of the total

Most state governments have budgets of more than a billion dollars each year. Such large amounts are needed because states provide many services for their citizens. For example, states pay for schools, police protection, and road repair.

In order to provide these services, states must get money from many places. Income taxes, sales taxes, federal **funds,** and gasoline taxes give states the money they need.

What Is Personal Income Tax?

A large amount of a state's income comes from personal income taxes. Citizens pay personal income tax on the income they earn from their jobs. Income taxes usually account for about 25 **percent** of the total money needed for a state to operate. However, some states do not collect income taxes at all.

What Is a Sales Tax?

Another source of income for many states is a sales tax. A sales tax is a set percentage of money that people pay on goods or services they buy. Sales taxes vary from state to state. In many states, items such as milk and bread are considered necessities and are not taxed. Other items, such as gasoline, cigarettes, and alcoholic beverages, have special taxes.

State sales taxes are highest in Mississippi, Rhode Island, Minnesota, Nevada, Washington, Illinois, and Texas. Colorado and Virginia have the lowest state sales taxes. Alaska, Delaware, Montana, New Hampshire, and Oregon have no state sales tax.

How Are Federal Funds Given to States?

Some of the money the federal government collects in taxes is used to aid the states. The amount of federal funds varies from state to state and from year to year. Federal support to a state is often given as a grant. In many states, grants are

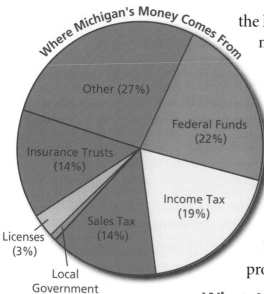

Where Michigan's Money Comes From

- Other (27%)
- Federal Funds (22%)
- Insurance Trusts (14%)
- Income Tax (19%)
- Licenses (3%)
- Sales Tax (14%)
- Local Government Funds (1%)

the largest source of state income. Such grants must, by law, be used in certain ways. The state must follow guidelines set by the federal government. For example, a federal grant for state education must follow rules set by the national government. Buildings or highways built with federal money must follow certain requirements set by the national government. The Americans with Disabilities Act of 1990 requires that buildings built with federal funds must provide access for people with disabilities.

What Are Other Sources of State Income?

In addition to personal income tax, sales tax, and federal funds, other **fees** are collected by the state. Citizens pay for driver's licenses and for automobile license plates and tags. There are fees for recording certain official papers, such as titles to property. Most businesses and many professionals pay fees to be licensed to perform their work in a state. Some states charge tolls for using certain roads and bridges. Some states permit racing or lotteries and receive a percentage of the money that is taken in from these activities.

SECTION 3 REVIEW On a separate sheet of paper, answer each of the questions using complete sentences.

1) Name three sources of income for a state.

2) What is a sales tax?

3) What is a federal grant?

4) What rules do states have to follow in using federal grants?

5) What are other ways states collect money to operate state government?

What do you think

What sources of income are important for your state?

Words to Know

Correctional
Intended to improve or to set right

Utilities
Companies that provide heat, telephones, electricity, or water to a community

What Is a State's Largest Expense?

In most states the largest part of the budget is spent on public education. Much of the money is used to operate the state colleges and universities. Some money pays for new school buildings, education for people with disabilities, and education for very young children. In most states, only a small portion of money goes to elementary and secondary schools because they are operated mainly on local tax money. Money is also provided by states to train people for new jobs. States offer financial assistance to people who qualify for such help.

Although the state sets some rules for schools, most of the decisions are made by local school officials. The state may decide how many days schools should be in session each year. The state also requires teachers to meet certain educational standards.

The largest part of most state budgets goes to public education.

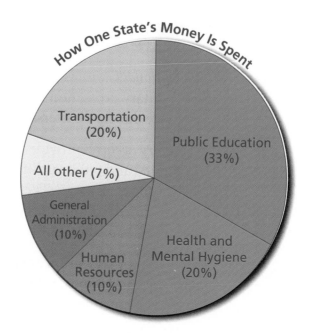

How One State's Money Is Spent

- Public Education (33%)
- Transportation (20%)
- All other (7%)
- General Administration (10%)
- Human Resources (10%)
- Health and Mental Hygiene (20%)

What Other Major Expenses Do States Have?

Building and maintaining highways, roads, and bridges take up 15 to 20 percent of the yearly budgets of many states. Many states have state hospitals that offer special kinds of treatment. States also help pay the costs of certain patients in nursing homes. States often have guidelines for hospitals and doctors to follow. There are also guidelines for the sale of medicine. Restaurants must follow certain health regulations in the handling of food. School children are required to have health exams. The state pays to see that its guidelines are followed.

What Are the Expenses of Running State Government?

Running the state government involves these expenses:

- *General administration* includes salaries and benefits for state employees and the maintenance of office buildings and equipment.

- The *state police force* provides protection and law enforcement. It assists other organizations in crime prevention.

- *Courts and prisons* handle civil and criminal cases. States usually have several **correctional** institutions and prisons.

- The *National Guard* is a citizens' militia that provides local military protection in emergencies. It gives assistance during disasters.

- *Regulatory agencies* provide rules for banks, insurance companies, and public **utilities,** such as telephone, gas, and electric companies. The state also watches over the safety standards and working conditions in factories, stores, and mines.

- *Park lands* for recreation are maintained by states. States buy land to be used for parks and spend money to improve existing parks.

State government requires billions of dollars each year and employs thousands of citizens. Strong state governments plan carefully to provide programs that their citizens need.

SECTION 4 REVIEW On a separate sheet of paper, write the correct word to complete each sentence.

1) The largest part of a state's budget is spent on ___.

2) Much of the state's education budget is spent on ___ and ___.

3) About 20 percent of a state's budget is spent on ___.

4) The citizens' militia that gives assistance during disasters is called the ___.

5) States buy land to provide ___ for recreation.

What do you think

Some states have a state lottery as a way to raise funds for education. What do you think of using a lottery as a way to fund education?

Words to Know

Exception
A case in which a rule does not apply or is not followed

Override
To reject or not accept

Preside
To act as leader or official

The legislative branch of each state has a lawmaking body that works nearly the same as the United States Congress. The main duty of this lawmaking body is to pass laws. In most states the name for this group is the legislature. Some states use names such as *general assembly* or *legislative assembly.* The name *general court* is used by the states of Massachusetts and New Hampshire.

How Many Houses Are in State Legislatures?

Like Congress, most state legislatures have two houses—the senate and the house of representatives. Nebraska is the **exception.** It has only one house in its legislature. While no state has a legislature as large as Congress, state legislatures all differ in size. The state house of representatives is always larger than the state senate.

Members of the state senate and house are elected by the voters in each state. The states are divided into voting districts. A voting district is an area where a certain number of people live and vote for their government leaders. There are smaller districts for the house and larger districts for the senate. In most states the senators serve a four-year term, and the representatives serve for two years.

How Often Do State Legislatures Meet?

Most state legislatures meet once a year for sixty to ninety days. These meetings of state lawmaking bodies are called sessions. If there is an emergency or a special need, the governor or the legislators themselves may call a special session.

When the legislature's regular session begins, the members form committees. Each of these small groups has a special task or job to do. These committees handle matters such as education, highways, courts, and local government needs. Bills, or ideas for new laws, are first discussed in committees. Sometimes bills are rewritten or rejected by a committee. When bills are ready, they are presented to the legislature for approval.

Organization of One State Government

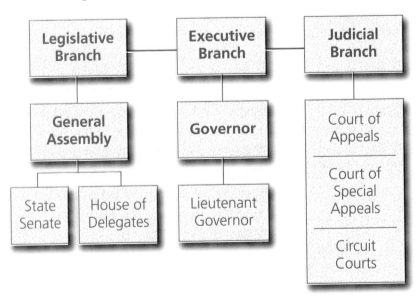

Each house of the state legislature has a **presiding** leader or official. The leader appoints committees and their leaders. She or he conducts meetings or sessions for that part of the legislature. The house of representatives elects a leader or speaker. In many states, the leader of the senate is chosen by state senators. In other states, the lieutenant governor is the leader for the senate. If the lieutenant governor cannot attend, a temporary president is elected by the members.

How Are State Laws Created?

In order for a bill to become a state law, it first must be introduced by a member of the state legislature in either house. A committee then receives the bill and begins working on it. Amendments may be made and parts of the bill may be rewritten. When the committee thinks the bill is in proper form, it is presented to all the members of the house where it was first introduced.

For approval most states require a majority vote in favor of a bill. If the bill is approved by that house, then it is sent to the other house of the legislature for consideration. The same steps for making amendments or changes are followed in the other house. If the bill is also approved by the second house of the legislature, it is sent to the governor for approval or veto.

If the governor approves the bill, it becomes law. If the governor vetoes it, the bill may return to the legislature for more work. If the legislature still thinks the bill is good, members of the lawmaking body can **override** the governor's veto by a certain vote, and the bill will still become law. In most states a two-thirds vote in favor of the bill is needed to override the veto. This is the same power that Congress has when the President vetoes a bill.

SECTION 5 REVIEW On a separate sheet of paper, write the answer for each question.

1) How many houses make up the legislature in most of the states?

2) Which state has a one-house legislature?

3) How are the members of the legislature chosen?

4) How often do most state legislatures meet?

5) What is the name of a small group of legislators who work on a special issue?

What do you think ?

Do you think the power for the legislature to override a governor's veto is a good power? Explain your answer.

Words to Know

Circumstance
An event or condition

★Pardon
To release or excuse someone from jail or prison

Rehabilitation
To help build or restore a person's physical or mental health and abilities

Riot
A public disturbance by a group of people

★Welfare
Programs set up to improve the lives of citizens who need special assistance

The executive branch of state government is made up of departments and agencies. It is headed by a governor. Other government officials assist with operating the state. As the chief executive, or leader, the governor has considerable power. A governor's duties are much like the duties of the President of the United States. The governor can:

- appoint heads of departments
- draw up the state budget
- act as commander in chief of the National Guard and call up the Guard in emergencies such as floods, hurricanes, or **riots.**

As the chief executive, the governor also has power in the legislative and judicial areas of state government. The governor may suggest bills to the legislature at any time. However, the governor usually does this when she or he meets with the legislature at the start of each session.

The governor has the power to appoint certain judges who serve in state courts. He or she may also shorten prison sentences, release prisoners, or even **pardon** a prisoner if special **circumstances** exist.

Because of their importance and power, many state governors have later become presidential candidates. Governors who have later been elected President include William McKinley, Theodore Roosevelt, Woodrow Wilson, Calvin Coolidge, Franklin Roosevelt, Jimmy Carter, Ronald Reagan, and Bill Clinton.

Powers and Duties of a Governor

- Chief executive of the state.
- Appoints people to fill important state jobs.
- Recommends how money is to be raised and spent.
- Commander in chief of state militia.
- Calls up state police and National Guard when they are needed.
- Pardons prisoners in certain cases.
- Proposes laws to the legislature.
- Leader of his or her political party in the state.
- Presides at important ceremonies.

Christine Todd Whitman is the governor of New Jersey.

How Are Governors Elected?

A statewide election is held to select a governor. The state constitution lists the qualifications for a person seeking the office, including the minimum age. Forty-seven states elect a governor for a four-year term. Only New Hampshire and Vermont limit their governors' terms to two years.

In most states, the governor lives in a governor's mansion that belongs to the state. Part of a governor's living expenses may also be paid.

What Other State Officials Do Most States Have?

There are many other key officials in the state executive branch. In most states they are elected at the same time as the governor. In a few states they may be appointed by the governor.

State Officials

- *Lieutenant governor*—The second most important official in a state. This person is elected in thirty-four states. He or she serves as the leader of the state senate in twenty-eight of the states.

- *Attorney general*—Chief legal officer in the state. She or he advises the governor on matters dealing with the law.

- *Secretary of state*—Keeps all official records, publishes laws passed by the state, and oversees much of the state's official business.

- *Comptroller or state auditor*—Controls the spending of state money and is in charge of keeping financial records for the state.

- *State treasurer*—Collects taxes due the state and pays bills owed by the state after they have been approved by the state auditor.

- *Superintendent of public instruction*—Top educational official of the state. She or he works with the board of education to carry out the laws and to set the qualifications for teachers in the state.

What State Agencies Help States Operate Smoothly?

Many departments and agencies exist within the executive branch of each state government. States have grown rapidly in population, and therefore departments have grown in size and number. Most states have a department of human resources, which takes care of such things as public assistance and **welfare.** It also handles health services and vocational **rehabilitation** programs.

Agencies to protect the environment and to control transportation are part of state governments. Every state has a board of education, with a superintendent or commissioner in charge. A labor board takes care of the problems of labor. A banking commission regulates the banks. Certain professionals and workers in the trades must obtain a license to work in a state. The state has special boards to give examinations to these people and to issue the licenses.

SECTION 6 REVIEW Match the sentence beginnings in Part 1 with the correct endings in Part 2. Write the complete sentences on a separate sheet of paper.

Part 1, Beginning of Sentence

1) The executive branch of a state government is . . .

2) The governor may . . .

3) The governor can suggest bills . . .

4) The lieutenant governor . . .

5) The attorney general . . .

Part 2, Ending of Sentence

a) . . . appoint heads of most state departments and agencies.

b) . . . is leader of the senate in twenty-eight states.

c) . . . headed by a governor.

d) . . . is the legal adviser to the governor.

e) . . . to the state legislature at any time.

What do you think

Why do you think governors have the power to pardon people for crimes in certain cases?

Words to Know

Disorderly conduct
Disturbing public peace

★**Domestic relations court**
A court that hears home and family disputes

★**Felony**
A serious crime

★**Juvenile court**
A court that hears cases of young people

★**Magistrate**
A minor law official similar to a justice of the peace

★**Misdemeanor**
A minor crime

★**Municipal court**
A court that hears civil cases, minor criminal offenses, and probate

★**Probate court**
A municipal court that makes decisions about wills

★**Small claims court**
A court that hears cases about small sums of money

Each state constitution gives the state government the power to keep law and order within the boundaries of the state. The legislative branch passes the laws, while the executive branch sees that the laws are carried out. The judicial branch explains the laws and has the power to punish those who break the laws.

State Courts

State courts follow the same principles as federal courts. Cases are divided into civil or criminal cases. Civil cases deal with disputes between two or more parties. Criminal cases deal with violations of state laws.

The organization of courts is almost the same in each state. Most state court systems have lower courts, trial courts, and a higher court, usually called the state supreme court.

Lower State Courts

In some small towns there are justices of the peace. A justice of the peace tries civil cases involving small sums of money, performs marriages, and settles minor offenses such as **disorderly conduct.**

In larger, more populated areas the role of the justice of the peace is taken over by **magistrate** courts or **municipal** courts. These lower courts are often separated into special **courts** that handle only one type of case. For example:

- *Juvenile courts* hear cases of young people who are accused of breaking the law.

- *Domestic relations courts* handle disputes or disagreements between husbands and wives and other family problems.

- *Small claims courts* settle disputes over small sums of money, usually without a lawyer. This allows people to seek justice without spending a great deal of money.

Some state judges are elected by the people. Elected judges can be voted out of office if voters don't agree with their decisions. Other judges are appointed by the governor. Some states combine both methods of judge selection. The governor appoints judges. After a period of time, the judges must win election to keep their jobs. This way judges must win the approval of voters to stay in office.

- *Municipal courts* deal with civil suits, minor criminal offenses, and probate. **Probate courts** settle questions about who should receive the property of someone who has died.

General Trial Courts

Criminal and civil cases are handled in trial courts. Most cases are heard by a judge and jury. A criminal case is a case brought by the state against a person who has broken a law. The crime may be a **felony** or a **misdemeanor.** A felony is a major crime, such as murder or arson. Misdemeanors are minor crimes, such as littering or some forms of stealing.

Civil cases are usually disagreements between two or more individuals or groups. The disagreement may be about money or property. One person or group sues another group for damages. The state is not involved in civil cases because no law has been broken.

Most criminal and civil cases are heard by a judge and jury.

Higher State Courts

The highest court in the state is usually called the state supreme court. An accused person who thinks his or her case was not tried fairly in a lower court may appeal to a higher court. When hearing or considering an appeal, the state supreme court does not hold a new trial. Instead the judges study the records and all the evidence. Then they vote on whether the accused person received a fair trial.

SECTION 7 REVIEW Choose a court listed in the Word Bank that matches the actions described below. Write your answers on a separate sheet of paper.

WORD BANK

general trial court

lower court

state supreme court

1) An accused person appeals her case to this court because she believes that her trial was not fair.

2) A serious criminal case involving murder is heard by a judge and a jury.

3) The judges study the evidence to decide if a case was tried fairly.

4) A girl of fourteen has broken the law. A hearing is scheduled.

5) A dispute between two people led to a serious injury of one person. The case is brought to trial.

6) The judge decides how to handle the property of a person who died.

7) A worker is charged with stealing tools worth sixty dollars. His case is being heard.

What do you think

Is it right for a judge who is appointed and not elected to make important decisions that do not require a trial?

Citizens & Government

The Miranda Rule

- You have the right to choose a lawyer and have the lawyer with you during questioning.

- If you cannot afford to pay a lawyer, you have the right to have a court-appointed lawyer.

In the 1960s, Ernesto Miranda sued the state of Arizona because he was not told his rights before he was arrested. This case went to the United States Supreme Court. In Miranda vs. Arizona, the Supreme Court ruled that arresting officers must read a list of rights to a suspect before asking the suspect to answer questions. The Supreme Court said that it would not uphold any conviction if a suspect had not been told of his or her rights. State and local police officers must follow the "Miranda Rule," as it is known.

Before police can question a suspect about a crime, they must tell the suspect:

- You have the right to remain silent.

- Anything you say may be used against you in court.

- You do not have to remain silent or have a lawyer. You may make any statements and answer any questions you wish. You have the right to stop and ask for a lawyer at any time.

Review

1) Why do you think the Supreme Court made this decision?

2) If a suspect chooses to talk with police and answer questions, can the statements be used against him or her?

3) How can knowing these rights help suspects protect themselves?

4) How do you think having a lawyer would help a suspect talk with police officers?

Media & Government

Television Trials

Herbert Wachtell
ATTORNEY FOR
QVC NETWORK

In the United States, courtrooms have always been open to the press and to the public. People can go into a courtroom and watch the court proceedings. But until the 1970's cameras were not usually allowed in courtrooms.

Each state decides whether to permit the use of cameras in its courts. In 1977, the state of Florida began to experiment with cameras in the courtroom. Today, 47 states permit television coverage of courtroom proceedings. The laws are different in each state, but they all require that the audio and video equipment be used in a way that does not interfere with the court. In Florida, cameras can show the jury. In California, the jury cannot be shown.

On July 1, 1991, Court TV began operating. Court TV is a twenty-four hour cable network that covers real courtroom trials from around the United States. Sometimes it covers trials while they are happening. Other trials are taped. Like C-SPAN, Court TV believes that people gain more understanding of an event by watching it rather than reading or watching reports about it from the media. Trials shown on Court TV are chosen for a number of reasons. Some things considered are the importance of the case, the issues being decided, the trials' educational value, and the expected length of the trial. A team of legal journalists uses a trial tracking system that helps the network choose which trials to broadcast. Usually the network covers one or two cases live each day and has a taped case or two ready to televise.

Review

1) Why do you think the laws for using TV cameras in a courtroom are made by the state?

2) How do you think having a camera in the courtroom affects how the defendant, lawyers, and judge act?

3) What do (don't) you like about the idea of watching a trial instead of hearing or reading a news report about it?

4) How does watching a trial help people understand the judicial system?

5) Why do you think Court TV has a case or two taped and ready to televise?

★ Congress has the power to admit new states to the United States. Many states were United States territories before becoming states. To become a state, territories must apply to Congress and write a new state constitution.

★ Each state has its own constitution. The power in states is divided among three separate branches—legislative, executive, and judicial.

★ Shared powers, such as the power to tax citizens, are powers that states share with the federal government. Reserved powers are powers only the states have, such as the power to establish schools.

★ The greatest source of income for states comes from federal grants. States also get money from income tax, sales tax, and fees. States use the money to run schools, build roads, and provide health and welfare programs. States also provide other services, such as police protection, recreation, cultural activities, National Guard, and courts of law.

★ The lawmaking branch of the state government is called the legislature in most states. It is divided into two houses—the senate and the house of representatives. The members are elected by the voters in each state.

★ A governor is the leader of each state executive branch. The governor appoints heads of departments and can suggest bills to the legislature. The state has other elected officials, such as a treasurer, an auditor, and an attorney general. Departments and agencies are run by the state to take care of services and the business of the state.

★ The judicial branch, with its system of courts, applies the laws and punishes criminals. There are three types of state courts: lower courts to handle lesser civil and criminal cases; general trial courts with a judge and jury for more serious cases; and state supreme courts to handle appeals from the other courts.

Comprehension: Identifying Facts

Choose the words from the Word Bank to complete the sentences. Write your answers on a separate sheet of paper.

WORD BANK

attorney general

branches

constitution

governor

grants

legislature

money

schools

serious

territories

welfare

1) Many states that were admitted to the United States were first areas called _____.

2) Each state in the United States operates under its own ___.

3) The power of the states is divided among three ___ of government.

4) These state governments need a great deal of ___ to run properly.

5) Federal ___ bring in the greatest amount of money.

6) States use most of their money to run the ___.

7) States also provide health and ___ programs.

8) Most state lawmaking bodies are called the ___.

9) The head of the executive branch of a state is called the ___.

10) Another elected official of the state who takes care of legal matters is the___.

11) The general trial courts handle ___ cases, both civil and criminal.

Comprehension: Understanding Main Ideas

On a separate sheet of paper, write the answers to the following questions using complete sentences.

1) What are three powers that the states reserved for themselves when writing the United States Constitution?

2) How do state governments spend money to protect the lives and property of its citizens?

3) Who is the chief executive of a state government? Name three of his/her duties.

4) What is the job of a state supreme court in appeals cases?

5) For a territory to become a state, who has to approve its state constitution?

6) What things change for citizens of U.S. territories if a territory becomes a state?

Critical Thinking: Write Your Opinion

1) States use several ways to obtain money to run their governments. Can you think of additional ways that states may obtain money?

2) Is the use of lotteries a good way for a state to raise funds for education? Explain your opinion.

3) Many state constitutions are very long—much longer than the United States Constitution. Why do you think this is true?

Test Taking Tip | When you review your notes to prepare for an exam, use a marker to highlight key words and example problems.

"If America discourages the locality, the community, the self-contained town, she will kill the nation. A nation is as rich as her free communities."

President Woodrow Wilson

Chapter

10

Local Government

When the colonists settled in America, they quickly elected leaders and made laws to keep peace and order. This was a form of local government. Today local government is still the level of government closest to people's everyday lives. Local government provides many services. It helps protect lives and homes, and provides citizens with schools, libraries, and other important services. In Chapter 10, you will learn more about how local government works.

Goals for Learning

★ To identify units of local government and name the powers each has

★ To describe the duties of various county officials

★ To describe three different types of city government

State governments decide what type of local government will exist in the state. Local governments receive a charter from the state legislature. The charter gives certain powers to the local government, such as the right to tax and to require licenses. Local governments are given responsibility for keeping law and order.

What Is County Government?

During the early history of the United States, counties existed to take care of the rural areas. For people in areas far from a town, the county government was the only government they had. Today, the county government usually serves an area that has several towns or cities. In most states, it is the largest unit of local government.

The number of counties varies from state to state. In each county, a city or town serves as the **county seat.** Like a state capital, the county seat is where county officials have their offices. These offices are often in a county courthouse or other building owned by the county.

Who Runs the County Government?

The county government is usually run by a county board, which is a group of elected officials. Some states use other names for this board. It may be called a board of commissioners, board of supervisors, or commissioners' court. This board passes laws about public health and welfare. The county board may also set the amount of taxes and may manage road construction in its area.

In many cases, the county board also makes **zoning** decisions. Zoning determines how and where homes and businesses may be built. For example, a place where many stores will be built is zoned for commercial use. Stores may not be built on land that is zoned for houses.

County boards supervise the use of libraries and other public buildings.

The county board also supervises the use of county buildings such as libraries, jails, and court buildings.

What Other Duties Are Handled by County Officials?

County officials are elected to carry out special duties:

- The *sheriff* is the chief county law enforcement officer. The sheriff carries out court orders. Sheriffs can arrest people who break the law. Most sheriffs are in charge of the county jail.

- A *county clerk* keeps records of births, deaths, and marriages in the county. The clerk also keeps copies of deeds, which are records of the sale of land or buildings.

- The *county treasurer* **supervises** how much money is collected and spent by the county.

- The *county auditor* examines county financial records and sees that they are correct.

• The *prosecuting attorney* or *district attorney* **prosecutes** people who have violated county or state laws.

In addition to these five officials, large counties often have a purchasing agent, public defender, park commissioner, public health nurse, and a **coroner**. A coroner is a person who investigates violent deaths and deaths where a doctor is not present.

SECTION 1 REVIEW On a separate sheet of paper, write the correct word to complete each sentence.

WORD BANK

charter
county
jail
money
road
seat

1) A __ is usually the largest type of local government.

2) Local governments receive a ____ from the state legislature.

3) The county board manages ____ construction and zoning regulations.

4) The sheriff carries out court orders and is in charge of the county ____ .

5) The treasurer supervises the collecting and spending of county ____.

6) County offices are located in the county ____.

What do you think

Which two of the activities of county government do you think are most important to individual citizens? Give reasons for your answers.

Words to Know

★**Assessor**
A person who sets the value of property

Cultural
Having to do with the values, attitudes, and customs of people in a community

★**Direct democracy**
Form of government in which all voters gather to conduct town business

Maintenance
Repair or upkeep of property or equipment

Trustee
A person who is given power to act for others

Urban
Having to do with living in a city

★**Ward**
A political division in a city

For many years most American citizens lived in rural areas on farms or in small towns. Today, the population of the country has shifted from rural to **urban** areas. So city governments must serve the needs of many people. This is sometimes difficult because some areas of large cities have become very crowded.

City governments are responsible for many things. Some of these duties include:

• police forces	• clean water
• fire protection	• public transportation
• road repairs	• trash collection

A city government also provides **cultural** and recreational activities that are an important part of city life. Libraries, museums, parks, gardens, art galleries, and theaters are supported with city funds.

Where Do City Governments Get Their Power?

State legislatures issue city charters to communities that want to become cities. A charter is a plan of government that outlines the powers given to a city. This charter permits a city to have a governing group separate from the areas around it.

Where Do Local Governments Get Funds?

Counties, cities, and other types of local government need money to provide services for their citizens. Three kinds of taxes are the chief sources of income for local governments: property taxes, sales taxes, and income taxes. Most local governments receive the largest income from property and sales taxes; only some local governments tax incomes.

Property includes the land and the buildings on it. The value of the property is determined by the town, city, or county **assessor.** The value of the property is called the assessed value. The assessed value can change as the condition of the property or buildings improves or gets worse. The local government sets the tax rate on the property, usually a certain dollar amount for every one hundred dollars of assessed value. If a town, county, or city needs more money, it can raise the tax rate.

Sales tax is a tax placed on certain items people buy. It is a percentage of the cost of the item. In some areas, foods and medicines are not taxed. Some people think that sales tax is not fair because everyone, rich or poor, pays the same amount of tax on an item.

Local governments get their money from other sources. Sometimes it sells bonds to raise money for building projects. Much money is raised in fees for licenses, such as automobile licenses. Another source of income may come from the federal and state governments. Sometimes as much as one-third of local income is received from the federal and state governments. Many poorer local governments could not operate without this additional financial aid.

How Are Cities Governed?

Cities are usually governed by one of three forms of government. The mayor-council is the most common type of city government. The two other widely used forms of city government are the commission and the council-manager types.

Mayor-Council

In a mayor-council city government, the chief executive or leader is called a mayor. Both the mayor and the council are elected by the voters. Each member of the council represents a small area or section of the city, called a **ward.** Either the mayor or the council appoints the heads of the departments that operate the city.

Sharon Sayles-Belton is the mayor of Minneapolis, Minnesota.

Three Forms of City Government

Mayor-Council

Mayor — City Council

Heads of Departments

Police Fire Parks Finance Public Works

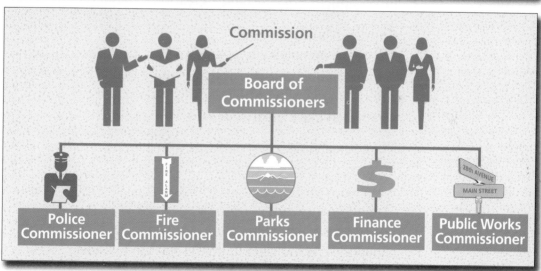

Commission

Board of Commissioners

Police Commissioner Fire Commissioner Parks Commissioner Finance Commissioner Public Works Commissioner

Council-Manager

City Council — City Manager — Heads of City Departments

Police Fire Parks Finance Public Works

Commission

Usually the commission form of city government has no elected mayor. The city is run by a group of commissioners that people elect. The commissioners work together as a group to run the city's government. Sometimes one commissioner will be chosen by the others to act as mayor. That person runs meetings and represents the commission at important ceremonies.

With the commission kind of government, each commissioner heads one of the city's departments. City departments may include finances, garbage collection, police and fire protection, health care, and recreation.

Council-Manager

A council-manager city government is also called the *city manager* plan. It has an elected council that acts as the city's lawmaking body. Under this system, the city is run very much like a business.

The council hires a city manager who handles the city's business under the direction of the council. The city manager appoints department heads who report to the city manager. The city manager does not belong to any political party and does not have to run for office. Many people think that this allows the city manager to do the best job possible.

Are There Other Kinds of Local Government?

Other forms of local government exist. Small communities may be called towns, townships, boroughs, parishes, or villages. Many of these local governments have received a charter from the state to operate. Because these communities are often much smaller than cities, their government is much simpler. They have fewer departments because not as many services are needed. Many of the mayors and council members are volunteers and are not paid. A mayor-council government is most often used in these communities.

New England Towns

Although the New England states are divided into counties, the towns are the basic unit of government. The town has a form of government called **direct democracy.** This means that all qualified voters meet to conduct the town's business. Meetings are held once a year or more often if necessary. The town's officers are elected at the yearly meeting.

This New England type of government began in colonial times. In those days the meetings were popular events, and almost everyone attended. Today these gatherings are poorly attended, even though the towns have grown. Some towns now elect representatives to attend rather than count on large numbers of citizens to participate.

City Governments Provide Police Protection

Of all the services provided by the city governments, police protection is probably the most important and most expensive. As cities grow in size and population, police departments must expand and improve to meet these new demands.

City police departments, with money from the federal government, are teaching police officers the latest crime-fighting and prevention methods. Police officers are now being taught how to investigate crimes, question witnesses, and gather the evidence the courts need to prove a case. When police officers spend more time investigating crimes, it helps detectives. As a result, more criminals are brought to justice. This makes cities safer and also reduces the cost of police protection.

Townships

About sixteen states in the Middle Atlantic and Midwestern regions of the U.S. have township governments. In general, townships are found in rural parts of counties. People of the township usually elect officials to serve on a board of commissioners or **trustees.** This board makes rules and regulations for the township. The board may include a tax collector, a clerk, and a justice of the peace.

Villages and Boroughs

Some states allow communities with about two hundred families to become villages or boroughs. They run their own government. They collect taxes, provide for street **maintenance** and fire protection, and other services as needed. Most officials of a village or borough serve part-time because there is not enough business for a full-time position. When villages become too large, they may ask the state legislature to grant them a city charter.

SECTION 2 REVIEW On a separate sheet of paper, write the word from the Word Bank that completes each sentence.

WORD BANK
commissioners
departments
mayor-council
rural
state

1) A city government has ___ that are responsible for providing services to the people of that city.

2) A city charter is issued by the ___ legislature.

3) The most common form of city government is the ___ type.

4) In a commission form of government the city is run by a group of ___ .

5) Townships are usually found in ___ parts of some counties.

What do you think

Why do you think the mayor-council form of city government is used more than other kinds?

Citizens & Government

Volunteering

Most communities have volunteers. Volunteers offer their time without pay to help others and to improve the community. Some people volunteer as individual citizens and some belong to organizations that do volunteer work.

Some volunteers are interested in helping elderly people or people with disabilities. *Meals on Wheels* is an organization that provides low-cost warm meals to people to see that they have a balanced diet. Some volunteers help with preparing the meals and others take the meals to people in their homes.

Schools and hospitals often use volunteers. In a school, a volunteer might help a teacher or help a student who has special needs. *Volunteers in Literacy* is a national organization that helps adults learn to read. The organization trains the volunteers who then work with individuals to help them learn to read or to improve their reading.

Sometimes people serve their communities by keeping a close watch on the activities of the local government. These people might gather signatures on a petition to protest a planned government action. They are looking out for the welfare of the citizens in the community.

During political campaigns, most of the people who work to help a candidate get elected are volunteers. They may deliver campaign literature to people, answer telephones, or help mail letters to voters.

There are opportunities for students to volunteer in most communities. Sometimes young people can learn about career opportunities and also discover their own abilities through volunteering. Volunteers usually get personal satisfaction from helping others and working to improve their community.

Review

1) Why are volunteers needed?

2) What are some of the benefits volunteering brings to the community?

3) What are some benefits of being a volunteer?

4) Which kind of volunteer activity do you think is most helpful? Give reasons for your choice.

Media & Government

Watching Local Government in Action

Local government is the level of government closest to people's everyday lives. Yet many citizens don't know much about their local government. Even though the public is welcome to attend city council meetings, few people go to them. To bring local government closer to citizens, some cable television networks broadcast local government meetings. Broadcasting city council meetings is a service to citizens. It can help citizens become better informed about their local government.

In many communities, cable television stations broadcast city council meetings, school board meetings, and other meetings of public interest. Cable channels often announce the meetings for several days before they happen. The meetings are broadcast live, or as they take place.

In a mayor-council form of government, the mayor leads the meetings. The meetings follow rules called Robert's Rules of Parliamentary Procedure. These rules tell how the meeting is to be run. For example, when a topic has been discussed, a council member may make a motion to take a certain action. If the motion is "seconded" by another council member, the whole council then votes on it.

Citizens who want the city council to take some action may ask to be on the agenda for a city council meeting. Citizens might protest a business that they think is harming the community. For example, if a local company is causing air or water pollution, citizens may ask the city council to take action against the company.

By watching these government meetings, citizens can learn about local issues that will affect them. People who watch the meetings can let the mayor or city council members know how they feel about the issues discussed.

Review

1) Why do you think more people don't go to city government meetings?

2) What are some issues that citizens might learn about from watching cable broadcasts of local government meetings?

3) How can citizens who watch the meetings let city officials know what they think?

4) Have you ever watched a local government meeting on TV?

★ Local governments protect the homes, lives, and environment of citizens who live there. They provide schools, libraries, and other services.

★ County governments are the largest units of local government. A county board runs the county, passes laws, collects taxes, and supervises construction.

★ City governments are growing in importance as the population in the U.S. shifts from rural to urban areas. City governments have special problems because of overcrowding.

★ Mayor-council is the most common form of city government. It has an elected mayor with several council members.

★ A commission is a form of city government that is run by commissioners. They may select one of the commissioners as leader.

★ A council-manager, or city manager, form of city government hires a city manager to run the city.

★ Towns and township governments are found in some parts of the country. They are smaller than cities and provide fewer services. Their elected officials may be unpaid or serve part-time.

Comprehension: Identifying Facts

On a separate sheet of paper, write the correct words from the Word Bank to complete the sentences.

WORD BANK

assessor
attorney
auditor
businesses
charters
Local
mayor
seat
sheriff
tax
treasurer
welfare
zoning

1) _____ governments are considered to be the closest governments to people's lives.

2) Local governments receive _____ from the state.

3) In most states, the county government takes care of public health and _____.

4) Counties collect taxes and make _____ rules.

5) Zoning rules say where homes and _____ may be built.

6) The _____ supervises how money is collected and spent for the county.

7) Financial records are examined by the county _____.

8) The _____ is the county's chief law enforcement officer.

9) A county _____ is the place where county offices are located.

10) The prosecuting or district _____ prosecutes people who violate laws.

11) The county _____ determines the value of property.

12) Sales _____ is placed on certain items people buy.

13) The mayor-council form of local government has a leader called a _____.

Comprehension: Understanding Main Ideas

On a separate sheet of paper, write the answers to the following questions using complete sentences.

1) What are two duties of a county board?

2) Why have city governments become more important over the years?

3) What is the most common type of city government? Who is the chief executive of this type of government?

4) What are three other types of local government, besides the county and city?

5) What is a charter and what does it allow a city to do?

Critical Thinking: Write Your Opinion

1) Cities provide police and fire protection and recreation facilities for citizens. What other services are not mentioned in the textbook that a city might provide for senior citizens, people with disabilities, or new U.S. citizens?

2) Why do you think there are so many different kinds of city government? Give at least two reasons.

Test Taking Tip When studying for a test, use the titles and subtitles in the chapter to help you recall the information.

" . . . More important than winning the election is governing the nation. That is the test of a political party—the acid, final test."

Adlai E. Stevenson

Chapter

11

Political Parties

Political parties are made up of groups of people who share common ideas or ways of thinking about government. These groups try to get their candidates into public offices where they will promote the group's ideas. Since the late 1700s, political parties have named most of the candidates for Congress, the vice presidency, and the presidency. Political parties are not mentioned in the Constitution. They exist by custom, not by law.

In Chapter 11, you will learn about the history of the U.S. two-party system, political parties today, and the election process. You will also learn about ways citizens can get laws changed through initiatives and referendums.

Goals for Learning

★ To explain the purpose of political parties

★ To identify the two major political parties and how they developed

★ To give reasons why minor parties are important

★ To describe the functions of political parties and the party platform

★ To name the types of primary elections

★ To describe the format of national political conventions

★ To explain how candidates campaign for office

★ To describe voting and the steps in the election process

★ To explain the uses of the initiative and referendum

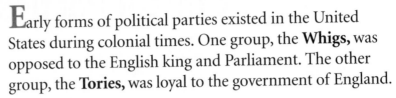

Words to Know

Dedicated
Devoted to; to give one's full attention to

★**Democratic party**
U.S. political party that stands for protecting rights of the individual

★**Republican party**
U.S. political party that stands for a limited government role in people's lives and limited change

★**Tories**
Colonists loyal to the King of England

★**Whigs**
Colonists who wanted independence from England

Early forms of political parties existed in the United States during colonial times. One group, the **Whigs,** was opposed to the English king and Parliament. The other group, the **Tories,** was loyal to the government of England.

After the colonists won the Revolutionary War, two other groups formed that had different political and economic beliefs. One group, the Federalist party, supported a powerful central government. The other, the Anti-Federalist party, wanted a less powerful central government with strong, independent states. In 1787 the Federalists held a Constitutional Convention in Philadelphia. The Anti-Federalists did not want to approve the Constitution until the Federalists added the Bill of Rights.

How Did the Political Parties Develop?

The Federalists supported George Washington, the first President of the United States. The Federalist party controlled the government until 1801 when Thomas Jefferson, an Anti-Federalist, was elected President.

As the country grew and changed, so did the political parties. By 1816, the Federalist party had weakened and its members left the party. The Anti-Federalist party also changed. It became known as the Democratic-Republican party. Later, in 1828, it was called the **Democratic party.** The Democratic party is still one of the major parties in the United States today. The other major party is the **Republican party.**

How Did the Democratic Party Begin?

In 1827, Andrew Jackson left the Anti-Federalist party that Thomas Jefferson started. Jackson felt that the party was being used for the good of rich people. He was **dedicated** to the idea that the federal government should represent the common people. Jackson was the first leader of the new Democratic party. He became President in 1829.

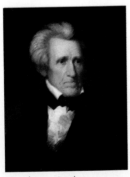

Andrew Jackson

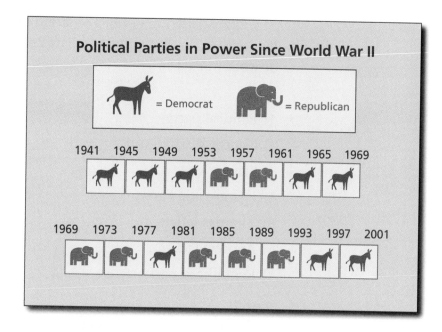

Political Parties in Power Since World War II

= Democrat   = Republican

1941 1945 1949 1953 1957 1961 1965 1969

1969 1973 1977 1981 1985 1989 1993 1997 2001

When Did the Republican Party Begin?

The Republican party is the other powerful political party in the United States. It began in 1854 when several groups combined. They did not have the same beliefs as the Democratic party. The Republican party was against slavery. Abraham Lincoln, who was strongly against slavery, was named presidential candidate for this new Republican party. In 1860 Lincoln was elected President of the United States.

When Did the Strong Two-Party System Develop?

A strong two-party system developed in the United States in the late 1800s after the Civil War. Many Northerners were Republicans. They included business people, farmers, soldiers from the Union army, and African-Americans. Many southerners were Democrats.

Over the years, each of the two parties has played an important role in governing the U.S. The strong two-party system still exists today.

SECTION 1 REVIEW On a separate sheet of paper, write the letter of the description in Part 2 that matches a name or word in Part 1.

Part 1

1) Political party

2) George Washington

3) Slavery

4) Democratic party

5) Thomas Jefferson

6) Andrew Jackson

7) Republican party

Part 2

a) first Anti-Federalist President

b) started by the Anti-Federalists

c) organization of people with the same ideas about government

d) wanted government to represent the common people

e) supported Abraham Lincoln for President

f) first Federalist President

g) opposed by the Republican party

What do you think

Why is it important for the government to represent all people equally?

Citizens & Government

Speaker Newt Gingrich

Newt Gingrich, United States Representative from Georgia, was elected Speaker of the House of Representatives in January 1995. Gingrich was the first Republican to serve as Speaker in over forty years.

The Speaker of the House is a position of political power. The Speaker of the House

- presides over Congress
- calls on members who wish to speak
- refers bills to committees
- decides with the help of party leaders which bills will be considered

One of the first things Gingrich did was to lead Republicans in Congress to make a pledge, called the *Contract With America*. The Contract With America promised to

- cut spending
- balance the federal budget
- get tough on criminals
- make the military stronger
- cut taxes for middle class people
- limit the number of terms members of Congress can serve

Gingrich and the Republican majority used their power to demand that a bill be passed requiring the federal budget to be balanced in seven years. President Clinton vetoed the bill, saying it would take too much money away from programs he felt were needed. This caused a government shutdown because the budget was not approved. Even though the Republicans had a majority in Congress, they did not have enough support to override the President's veto.

Review
1) Which of the promises in the Contract With America do you think is most important? Why do you think so?

2) Why is it hard to choose between having a balanced budget and cutting government programs?

Words to Know

★Coalition
A group of several political parties

★Minor party
A political party whose electoral strength is usually too small for it to gain control of the government

★Multiparty
Many parties

★Nominate
To select someone for a job or office

Obstacle
Something that stands in the way

★Progressive
In favor of changing government

★Third party
A major party that exists for a period of time in a nation or state that usually has a two-party system

The United States has a two-party system, where each party tries to get control of the government. Great Britain and about twelve other nations also have two-party systems. Many countries have a **multiparty** system. For example, France has five major political parties. In a multiparty system, one party usually does not get enough candidates elected to control the government. Several parties often combine, or make a **coalition,** in order to have a voting majority.

In the United States, there are a number of **minor parties.** These parties do not have the power of the Democratic party or the Republican party, but they have had an important place in the country's political history.

How Are Minor Parties Created?

Sometimes people who have different political beliefs from those of the Democrats and Republicans want to run for office. To run, these people have to be **nominated** by another party. Even though these candidates have little chance of being elected, they do have an influence on the election outcome. It is possible for them to take votes away from one of the major candidates and swing the election in favor of the other party.

This happened in 1912 when the **Progressive** party nominated Theodore Roosevelt as the **third-party** candidate for President. Roosevelt did not win but he took votes away from William Taft, the Republican candidate. Because of this, the Democratic nominee, Woodrow Wilson, won the election.

Most minor parties are created to promote ideas. Libertarians are in favor of limited government. The Socialist party was organized in 1901 to promote collective ownership and equal distribution of wealth. The Socialist Labor

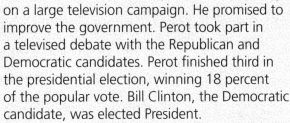

Ross Perot, Independent Candidate

In 1992, Ross Perot, a Texas businessman, was an independent candidate for President. Perot spent his own money on a large television campaign. He promised to improve the government. Perot took part in a televised debate with the Republican and Democratic candidates. Perot finished third in the presidential election, winning 18 percent of the popular vote. Bill Clinton, the Democratic candidate, was elected President.

Perot was also a presidential candidate in the 1996 election. He was nominated by the Reform party. Once again, he did not win the election.

party wants workers to control business. These three parties have never had a successful presidential candidate, but they continue to promote their beliefs.

The American Independent party was formed in 1968 to support George Wallace, former governor of Alabama, for President. In 1996, Steve Forbes, a businessman, spent millions of dollars campaigning for President. Forbes was in favor of a flat tax, where everyone would pay the same amount of income tax. He eventually dropped out of the campaign.

What Influence Do Minor Parties Have?

Minor parties sometimes hold beliefs that the major parties do not support. This brings the beliefs to the attention of the major parties. They may then support those beliefs. Usually this happens when many citizens see the need for change and support the minority ideas.

Why Is It Hard for Minor Parties to Succeed?

Minor parties have many **obstacles** to overcome. They usually do not have the money needed to promote their candidates and programs. Newspapers, television, and radio usually do not give minor party candidates much attention. In most cases a minor party stands for only one issue. It may depend on the name of one person who is known for some popular issue, such as states' rights or religious concerns.

SECTION 2 REVIEW Match the beginning of the sentence in Part 1 with the correct ending in Part 2. Write the complete sentences on another sheet of paper.

Part 1, Beginning of Sentences

1) Minor parties are referred to as . . .

2) In 1912 the Progressive party . . .

3) Third parties have dealt with issues like . . .

4) Some obstacles standing in the way of third parties are . . .

5) In 1992 and 1996, Ross Perot . . .

6) The United States is one of a number of countries that has . . .

Part 2, Ending of Sentences

a) states' rights and religious concerns.

b) the lack of financial support and little attention from the newspapers and television.

c) third parties.

d) ran for President.

e) nominated Theodore Roosevelt for President.

f) a two-party political system.

What do you think

Why do you think the Libertarian and Socialist parties still exist today?

Words to Know

★Conservative
A person who opposes or resists change

★Constituent
A member of an office holder's voting district

Fund raiser
An activity held to raise money

★Incumbent
A person who holds an office

★Liberal
A person whose political views are open to change and who supports individual rights

★Opposition party
A political party that does not have a majority in the government

★Platform
A statement of the ideas, policies, and beliefs of a political party in an election

Traditional
An established or customary way of doing things

P olitical parties exist for many reasons. They believe in certain policies. They try to present candidates who will support these beliefs.

Of the two major parties, the Republicans **traditionally** have been politically **conservative.** Conservatives are usually interested in keeping things the way they are. The Democrats have been more **liberal.** Liberals tend to be more open to change and concerned with protecting individual liberties. Both political parties include people who have a wide range of beliefs.

What Is the Party Platform?

Every four years, in the summer before a presidential election, party members come together for a national convention. At this convention, the party nominates candidates for President and Vice President. Each party agrees on a set of statements about what the candidates will do if elected. These statements of policy and promises are known as a **platform.**

A platform committee is made up of delegates from each state and territory of the country. They listen to suggestions and ideas before the convention begins. They put these ideas together. During the convention, they present the platform. Sometimes it is accepted as presented. Sometimes parts of it are debated and changed before the convention accepts it.

What Other Functions Does a Political Party Have?

Besides nominating candidates and writing party platforms, political parties also have a number of other functions. Political parties are most active during political campaigns in election years. Then they work hard to get their candidates elected.

Some 1996 Political Party Platform Issues

National Debt

Republican Party
Wants to make a constitutional amendment that will require the country to pay off its national debt.

Democratic Party
Wants to pay off the national debt by the year 2002.

Economy

Republican Party
Believes there is too much wasteful spending and that the high national debt will be harmful to future citizens.

Democratic Party
Believes the country's economy is getting stronger because more jobs are being created, more small businesses are being started, and the U.S. is selling more goods and services to other countries.

Education

Republican Party
Wants to do away with the Department of Education and put more control of schools at the state level. Believes spending more on education is not the only way to improve it. Supports creating government grants for private or home schooling.

Democratic Party
Believes education is key to the country's success. Supports making public schools stronger, safer, better at preparing students for jobs, and more equipped with technology. Believes each American should have the right to go to college.

Environment

Republican Party
Believes states and private industry are key in protecting the environment. Wants the rights of private property owners considered when an environmental decision could affect them.

Democratic Party
Believes that the federal government is responsible for enforcing laws that protect the environment. Believes that it is possible to protect the environment and create more jobs in the process.

Defense

Republican Party
Believes that the U.S. is not prepared to defend itself from missile attacks. Believes defense spending reductions have damaged the military. Wants to make military spending more efficient and with long-term goals in mind.

Democratic Party
Believes in small increases in spending for the military and in finding ways to make military spending more efficient. Wants to reduce the threat of dangerous weapons.

Between elections, political parties work to see that party **incumbents** will be re-elected in the next election. They may hold **fund raisers** to help pay for campaigns. They may also send newsletters to **constituents** to tell them about how the office holder is working to help them.

What Is the Opposition Party?

When a party's candidate is in office, that party is in power. It helps govern by seeking support for the official as he or she tries to put party policy into action. When a party is not in power, it is called the **opposition party.** Members of the opposition party watch the party in power very closely. They point out changes in government they would like to see made, and suggest how this might be done. They always hope this will help their party in future elections.

SECTION 3 REVIEW On a separate sheet of paper, write the correct word from the Word Bank to complete each sentence.

WORD BANK
conservative
differing
election
four
ideas
parties
platform
power
state

1) Republicans traditionally have been more ___ than Democrats.

2) Sometimes members of the same party have ___ beliefs about good government.

3) National party conventions take place every ___ years.

4) A ___ is made up of statements of beliefs, policies, and candidates' promises.

5) The platform committee is made up of delegates from each ___ and territory of the country.

6) Political parties often are most active during an ___ year.

7) The opposition party closely watches the actions of the party in ___.

8) Political ___ have certain policies that they believe in.

9) The platform committee listens to ___ for the platform before the convention begins.

What do you think

Why do you think the opposition party suggests changes to be made in government? Why do you think political parties are more interested in having an incumbent run for re-election than in having a new candidate?

Words to Know

★Direct primary
Kind of primary where voters choose a candidate to support

★Indirect primary
Kind of primary where delegates choose candidates

★Nonpartisan primary
A primary not influenced by a particular political party

Preference
Choice

★Primary election
An election to choose candidates or select delegates to a party convention

A state **primary election** is an election that is held before the general election. Political parties use the primary election method to choose members of their party to run for public office in the general election. Many candidates may want to be nominated in a primary. Only one candidate from each party is chosen to run for an office in a general election. Then, in the general election, voters choose between the candidates who won the primary election.

Direct Primary

There are several types of primaries. The form most often used is the **direct primary.** In a direct primary, party members who wish to run for office ask to have their names put on the ballot. Then the voters choose the candidate they support. There are two kinds of direct primaries: open and closed. An open primary has ballots for all the candidates. Voters may choose both the party and the candidate of their choice when they are in the privacy of the voting booth. A closed primary requires voters to declare in advance which party they want to vote for. They can vote only for candidates of that party.

Indirect Primary

In an **indirect primary** members of a political party elect delegates to party conventions. At the party convention, the delegates elected at the primary choose the candidates who will represent that party in the election. This is called indirect because party members and then the delegates do the selecting instead of the voters.

Nonpartisan Primary

Nonpartisan primaries are not connected to a political party. This type of primary is generally used for smaller local elections. Voters consider a candidate's qualifications and are not concerned about the candidate's political party.

Kinds of Primaries

Direct
Voters choose candidates they support

   Open Primary—All candidates are on the ballot

   Closed Primary—Voters choose party and then vote for candidates from that party

Indirect
Convention delegates choose candidates

Nonpartisan
Candidates' parties not important

Presidential
State election to choose delegates for national convention

Presidential Primary

Some states use a presidential primary to select delegates for the national convention. The delegates promise to support a certain candidate. The candidate presents his or her delegates at the national convention. A vote for those delegates is the same as a vote for the candidate who presents them. A similar method is the presidential **preference** primary. In this primary voters choose delegates in the same way, but the delegates do not have to support certain candidates.

SECTION 4 REVIEW On a separate sheet of paper, write the kind of primary from the Word Bank that each statement refers to.

WORD BANK

direct, closed primary

direct, open primary

indirect primary

nonpartisan primary

1) The voters choose the party and the candidate.

2) Only delegates to a party convention are chosen.

3) No political party is involved. This type of primary is used for small, local elections.

4) A voter declares which party he or she is voting for and then votes for the candidates of that party.

What do you think

Why do you think most states use the direct primary form of selection for candidates?

Words to Know

*Acceptance speech
A speech agreeing
to accept a
nomination

*Alternate
Someone who is
appointed to
substitute for a
delegate at a
political convention

*Keynote address
A speech that
presents the main
issues of interest
and promotes
enthusiasm and
party unity

*Nominee
A person who has
been chosen to run
for election

Predict
To state what will
happen before it
happens

*Roll call
To call off the name
of each state

Unity
Having agreement
of purpose and a
feeling of oneness

*Unpledged
Not promised
to a particular
candidate

Every four years political parties hold national conventions to select their candidates for President and Vice President, and to develop a party platform. These conventions are held in large cities and take place in the summer before the November presidential elections. Citizens can follow the proceedings of the convention on television, on radio, and in newspapers.

At the convention, the party will have delegates vote for a candidate for President. The party also tells each state and territory how many delegate votes it will have.

How Are Convention Delegates Chosen?

Convention delegates are chosen in different ways: presidential preference primary elections, or state or district conventions. A delegate and an **alternate** are selected for each vote that a state or territory has. If the delegate is unable to vote, the alternate votes instead.

The candidates have already worked hard before the national convention. They have campaigned across the country to win the support of delegates. At the convention these candidates work to win **unpledged** delegate votes until the moment votes are cast. The successful candidate becomes the party's **nominee** for the national election for President.

What Is the Keynote Address?

After the national committee chairperson calls the convention to order, a special speech is given. This is called the **keynote address.** This speech is made by an important party member who usually praises the party, asks for cooperation among its members, and **predicts** party victory in the coming national election.

Susan Molinari, Republican representative for New York, was the keynote speaker at the 1996 Republican National Convention.

How Are National Conventions Organized?

Four committees organize and run each party's national convention. Each state and territory is allowed one member on each committee.

The *Organization Committee* selects the permanent chairperson and convention site.

The *Rules Committee* sets the rules and procedures for running the convention.

The *Credentials Committee* settles any dispute about which delegates from a state or territory may vote.

The *Platform Committee* develops and writes the principles and policies for the party platform. In writing the platform, the committee members usually try to include the ideas and views of the person who is most likely to be named the party's presidential candidate.

What Happens at a National Convention?

When the party platform and the committees are ready, the nominating for the party's presidential candidate begins. Many people give speeches explaining why each person should be the nominee. Presidential candidates who will not get the party's nomination also give speeches to support the person who will most likely be the party's nominee. Other people hold loud demonstrations to get other delegates to vote for a candidate.

Then, the party chairperson calls the roll to begin the balloting. Delegates from each state and territory are asked to vote. Sometimes a candidate will win the party's nomination on the first **roll call,** or vote. This is often the case when a popular President is nominated for a second term. If there is no candidate to receive the majority of votes, the chairperson calls for a second ballot. This happens sometimes when there is more than one popular candidate. Usually only one roll call is needed, however.

Once a presidential candidate is named, the candidate meets with advisers and selects a vice presidential candidate. The presidential candidate usually has a vice presidential candidate in mind before the convention.

The convention ends with the **acceptance speeches** of the new candidates. Acceptance speeches are given to bring the party together. Primary elections and the national conventions can cause differences that need to be calmed. The speeches can sometimes help. After the convention, these candidates and their supporters face several more months of campaigning. Presidential candidates usually try to bring together all the candidates who did not receive the party's nomination. This helps the party to show its **unity** to the nation's voters.

SECTION 5 REVIEW On a separate sheet of paper, write the answers to the following questions using complete sentences.

1) What is the main duty of a delegate to a political convention?

2) What does the Credentials Committee do?

3) What is one way supporters show that they favor a candidate?

4) What is an acceptance speech?

5) Why is it sometimes necessary to have several roll calls when voting at a convention?

6) Who chooses a party's candidate for Vice President?

7) What does the Rules Committee do?

8) Why are alternate delegates needed at conventions?

9) What does the Platform Committee do?

10) How does an acceptance speech show party unity?

What do you think

Which is more important to voters—the party platform or the candidate? Give reasons for your answer.

Words to Know

Donation
A gift or contribution

*★***Political Action Committee (PAC)**
A group that collects money to spend for political purposes

*★***Propaganda**
Ideas, facts, or information spread deliberately to help or harm a cause

*★***Publicity**
Information that is presented to call attention to a candidate's activities in order to get votes

Once a candidate receives the support of a major political party at the party convention, the busiest time of the campaign begins. It takes a candidate and his or her supporters a great deal of time and effort to win votes.

A successful campaign also requires a large amount of money. The most expensive campaigns are those carried on by candidates for national offices such as the presidency.

Why Is So Much Money Needed?

Money is needed for many campaign activities. A national campaign must have offices and staffs all over the country. The cost of running these offices is high. Candidates also need **publicity.** Advertising on radio and television, in newspapers, and on posters costs a great deal of money. Mailing letters to ask for financial support is another expense. Candidates travel from place to place to talk to voters and must pay for travel costs. Often candidates have planes, trains, or buses to take them and their workers all over the country.

How Do Candidates Get the Money They Need?

Many committees are involved in a political campaign. A fund-raising committee is one of the most important. This committee may seek money by appealing to supporters by mail. They may plan dinners or picnics and sell tickets to people who wish to attend. A candidate's own political party contributes some of the money to the campaign. Many candidates spend their own money on their campaigns. Because of the expense, it is difficult for many people to run for public office.

Many people who support a candidate work as volunteers without being paid. Candidates may receive **donations,** but they are limited as to how much money they may accept and how much they may spend on their campaigns. This makes it difficult for any group to contribute a large amount of money to a candidate and then to expect the candidate to vote for laws that serve the group's special interests.

Another way that candidates receive money is through interest groups that set up committees known as **Political Action Committees (PACs).** They collect money to spend for political purposes. A federal law limits the amount that can be given directly to a candidate's campaign fund. But a PAC can spend an unlimited amount on its own to support a candidate. PACs buy television time and newspaper advertisements, and send letters to their members urging them to vote for a candidate. For example, the tobacco industry spends thousands of dollars to support certain candidates. Some people feel that PACs should be limited in the amount of money they contribute and spend. They believe money given to a candidate by a large industry will pressure the candidate to vote for laws that favor that industry.

Who Is on a Candidate's Campaign Staff?

A campaign staff is usually made up of men and women who have worked with the candidate for a long while. They may even be personal friends. Volunteers are very important to the campaign. They do a great deal of work to try to get their candidate elected.

Organization of a Typical Campaign Staff

Campaign Manager Plans and runs the campaign.	**Treasurer** Pays the bills of the campaign.
Press Secretary Handles contacts with news media.	**Media Director** Directs advertising and publicity.
Fund Raiser Seeks money contributions.	**Poll Taker** Conducts surveys to see how popular the candidate is.

SECTION 6 REVIEW On a separate sheet of paper, write the answers to the following questions using complete sentences.

1) What are two things needed to run a big national campaign?

2) What are three ways money may be raised to run a political campaign?

3) What are some expenses of a national campaign?

4) Who makes sure that a candidate becomes well known?

5) Who decides on the plan for running the campaign?

6) Who conducts polls to find out how popular the candidate is?

7) Who pays campaign bills?

8) Who gets money for a political campaign?

9) What is a Political Action Committee?

10) Why do some people think PACs should have a limit on the amount of money they can contribute to a campaign?

What do you think

How does the cost of a political campaign limit who can run for political office?

What Is Political Propaganda?

During a political campaign, candidates use newspapers and television ads to persuade citizens to vote for them. They present their beliefs and ideas as the best answer to the country's problems. They also attack other candidates' views. These methods are sometimes called **propaganda**. Its goal is to influence voters. Here are some of the propaganda methods used in political campaigns.

A *get-on-the-bandwagon* message tries to show that everyone else will vote for the candidate, so you should too.

Name calling happens when a candidate calls another candidate names, such as "radical," "racist," or "extremist." That

makes voters think that other candidates can't be trusted. It promotes fear of what would happen if the other candidate gets elected.

Card stacking is when a candidate presents only the facts that support his or her point of view.

Plain folks is used by candidates who are trying to convince voters that they are just ordinary working people. Candidates dress in working clothes and are seen visiting farms and talking with people.

Candidates may use *testimonials,* or statements from famous people, to win support. Often the famous person or celebrity knows very little about the candidate.

Sometimes it is very hard for voters to decide who will be the best senator, governor, or President. These misleading messages appeal to people's emotions and fears and make it hard to decide who to vote for.

Review

1) What do voters believe when they hear a testimonial—when a famous person says good things about a political candidate?

2) What is misleading about presenting only the facts that support a candidate's stand on an issue?

Words to Know

★Absentee ballot
A ballot that is mailed in before an election

★Dishonorable discharge
To be put out of the armed forces for shameful or disgraceful reasons

Eligible
Someone who qualifies to do something

Incompetent
Lacking qualities needed to do something

★Poll
Place where people vote

Privacy
Being alone, where no one can observe you

★Redistricting
Changing the borders or boundaries of an area

★Register
To fill out a form so one can vote

The right to vote is protected by the Constitution. This freedom to have a voice in choosing leaders is considered to be a privilege. Unfortunately, many citizens do not take advantage of their right to vote. They may lack interest. They may feel that their vote would not make any difference. They may not know how to register to vote. Some people may feel that the government is running well and no change is needed.

Although the United States is a government of the people, the number of people who vote in elections is low. Most democratic countries have higher voter turnouts than the United States. In 1988, there were over 170 million **eligible** voters in the U.S. Only 102 million people, or 57 percent of the voters, voted. In 1992, a similar percentage of voters voted. People over 64 years old had the highest voter turnout. People between the ages of 18 and 24 had the lowest voter turnout.

The qualifications to be a voter are few and simple. No one may be denied the right to vote because of race, color, sex, or religion. These rights are called *civil rights.*

Who May Register to Vote?

In most states, a voter must **register** in his or her own county. Any United States citizen has the right to vote if he or she is at least eighteen years old and has lived in a state for a certain period of time. Although the length of time varies from state to state, it is generally thirty days.

Persons who have been convicted of certain serious crimes may not be permitted to vote. Some states will not permit anyone to vote who has received a **dishonorable discharge** from the armed forces. Most states will not allow people to vote who have been judged mentally **incompetent.**

Do 18 Year Olds Vote?

There are more than 26 million Americans between the ages of 18 and 24. The Twenty-Sixth Amendment to the Constitution, passed in 1971, gave any person 18 or older the right to vote. Before that the voting age was 21.

At the time the Twenty-Sixth Amendment was passed, many young people under 21 were fighting in the Vietnam War and many were involved in the Civil Rights movement. These young people lobbied for the amendment and were enthusiastic about having the right to vote.

In 1972, 48 percent of 18 to 20 year olds voted in the presidential election. In 1988, only 33 percent of the people in this age group voted for President. In 1992, 42 percent of 18 to 24 year olds voted.

Federal, state, and local government employees may vote, but some must follow certain rules when taking part in political activities. Some government workers may not hold public office, serve as a delegate to a political convention, or serve as a candidate's campaign manager.

How Does Registration Work?

Qualified persons who wish to become voters must register in the voting district where they live. A person may register at the courthouse of the voting district. Sometimes other places of registration will be set up. The names of persons who register are recorded on the district's list of qualified voters. These lists of voters are important. They help prevent people from voting more than once in different places. Another reason for registration is to have a record of where voters live and who may legally vote on local matters.

Any citizen who votes regularly is considered an active voter. If a citizen fails to vote in a certain number of elections, his or her name will be taken off the list of active voters. The person would have to register again in order to vote. Some states require voters to reregister from time to time, even if they do vote. Officials feel that they can keep more accurate records of active voters this way. They can then drop from their lists the names of inactive voters who fail to register.

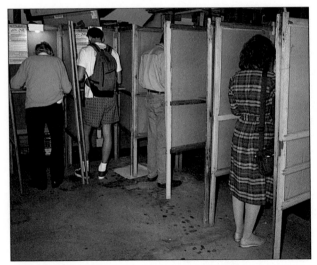
People can vote in the privacy of a voting booth.

How Does Voting Work?

Special places, called **polls,** are set up where people can vote. Often schools or church halls are used for this purpose. Officials working at the polls check their records for a voter's name before they allow him or her to vote.

Votes may be cast on a paper ballot or with a voting machine that shows the ballot. A ballot is a list of candidates and the parties they represent. Sometimes suggested bills or amendments are also on the ballot.

Privacy is an important part of the election process. Early in the country's history, people were required to vote by voice or by raising their hands. Later, when ballots were first used, different sizes and colors were made for each candidate, so others were able to see a voter's choice. Today, voting is done in the **privacy** of a voting booth.

What Are Absentee Ballots?

A person who is going to be away from the voting district for a primary or general election may use an **absentee ballot.** An absentee ballot may be requested in person or by mail. This is a ballot available for a certain length of time before the election day. The ballot must be marked and turned in ahead of time.

What Are Voting Districts?

Boundaries of voting districts are set according to the number of people living within them. Each district within a state must have the same population. As populations change, these boundaries may have to be redrawn. This is called **redistricting.** The United States' population is shifting from rural areas to cities. Urban areas need more representatives than rural areas. This redistricting has not always been done fairly. Certain court cases during the past thirty years have pointed out this problem. Some states were found to have divided their districts unfairly. These states had to redraw their district lines more fairly. Unfair division of political districts is called *gerrymandering*.

Great effort has been made to organize the districts so that each citizen will be fairly represented in both federal and state governments. Each member of the House of Representatives in Washington, D.C., represents about 500,000 people in his or her state.

SECTION 7 REVIEW   On a separate sheet of paper, write the correct word from the Word Bank to complete each sentence below.

WORD BANK
absentee
ballot
polls
population
privacy
qualifications
record

1) A person must have certain _____ in order to vote.

2) One reason for registration is to have a ___ of people who may legally vote.

3) Special places set up for people to vote are called ___.

4) A ___ contains the names of all candidates to be voted on.

5) Today voting is done in the ___ of a voting booth.

6) Redistricting is necessary when ___ changes occur.

7) An ___ ballot is used by people who are not going to be in their own voting district at election time.

What do you think ?

Why do you think it's important for people to have privacy when voting?

Words to Know

Affirmative action
A policy to increase employment for minorities

Circulate
To pass from person to person

★**Compulsory referendum**
A referendum that requires voter approval

★**Initiative**
The process of proposing a law through a petition and then voting on it

★**Optional referendum**
A referendum that a legislature sends to voters willingly

★**Petition referendum**
A referendum that is placed on a ballot to protest a law

★**Recall**
The process of removing a public official from office by voting

★**Referendum**
Having voters vote on a law proposed by popular demand or by a legislative body

In addition to voting for candidates for public office, citizens may also vote on certain issues. Their votes can bring about new laws.

What Is a Referendum?

Certain bills are presented to voters at the polls. This process is called a **referendum.** A referendum takes place only at the state level. There are different kinds of referendums.

Petition Referendum

After a law is passed by the state legislature, citizens may use a petition to protest the law. Someone who objects to the law may **circulate** a petition for others to sign. If enough people sign the petition, a **petition referendum** will be placed on the ballot. Voters can vote for or against the law at the polls. If enough votes are cast against the law, the law will be rejected.

Optional Referendum

In some states the legislature may refer a proposed law to the public for acceptance or rejection. This is called an **optional referendum.** In this case, the legislature is not forced by law to refer the law to the voters, but it does so willingly. Usually the issues referred to the public are ones that have caused a great deal of controversy.

Compulsory Referendum

When state laws require that certain issues be sent to the voters for their approval or rejection, a **compulsory referendum** is used. For example, a state may use a compulsory referendum to get voter approval to change the state constitution. Delaware is the only state that may change its constitution without public approval.

What Is an Initiative?

In some states citizens can suggest a new law to be presented to voters. This suggested law is called an **initiative,** or a proposition. A petition must be signed by a certain number of people before the initiative can be voted on by the legislators or by the citizens. If a majority are in favor of the law, it goes into effect.

Recall

Sometimes citizens want to remove an elected official from office before his or her term has expired. Usually this happens when the official has done something disgraceful while in office. For example, an official might be accused of committing a certain crime such as using public funds for the official's personal life. To remove the official, citizens may use the **recall** process. They draw up a petition, get a large number of signatures, and meet certain legal requirements. Then the recall issue is placed on the ballot. If a majority of the voters are in favor of the recall, the elected person must leave office.

SECTION 8 REVIEW On a separate sheet of paper, write *Yes* or *No* to answer each question below.

1) Are referendums used at the state level?

2) Do voters ever have a chance to approve or reject suggested laws?

3) May states change their constitutions?

4) Is the legislature required to refer an optional referendum to the public?

5) Can an elected official be voted out of office?

6) Does a compulsory referendum need to go to voters for approval or rejection?

7) Can the state of Delaware change its constitution without public approval?

8) Is an initiative also called a referendum?

9) Elected officials can only be removed from office in Delaware.

What do you think

How are initiatives and referendums important to U.S. citizens?

★ Political parties are groups of citizens who share many of the same beliefs about government.

★ The purpose of political parties is to support candidates who agree with the ideas of party members.

★ The two major political parties in the United States since the 1800s are the Democratic and Republican parties.

★ The Democratic party was formed by the Anti-Federalists. Two of its early leaders were Thomas Jefferson and Andrew Jackson.

★ The Republican party grew out of the anti-slavery movement. In 1860 Abraham Lincoln was the first President elected by the Republican Party.

★ Minor, or third, parties appear from time to time. Although no third-party candidate has ever been elected President, minor parties do affect election outcomes. They take votes from major parties and they call attention to certain issues.

★ Most states hold primary elections where voters choose candidates for the general election and delegates to political conventions. The delegates usually support a certain candidate. These conventions are followed by the general election, where the voters actually choose the office holder.

★ Every four years, national conventions are held where delegates decide on the party platform and presidential and vice presidential candidates for the coming election.

★ After conventions, the candidates campaign for several months to convince voters that they should be elected to office.

★ The Constitution guarantees citizens the right to vote. Many citizens are not active voters.

★ A person must register before he or she can vote. Voters must be at least 18 and have lived in an area for a certain amount of time.

★ Voting is done on a voting machine or by paper ballot in the privacy of a voting booth.

★ Voting districts are set up according to population. As population changes take place, redistricting is necessary.

★ Sometimes citizens vote on laws. The referendum and initiative are ways of presenting laws directly to the voters to approve or reject.

★ Voters may use the recall process to remove an elected official from office.

Comprehension: Identifying Facts

On a separate sheet of paper, write the answers to the following questions using complete sentences.

1) What is the purpose of political parties?

2) What do political parties do?

3) What are the two major political parties?

4) Why are third parties important?

5) Which election takes place first: the primary election or the general election?

6) What is an indirect primary?

7) How often are national political conventions held?

8) What is the purpose of a national political convention?

9) Why are political campaigns expensive?

10) Do all voters have to register to vote?

11) Do voters in all the states have to meet the same requirements?

12) Why do U.S. citizens value their right to vote?

13) Citizens can vote for the candidate of their choice. What else might be on a ballot for a voter to consider?

14) What is an initative?

15) What is a referendum?

Comprehension: Understanding Main Ideas

On a separate sheet of paper, write the answers to the following questions using complete sentences.

1) What issue led to the creation of the Republican party? What famous American was supported by the Republican party in 1860?

2) What is the purpose of a state primary election?

3) How is the vice presidential candidate chosen?

4) All citizens who are at least 18 years old may vote in elections if they are registered. Which groups of people are not allowed the privilege of registering to vote?

5) What is a ballot? What are two ways that voting may be done?

6) What is a platform? How is it used?

7) What is the purpose of an absentee ballot?

8) Why is a political campaign so expensive?

Critical Thinking: Write Your Opinion

1) It takes a great deal of money to run a national political campaign. Each year the costs increase. What are some ways the cost of running a national campaign could be limited or decreased?

2) Although citizens are strongly encouraged to vote, many do not. What do you think can be done to encourage more people to vote?

Test Taking Tip | When taking a test where you must write your answer, read the question twice to make sure you understand what is being asked.

"*Ask not what your country can do for you— ask what you can do for your country.*"

President John Fitzgerald Kennedy

Chapter

12

Citizenship

The United States is a nation of immigrants. When the first immigrants came, Native American Indians were scattered across North America. Now people of many different races and nationalities live in the U.S. Today, people who are born in the United States become citizens at birth. A person who was not born in the United States may become a United States citizen through a special process.

In Chapter 12, you will learn more about the immigrants who have come to the United States. You will also learn about how people become citizens and the rights and responsibilities of citizens.

Goals for Learning

★ To identify reasons why people immigrated to the United States

★ To explain immigration quotas today

★ To describe how people become U.S. citizens

★ To identify the requirements for naturalization

★ To describe political asylum

★ To explain the rights and responsibilities of citizenship

Words to Know

Famine
A shortage of food so severe that people may starve

★Immigrant
A person who comes to live in a new country

★Nationality
The state of belonging to a certain country

★Persecution
The act of punishing people for their religious or political beliefs

Quota
An assigned number

Refuge
Protection or shelter

★Refugee
A person who flees from a country to a safer place

People have immigrated to the United States at different times and for different reasons. Through the years **immigrants** have come to the U.S. in great numbers.

Why Did People Come to America?

The first settlers came to the United States to gain the freedom they did not have in the countries of their birth. Since that time, many immigrants have come to escape unfair treatment or to seek the freedoms guaranteed by the U.S. Constitution. Wars and **famines** drove some people to leave their countries. These people chose the United States as the land of **refuge** and opportunity. Large numbers of immigrants came as laborers, or workers. Most of the early immigrants to the U.S. came from European countries. Today most immigrants come to the United States from Asia and Latin America.

When Did Most Immigrants Come to the United States?

There have been four major waves of immigration to the United States since the 1600s. The first wave began with the colonists who came from Europe between 1600 and the beginning of the Revolutionary War in 1775.

The second wave of immigrants came between 1820 and the 1870s. During that time, many people came from Europe to escape famine and hard economic times. After gold was discovered in California in the mid-1800s, many people came from across the Pacific Ocean to get rich.

The third wave of immigration came between 1880 and 1920. Many of these people came from Europe and entered the United States at Ellis Island in New York.

The fourth wave of immigration began in 1965 when the U.S. immigration laws were changed. The change made it possible for more people to immigrate to the U.S.

The Statue of Liberty

The Statue of Liberty stands on Liberty Island in New York Harbor. Made of copper hammered on iron, it stands 151 feet tall. A newly restored "Miss Liberty" was given a one hundredth birthday celebration on July 4, 1986. The statue was a gift to the United States from France. It has greeted thousands of immigrants as they sailed into New York Harbor.

A bronze plaque on the Statue of Liberty contains these words from the poem, "The New Colossus," by Emma Lazarus:

> *Give me your tired, your poor,*
>
> *Your huddled masses yearning to breathe free,*
>
> *The wretched refuse of your teeming shore.*
>
> *Send these, the homeless, tempest-tost to me,*
>
> *I lift my lamp beside the golden door!*

Near Liberty Island is Ellis Island. It was an immigrant station until 1954. Many immigrants to the United States were required to stay there for a period of time to determine whether they were eligible to enter the country.

During the immigration wave of the early 1900s, many Europeans arrived at New York Harbor. The Statue of Liberty was a symbol of refuge and freedom for the immigrants.

What Laws Affect Immigration?

In 1921, a law was passed to limit the number of people who could come to the United States. It set **quotas** by country. In 1965, the Immigration and **Nationality** Act ended quotas based on nationality. This law set an annual quota of 170,000 people from the Eastern Hemisphere and 120,000 people from the Western Hemisphere. In 1995, the total number of immigrants allowed to enter the United States each year was set at 675,000. Sometimes more immigrants come to the U.S. than what the quota sets up. Sometimes **refugees** from political or religious **persecution** are also allowed to come. For example, after the Vietnam War many Vietnamese and Cambodian refugees came to the United States to escape the war in their countries.

Chang-Lin Tien

When the Communist government took over China, a boy named Chang-Lin Tien and his family fled the country. Tien sought refuge in the United States in the 1950s when he was 21. He became a U.S. citizen in 1969.

Tien received scholarships to study at the University of Louisville in Kentucky and at Princeton University in New Jersey. After receiving his Ph.D., Tien joined the faculty of the University of California at Berkeley. In 1990 Chang-Lin Tien was named chancellor of the University of California at Berkeley. He is an example of the many immigrant success stories.

Often more people wish to come to the United States than the yearly limit allows. People who have relatives in the U.S. have a better chance of being admitted than those who do not. Then each case is judged by itself. People who have special talents or job skills may qualify over those who do not.

SECTION 1 REVIEW On a separate sheet of paper, match the sentence beginnings in Part 1 with the endings in Part 2. Write the correct letter next to each number.

Part 1

1) Most of the early immigrants to the U.S. came from . . .

2) Today many people immigrate to the United States from. . .

3) Many immigrants have come to the United States to . . .

4) People who have relatives in the U.S. or have certain skills . . .

5) After the war in Vietnam, many Vietnamese and Cambodians . . .

Part 2

a) Asia and Latin America.

b) escape mistreatment, famines, and revolutions in other countries.

c) are more likely to be admitted to the U.S.

d) European countries.

e) came to this country as political refugees.

What do you think

Should there be a limit on the number of immigrants who can come from one country? Give reasons for your answer. Did your family immigrate to the United States from another country? If they did, tell when they came to the United States and why.

Most Americans are **native**-born. A person who is born in the United States or in one of its territories automatically becomes a U.S. citizen. A person born to American parents in a foreign country is also a United States citizen. In most cases, a child born to foreign parents in the United States is considered a United States citizen. The parents of these children must be living in the United States at the time of the child's birth. Sometimes there are questions about whether a person is legally a United States citizen. These matters must be settled by the Department of Justice. The Immigration and Naturalization Service is an agency of the Department of Justice. It is in charge of laws that have to do with **aliens.** The agency says who may enter this country, who may become a citizen, and who is to be **deported.**

Why Do Citizens of Foreign Countries Live in the U.S.?

Aliens are people who are citizens of another country but who are in the United States for a particular reason. They may be visitors or they may have temporary jobs in the United States. While aliens are in the United States, they must follow the laws of the country. They enjoy most of the rights of American citizens. Aliens must register once a year in January with the United States Immigration and Naturalization Service. This is done so that immigration officials have a record of the location and activities of aliens. Some aliens may decide to become citizens. If they become citizens they no longer have to report to the agency. They gain full rights as a citizen, such as the right to vote, serve on a jury, or hold a public office. Aliens who have broken laws or have failed to pay taxes may be deported.

An alien who is deported must leave the United States and return to the country of his or her birth. There are many reasons why an alien might be deported. The person may have committed a serious crime. Perhaps the person is loyal to some government that is unfriendly to the United States.

Many aliens hope to become citizens of the United States. They can do this by a process called **naturalization.**

What Is Naturalization?

Congress has made rules for aliens to follow in order to become citizens of the U.S., or naturalized citizens. The rules for citizenship say that aliens must:

1. be at least 18 years old
2. have lived in the United States for
    a. five years, or
    b. three years if married to a U.S. citizen, or
    c. less time if the person has served a year in some branch of the armed services
3. make an application, or a request, for naturalization to the immigration authorities
4. be able to speak, read, and write English reasonably well
5. have two witnesses testify that they are good, honest people
6. know about the history of the U.S. and its government
7. take an examination about U.S. history and government
8. promise not to support any government or belief that would overthrow the government of the United States
9. make an oath of loyalty to the U.S. in court before a judge

After aliens have successfully done these things, they become citizens of the United States. They gain all the rights and privileges of citizens by birth. The children of naturalized U.S. citizens automatically become U.S. citizens when their parents do. These children must be under the age of 18 and living in the United States at the time.

It is possible for naturalized citizens to lose their citizenship. This can happen for a number of reasons. Usually it is because the aliens were dishonest about themselves when they became naturalized citizens. Taking away citizenship has to be done by court order.

What Is Political Asylum?

The United States also offers protection called **political asylum** to aliens. The word "asylum" refers to a place of safety. Political asylum means a place where a person is safe from the dangerous actions or beliefs of his or her own country or government.

Political asylum may be given to visitors, athletes, artists, sailors, or workers from another government. It is given to these people because they feel mistreated by their own

The Oath of Allegiance

People who want to become citizens of the U.S. must take this oath:

"I hereby declare, on oath, that I absolutely and entirely renounce and abjure all allegiance and fidelity to any foreign prince, potentate, state, or sovereignty, to whom or which I have heretofore been a subject or citizen; that I will support and defend the Constitution and laws of the United States of America against all enemies, foreign and domestic; that I will bear true faith and allegiance to the same; that I will bear arms on behalf of the United States when required by the law; that I will perform noncombatant service in the armed forces of the United States when required by law; that I will perform work of national importance under civilian direction when required by the law; and that I take this obligation freely without any mental reservation or purpose of evasion, so help me God."

countries. The United States offers them protection until it is clear why they wish to leave their native lands. If their reasons are strong enough, the aliens are allowed to stay. They may apply for United States citizenship.

SECTION 2 REVIEW On a separate sheet of paper, write the correct word from the Word Bank to complete each sentence.

<table>
<tr><td>

WORD BANK

aliens

asylum

birth

citizen

country

deported

Immigration

January

Justice

naturalization

</td><td>

1) Most Americans are citizens by ___.

2) A person born to American parents in a foreign country is a United States ___.

3) Children born in the United States to parents who represent another government become citizens of their parents' ___.

4) Questions about who is legally a United States citizen are settled by the ___ and Naturalization Service.

5) Citizens of other countries who are in the United States are called ___.

6) Aliens must register with the Immigration and Naturalization Service each ___.

7) The Immigration and Naturalization Service is an agency of the ___ Department.

8) An alien who is ___ is forced to leave this country and return to his or her own country.

9) The legal process a person must go through to become a United States citizen is called ___.

10) A person seeking ___ is looking for a safe place to live.

</td></tr>
</table>

What do you think

Do you think an alien who commits a serious crime should be sent back to her or his country? Why, or why not?

Words to Know

Equality
Having the same rights as others

★Patriotism
Love or devotion to one's country

Each person is born with different talents and abilities. In school, everyone does not make the same grades. Not everyone has the same athletic ability or the same artistic or musical talent. In the business world, not everyone is able to do some jobs. So what does the Declaration of Independence mean when it says, "All men are created equal"?

Equality among citizens is based on opportunities and rights. All American citizens have the rights described in the Constitution and its amendments.

The chart on page 237 shows some rights given to American citizens by the First Amendment to the U.S. Constitution. It describes what citizens may and may not do in practicing these rights.

What Duties Do Citizens Have?

Rights and protections could not survive unless citizens took their duties seriously. To help protect and preserve the rights of citizenship, Americans have these duties:

Civic duties	**Political duties**
• support the government	• vote in elections
• observe laws	• keep informed about government
• defend the country	

An important duty for all citizens is to learn about laws that affect them and their communities. Citizens are expected to obey the laws. Citizens are also expected to express their opinions about laws that should be changed.

Young people can prepare for the day when they will be voters. They can do this by keeping up with current events in local, state, national, and international communities.

How Some Rights May or May Not Be Used

Right:	Freedom of Religion
Citizens May:	Worship as they please and join any church they wish.
Citizens May Not:	Get in the way of anyone else's religious freedom.
Right:	Freedom of Speech
Citizens May:	Speak their feelings, even about government, without fear of punishment.
Citizens May Not:	Harm others with their speech or prevent others from speaking freely.
Right:	Freedom of Assembly
Citizens May:	Gather in groups to discuss issues or to demonstrate peaceably.
Citizens May Not:	Assemble to cause a riot, hurt people, or damage property.
Right:	Freedom of the Press
Citizens May:	Publish opinions of issues without fear of punishment.
Citizens May Not:	Publish false statements or pictures that would harm an individual or group.

Before citizens are old enough to vote, they serve their country and community by studying about their government. People also practice citizenship by participating in school and community projects. These projects often have a goal of improving the community or correcting a problem. The projects usually require cooperation and a democratic attitude. At school, these projects might include playing in the band or taking part in student government. Respecting school rules, teachers, and fellow classmates is another way to support our rights and freedoms.

In the community, young citizens can belong to clubs that promote **patriotism.** They can also volunteer time to one of many community groups that help other people achieve a better quality of life.

For many years young men have been required to register for the military draft when they become 18 years old. Sometimes they were even required to serve in the military for about two years. Today, the United States has a volunteer military.

Some government leaders think that all young people should be required to give some service to their community. The service could be military or civilian. Some schools and colleges require students to provide a number of hours of community service before they can graduate.

Some people feel that young people should be paid for the community service they do. Others think it should be unpaid. They believe that young people will take pride in giving service to their community. Young Americans have many talents to share with other people. Some people believe that the country would be stronger if more people shared their talents with others.

SECTION 3 REVIEW On a separate sheet of paper, answer the following questions with a *yes* or *no*.

1) May citizens worship as they please?

2) May citizens assemble to start a riot?

3) May citizens say how they feel about the government without fear of punishment?

4) May citizens write a letter to the newspaper about government?

5) May citizens publish lies in order to hurt a certain group?

6) May citizens gather for peaceful demonstrations?

7) May citizens publish their opinions and criticisms of issues without fear of punishment?

8) May citizens use their rights to break a law?

9) May citizens enjoy rights that are not listed in the Bill of Rights?

What do you think Do you think young Americans should be required to do community service? Why, or why not? Do you think that citizens should be required by law to vote? Why, or why not?

Public Service Advertising

Once this man dreamed of going to college.
Today he finally made it.

For more than fifty years, The College Fund has helped
thousands of young men and women achieve goals their grandparents
could only dream of. We are proud to have made a critical difference
in the lives of so many. But our job is not done. With your help,
we will continue to bring many more dreams within reach.

SUPPORT THE COLLEGE FUND/UNCF.
A MIND IS A TERRIBLE THING TO WASTE.

1-800-332-UNCF

The slogan "A mind is a terrible thing to waste" was used to promote contributions to the United Negro College Fund. It is what is called a public service advertisement, or PSA. The United Negro College Fund is an organization that provides scholarships for African-American students.

Public service advertising began during World War II. In the early 1940s, an organization known as the War Advertising Council worked to help the U.S. government's war effort. The council created advertisements to encourage Americans to buy war bonds. Other ads helped recruit men into the armed forces and persuaded women to work in factory jobs to help.

Later this council was named the Advertising Council. It has created ads that promote safety and education. These ads are printed in newspapers, magazines, and on advertising billboards. They are also broadcast on TV and radio shows. The advertisements are created by volunteers. The media donates the time or space to run these ads.

A number of public service ads have used characters, such as Smokey the Bear and McGruff the Crime Dog. Smokey the Bear has become a symbol of the importance of preventing forest fires. McGruff the Crime Dog is a crime prevention symbol. The council created the slogan "Buckle Up for Safety" to promote use of automobile seat belts.

Public service announcements and advertising are a way that the mass media serves citizens to create awareness of important public issues.

Review

1) Advertisements usually are shown to sell a product or service. What do public service ads sell?

2) How do you think public service ads help citizens?

3) Why do you think advertisers and the mass media are willing to donate their creativity, time, or space to public service ads or announcements?

Citizens & Government

Two Famous Children of Immigrants

Cesar Chavez

Cesar Chavez was born in Arizona in 1927. His parents were born in Mexico and had come to the United States. When Cesar was a boy, he and his family became migrant farmworkers in California. Migrant farmworkers harvest crops and move from place to place as crops need picking.

Chavez dedicated his life to helping farmworkers. He organized the poor and under-paid workers. By using peaceful means, he helped them get better pay and working conditions. Change did not always come easily. For example, it took five years for Chavez to get better working conditions for grape pickers in California. Under Chavez's leadership, the grape pickers refused to work for almost five years. These workers did this to make the grape farm owners give in to the workers' needs. Finally the farm owners agreed to give the workers contracts and higher pay.

Cesar Chavez

Colin Powell

General Colin Powell

Colin Powell is the first African American to serve as chairman of the Joint Chiefs of Staff. This is one of the most important positions in the Department of Defense.

Powell was born in the Harlem area of New York City in 1937. His parents were immigrants from Jamaica. They had little education. Powell attended the City College of New York. He enrolled in the Reserve Officers Training Corps (ROTC). When he graduated, he was the top student in his ROTC class.

After many years in the army, Powell became a four-star general. He worked very hard to settle problems in peaceful ways. President Bush invited him to serve as chairman of the Joint Chiefs of Staff. Powell led the Joint Chiefs of Staff during Operation Desert Storm in 1992. During this time, the American people came to admire Powell. In 1996, many people encouraged Powell to run for President. He decided he would not be a candidate.

Review

1) What type of work did Cesar Chavez and his family do? What success did he have?

2) In what way is Colin Powell's life a success story?

★ The United States is a nation of immigrants. Immigrants have come to the United States from all parts of the world.

★ The first settlers were escaping what they felt was unfair treatment in their own countries. Other settlers came to escape famine and revolutions or to have an opportunity to improve their lives.

★ For many years, most of the immigrants came to the United States from Europe. More recently the largest number of immigrants have come from Asia and Latin America.

★ The United States offers a home to refugees. It grants political asylum to people who leave their countries because they are being mistreated by their country or government.

★ Anyone born in the United States or its territories becomes a United States citizen. Anyone born of American parents anywhere in the world also becomes a U.S. citizen.

★ An alien is someone who was born in another country but who is in the United States as a visitor, worker, or student. An alien may become a naturalized U.S. citizen by meeting certain requirements.

★ U.S. citizens are guaranteed special rights by the Bill of Rights.

★ Responsible citizens take an interest in government. They take part in community activities, and they vote regularly.

★ When people carry out their duties as citizens and respect the rights of others, the quality of life improves for everyone.

U.S. Immigration Waves

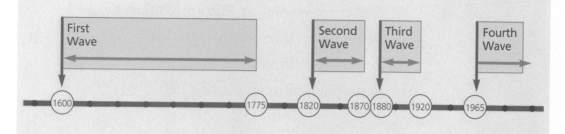

Comprehension: Identifying Facts

On a separate sheet of paper, write the words from the Word Bank to complete the sentences.

WORD BANK

alien
Asian
asylum
duties
European
famine
government
law
political
protected
rights
student
unfair
vote
war
wisely
world

1) The first settlers came to America to escape ____ treatment.

2) Early settlers also came to America to escape ____ or ____.

3) Before 1930 most of these immigrants came from ____ countries.

4) Today, most immigrants come from ____ and Latin American countries.

5) America also offers a home to religious or ____ refugees.

6) An ____ is someone born in another country and who is in the United States as a visitor, worker, or ____.

7) An alien is required to do certain things by ____ in order to become a United States citizen.

8) People born in the United States or born of American citizens anywhere in the ____ are United States citizens.

9) Foreigners who feel that they are mistreated by their government may seek a place of safety, or political ____, in the United States.

10) People who seek asylum are ____ by the U.S.

11) United States citizens have certain ____ given by the Bill of Rights.

12) Citizens also have ____ that are required by law.

13) Responsible citizens learn about their ____.

14) Responsible citizens ____ regularly.

15) Responsible citizens use their rights ____.

Comprehension: Understanding Main Ideas

On a separate sheet of paper, write the answers to the following questions using complete sentences.

1) If a person is not a citizen of the United States by birth, how else can he or she become a citizen? Name two requirements for a person to become a new citizen.

2) What are immigration quotas?

3) What are two duties of every good citizen?

Critical Thinking: Write Your Opinion

1) Do you think the United States government should increase the limits on the number of people who may immigrate to the United States? Why or why not?

2) All U.S. citizens have basic rights that are guaranteed by the Constitution. Which do you think is the most important right you enjoy as a citizen?

Test Taking Tip If you don't know the answer to a question, put a check beside it and go on. Then when you are finished with the other questions, go back to the checked questions and try to answer them.

"...America's leadership and prestige depend, not merely upon our unmatched material progress, riches, and military strength, but on how we use our power in the interests of world peace and human betterment."

President Dwight D. Eisenhower

Chapter

13

The United States and Governments of the World

Our country is part of a large, global community that is made up of all the countries of the world. These countries, including the United States, depend on one another for trade, services, and protection. Many countries view the United States as the world leader. The United States is a wealthy and important nation in the world.

In Chapter 13, you will learn about U.S. foreign policy, the United Nations, and the governments of other countries.

Goals for Learning

★ To identify the goals of United States' foreign policy

★ To explain the purpose and work of the United Nations

★ To describe the governments of Great Britain and France

★ To describe changes that have happened in the former Soviet Union

★ To identify the types of government in China and Japan

★ To identify the types of government in Mexico, Cuba, Brazil, and Argentina

★ To describe the governments of Israel and other areas of the Middle East

Words to Know

★Ally
A country joined to another country by a treaty or agreement

Cooperative
Willing to work together

★Embassy
A country's headquarters in a foreign country

★Free trade
Trade between countries without legal barriers on imports or exports

★North American Free Trade Agreement (NAFTA)
An agreement that took affect in 1994 that lowers tariffs and increases trade between North American countries

Participate
To take part in

★Tariff
A charge for bringing products or goods into a country

Foreign policy today includes a wide range of activities. U.S. leaders **participate** in diplomatic meetings with other world leaders. The country has trade agreements with other countries and is a member of many world organizations. The United States also participates in peacekeeping military actions with other countries. All of these activities are part of the United States' foreign policy.

The federal government is in charge of making and carrying out U.S. foreign policy. The power to do this is shared by Congress and the President. Congress has the power to regulate foreign trade, support the armed forces, and declare war. The President is commander-in-chief of the armed forces and oversees relations with other countries.

What Are the Goals of U.S. Foreign Policy?

Maintaining **cooperative** relationships with other countries and keeping the country safe are two goals of U.S. foreign policy. Another goal is to promote trade in order to keep business strong and the economy growing.

Foreign policy also works to promote democracy. The U.S. helps some nations with their economies and sometimes offers military aid.

Another goal of foreign policy is to protect human rights. The U.S. has provided relief to victims of disasters, and refused aid to countries that deny basic human rights to their people.

How Is Foreign Policy Carried Out?

Although the President is in charge of foreign policy, the President receives assistance from many agencies and advisers to carry it out. The secretaries of state and defense both play a major role in foreign affairs. The Vice President is also sometimes called on to assist the President.

The State Department is led by the secretary of state. Warren Christopher (right) was appointed secretary of state by President Clinton in 1993.

The State Department's Role

The State Department maintains over 140 **embassies** throughout the world. A U.S. embassy is our headquarters in a foreign country. This is where an ambassador works.

The United States provides millions of dollars in aid to developing countries. This foreign aid is distributed by the Agency for International Development (AID), which acts in cooperation with the State Department.

The Defense Department's Role

National security is an important part of American foreign policy. The Department of Defense carries out national security policies. This includes protecting the countries that are our **allies.** The United States helps to solve conflicts in other countries that may threaten world peace. The Defense Department maintains the army, navy, and air force.

What Are Trade Policies?

Our economy depends on trade with other countries. Many U.S. businesses want to sell their goods throughout the

What Is NAFTA?

On December 17, 1992, President Bush, Canadian Prime Minister Mulroney, and Mexican President Salinas, signed the **North American Free Trade Agreement (NAFTA).** It was signed into law by President Clinton on November 17, 1993, and it took effect January 1, 1994. The agreement lowers **tariffs** in order to increase trade between Mexico, the United States, and Canada. This trade agreement forms one of the largest free-trade zones in the world. It includes a market of about 400 million people. It provides about $6.5 trillion worth of goods and services per year.

People in favor of NAFTA believe that more jobs will be creatd in the U.S. They think this will happen because more goods from the U.S. will be sold.

Some people are not in favor of NAFTA. Labor unions think that U.S. companies will move to Mexico where they can pay workers lower wages. Union members believe Americans will lose jobs if this happens.

world. Our foreign policy sets up trade policies to allow this. Trade policies also protect U.S. companies from losing too much business to other countries.

Sometimes the government imposes tariffs or sets quotas on items coming into the country. These tariffs, or fees for importing goods, help to protect products made in the U.S. When a quota is placed on a foreign product, only a certain number can be sold in the country.

The United States helps foreign businesses by offering low-cost loans. Sometimes foreign countries use these loans to buy goods made in the U.S. In 1988, the U.S. loaned more than 700 million dollars to foreign countries, with the condition that some of the money be used to buy U.S. steel and machines.

Agreements are sometimes made to promote **free trade.** The United States and another country will agree to reduce trade barriers to help businesses in both countries.

SECTION 1 REVIEW On a separate sheet of paper, write the correct word from the Word Bank to complete each sentence below.

WORD BANK

federal

human

national security

safe

State

Tariffs

trade

1) The _____ government is in charge of foreign policy.

2) Keeping the country _____ and protecting _____ rights are two goals of U.S. foreign policy.

3) The _____ Department has embassies in other countries.

4) The Defense Department is responsible for _____.

5) _____ that protect products made in the U.S. are a part of our _____ policy.

What do you think **?**

Will NAFTA create more jobs in the United States? Explain your answer.

Words to Know

Humanitarian
Having to do with promoting human welfare and social reform

Mediator
A person or group who talks with people on both sides of an argument to settle their differences

★**Sanction**
An action taken to force a country to obey a law or rule

The United Nations (UN) is an international organization of about 185 countries. It is the world's most influential organization. It formed in 1945 when representatives from fifty countries met in San Francisco, California. They wrote a charter with these main purposes:

- to keep the peace
- to bring about good world relations
- to help find answers to world economic, social, cultural, and **humanitarian** problems
- to protect basic human rights and freedoms throughout the world

The UN meets in the UN building in New York City. At a fiftieth birthday celebration in 1995, world leaders praised the work the UN has done. They praised its peacekeeping efforts and its work to help people of the world.

How Does the United Nations Work?

The UN is a world organization, but not a world government. Each country in the UN has its own government. The UN has six main divisions:

- General Assembly
- Security Council
- Economic and Social Council
- International Court of Justice
- Secretariat
- Trusteeship Council

Every country that belongs to the UN is a member of the General Assembly. People from each country are elected to serve in the other five divisions. The daily business of the UN is carried out by a Secretary-General who is the head of the Secretariat. The Secretary-General is responsible for United Nations business. The Security Council decides

Trygve Lie of Norway, the first Secretary-General of the UN, served from 1946-1953.

what actions the UN will take. It is made up of fifteen member nations. Five countries have permanent seats on the Security Council. These are the United States, Great Britain, France, China, and the former Soviet Union. Other members are selected for two-year terms by the General Assembly.

The UN acts as a **mediator** between countries and groups within countries that are having disagreements. It can place **sanctions** on a country that breaks rules. It cannot make a country obey. It can call on UN countries to send out troops to act as peacekeepers in troubled areas. Their goal is to keep peace, but they have sometimes become part of the conflict. The United Nations has used its military in Korea, Israel, Palestine, Congo/Zaire, Iran, Iraq, and Bosnia.

Sometimes countries that are members of the UN do not agree with the actions that are taken. However, the UN has given hope for world peace and human rights as no other world organization has been able to do in the past. Today the UN has financial problems. Many members are not paying their dues to keep the organization going.

SECTION 2 REVIEW On a separate sheet of paper, write the answers to the following questions.

1) How many countries belong to the UN?

2) Name one purpose of the UN stated in its charter.

3) What is a sanction?

4) Which countries are permanent members of the UN Security Council?

5) Why does the UN have financial problems?

What do you think

What do you think the UN should do if a country does not pay its dues?

Words to Know

*Common law
*Group of laws
based on customs*

*Common market
*A group of
countries that
has come together
to remove trade
restrictions*

*Constitutional
monarchy
*A government run
by a constitution
and a single royal
family*

*European Economic
Community (EEC)
*A group of twelve
European nations
that is becoming a
common market*

*North Atlantic
Treaty Organi-
zation (NATO)
*An organization
of sixteen nations
joined together to
create a common
defense*

*Prime minister
*The chief executive
in some countries*

Most of the people who originally settled the United States came from European countries. Many of the countries of western Europe were allies with the United States during the world wars. The United States has close ties with the countries in western Europe, especially with Great Britain and France.

What Kind of Government Does Great Britain Have?

In Great Britain all the power is given to one central group of people. This is called the Parliament. Although the British government is really a **constitutional monarchy,** the Parliament holds the power. It makes the laws and elects the **prime minister**.

Comparing the Governments of the United States and Great Britain

Although Great Britain's government is based on a constitution, the constitution is quite different from the United States Constitution. Only part of Great Britain's constitution is in writing. The constitution is made up of laws passed by Parliament, old documents, and **common law.** Common law is a group of laws based on the customs of the people. The unwritten part of the constitution is based on tradition. This includes the way the Parliament and monarch work together.

Who Is the Chief Executive of Great Britain?

The chief executive of Great Britain is the prime minister. The prime minister is elected by the controlling party in Parliament, and is formally appointed by the monarch. She or he is not elected directly by the people like the President of the United States. The British prime minister does not have the power to veto a law as the U.S. President does.

The British Parliament is one strong central branch of government. It makes the laws and sees that they are enforced. The Parliament is made up of two houses: the House of

Lords and the House of Commons. Parliament works much like the United States Congress. However, only members of the House of Commons are elected. Members of the House of Lords receive their membership by inheriting it, or as an honor. In the U.S. Congress, both houses are elected.

What Kind of Government Does France Have?

France is a republic form of government with a constitution. It has had this type of government since the French Revolution in 1789. Although France has a parliamentary form of government, it is quite different from the governments of the United States and Great Britain.

President Clinton (left) meets with French President Jacques Chirac (center) and German Chancellor Helmut Kohl.

The government of France is led by a strong president, supported by a parliamentary system. The French president is elected to a seven-year term and may be re-elected to an unlimited number of terms. The government also includes a prime minister, appointed by the president, and cabinet ministers who head each government department.

The Parliament is made up of two houses, the Senate and the National Assembly. The National Assembly makes the laws. Even though it is similar to the United States Congress, the National Assembly is very limited in the laws it may make. The president makes all foreign policy laws and laws about other national matters. The Assembly takes care of such things as education, crime, and civil rights. The French president can break up Parliament at any time and call for new elections. In the United States, laws must go through the legislature and Congress cannot be broken up by the President.

What Is the European Economic Community?

Twelve European nations formed the **European Economic Community (EEC)** in 1957. It has been slowly moving toward forming a **common market.** In a common market,

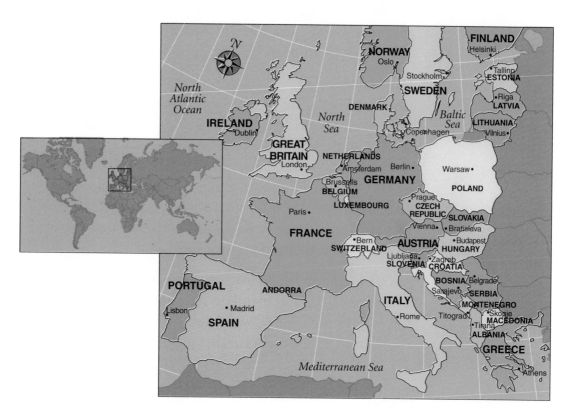

the members combine their economies for the good of all members. Tariffs among the nations are dropped. A common tariff for all other countries has been adopted by the EEC. By 1992, the EEC ended all economic restrictions among its members. The countries are gaining the freedom to trade and move goods easily through the member countries. Countries that belong to the EEC are Belgium, Denmark, France, Germany, Greece, Ireland, Italy, Luxembourg, the Netherlands, Portugal, Spain, and the United Kingdom.

The United States is working with the EEC to see that restrictions against American goods are not increased. Some members of the EEC do not want to trade with the United States because of high U.S. tariffs.

As a result of its economic success, the EEC hopes to improve political and military relations between countries within the organization. Some countries of Eastern Europe that are moving toward democracy are receiving aid from the Western European EEC nations.

What Is NATO?

The **North Atlantic Treaty Organization (NATO)** was formed after World War II. It is an organization of sixteen western nations to provide a common defense against a possible military attack by the Soviet Union. The United States has been a leading member. The U.S. had a large supply of atomic weapons. The NATO countries agreed that an armed attack against one or more of them would be considered an attack against them all.

NATO members held a fortieth anniversary meeting in 1989. At this time all members agreed to reduce armed forces in Europe. NATO was later involved in peacekeeping missions in the Bosnian conflict in 1994.

SECTION 3 REVIEW On a separate sheet of paper, write the correct answer to complete each sentence.

1) In Great Britain, power is given to one central group known as the (prime minister, constitution, Parliament).

2) The (monarch, prime minister, president) of Great Britain is elected by the party that controls Parliament.

3) The French government is led by a strong (party, president, monarch).

4) Countries that belong to the (EEC, UN, NATO) are able to trade with each other without tariffs.

5) NATO was formed to protect its members from (China, trade policies, the Soviet Union).

What do you think

Why do you think NATO reduced its number of armed forces in Europe?

Words to Know

★Communism
A plan for government that seeks to eliminate private property

Russia, formerly part of the Soviet Union, was ruled by the Communist party for many years. The communists took over the country in 1917. **Communism** is based on the idea that there should be no private property but that the state should own everything. The communists overthrew the leader, or czar, and took over all business, industry, and farm land. The "Supreme Soviet" ran the government. A premier led the government and operated much like a dictator. All of the government power was held by one political party.

Boris Yeltsin, the first elected leader in Russian history, became president of Russia in 1991.

How Has Government Changed in Russia?

In 1991 the leaders of the Communist party lost power. The fifteen republics that made up the Soviet Union began to break away and form independent states. The economy was in serious trouble. People could not buy food or other necessary products. Eleven republics joined together with Russia in an effort to improve conditions. This new union is called the *Commonwealth of Independent States* (CIS).

Today, free elections are being held in Russia and in the independent republics. They are trying to make new laws and to improve industry and trade. People are trying to improve their daily lives. They are hoping there will soon be more food, jobs, and lower prices.

The United States wants these developing countries to succeed. It encourages trade and friendly relations with Russia and the other republics. Some U.S. companies are starting businesses in the republics of the CIS.

The people of the new republics, including Russia, believed their countries would improve quickly when communist rule ended, but they have not. Crime has increased in Russia and factories have closed in other republics. Prices have risen, and jobs are still scarce. The problems caused by some economic and political changes have made leaders unpopular. Leaders disagree on how quickly changes should be made.

Even with the problems, the people are enjoying new freedoms. They can own private property and buy consumer goods, even though prices are high. There are still people in the governments of the republics and Russia who would like to return to a communist government.

Today people have the freedom to vote for the kind of leadership they want. The new countries will depend on support from democratic countries, such as the United States, Great Britain, and France to remain strong.

SECTION 4 REVIEW Choose the correct ending for each sentence. On a separate sheet of paper, write the complete sentence.

1) Communism is based on the idea that the
   (a) state owns all property.
   (b) people should own everything.

2) Some of the republics that were part of the Soviet Union joined to form the
   (a) Communist Republics.
   (b) Commonwealth of Independent States (CIS).

3) Since 1991
   (a) the communists have controlled the government.
   (b) free elections have been held.

4) The twelve republics
   (a) are working to improve the economy.
   (b) want to go back to communism.

5) The United States is encouraging
   (a) the return of communism to Russia.
   (b) trade and friendly relations with the Commonwealth of Independent States.

What do you think

Do you think Russia and the Commonwealth of Independent States will return to communism? Why, or why not?

Words to Know

★Diet
Japan's legislative body

Diplomatic relations
When a country sends an ambassador to another country

★Politburo
The policy-making body of a communist government

China and Japan are important countries in Asia. The People's Republic of China is a huge country with over a billion people. It is a poor country that is becoming modernized. China is trying to build industries and to improve its economy. By contrast, Japan is a small island country. It also has a large population. Japan has a strong economy and is highly industrialized.

What Kind of Government Does China Have?

China has a communist government. It is the largest communist country in the world. The Communist party gained power in 1949 under the leadership of Mao Tse-tung. Under Mao, China kept out of world affairs,

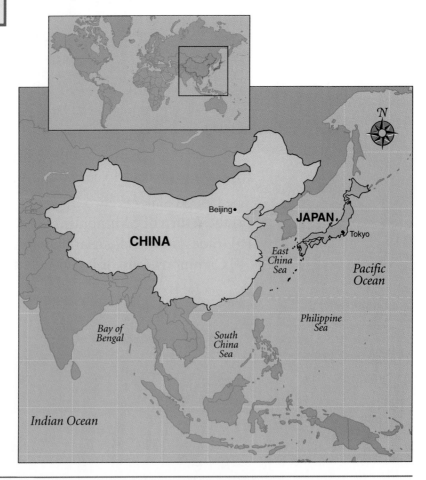

Mao Tse-tung was the leader of China from 1949-1976.

and private ownership was discouraged. Government controls much of the country's industry.

The highest legislative body in the government of China is called the *National People's Congress.* It elects the president and vice president. It also appoints members of the court, the military commission, and the state council.

The Central Committee, another part of the communist government, is made up of high ranking officials. The Central Committee selects members of the **Politburo.** This group makes policies for the People's Republic of China. The highest ranking Communist party member is the general secretary. The general secretary and staff supervise the government and command the military.

The Chinese government has given its military leaders great power. The government depends on these military leaders to maintain a powerful army and navy. China spends large amounts of money on nuclear weapons. Other countries that are friendly to China, such as Pakistan and Iran, are sharing in the nuclear knowledge. China is also trying to expand its influence by claiming small islands in the South China Sea.

What Rights Do Chinese Citizens Have?

Many Chinese citizens are unhappy with the lack of individual freedoms and rights within their country. Recently, some citizens have spoken out against the government and asked for changes. They want certain rights and freedoms, such as free elections, freedom of speech, and individual rights.

What Is Taiwan?

When the Communists took control of China's government from the Nationalists in 1949, the Nationalists retreated to the island of Taiwan off the coast of China. They still remain there today. Both Taiwan and the People's Republic of China claim to be the true government of all the Chinese people. Unlike China, Taiwan continued to carry on trade with Europe and the United States. As a result, Taiwan's economy has grown.

What Are U.S.-Chinese Relations Like?

The United States has had a friendly relationship with the government of Taiwan. Between 1949 and the early 1970s, the U.S. had **diplomatic relations** with Taiwan. In the early 1970s, President Nixon visited China to establish diplomatic relations. Because both Taiwan and China claim to be the true Chinese government, the U.S. could not have a diplomatic relationship with both countries. The U.S. broke off its diplomatic relationship with Taiwan. In 1971, the People's Republic of China was admitted to the United Nations, and Taiwan was expelled from the United Nations. China is one of the five members of the UN Security Council. While the government leaders of Taiwan and China have talked about ways to reunite, they continue to exist as separate countries.

Tiananmen Square

In 1989, a group of Chinese students gathered in Tiananmen Square in Beijing to begin a hunger strike. One student called it a protest "for democracy, for freedom." The students hoped to gain the attention of the Chinese leaders. It was a peaceful gathering, but the military leaders of the Chinese government thought of it as a revolt. At first they sent unarmed guards to move the students. When that did not work, they sent tanks and soldiers with guns. In the hours that followed, many people were killed or wounded as the demonstrators tried to run from the square. This action shocked the world. Since Tiananmen Square, the government has imposed strict rules on students and young people.

The U.S. buys much of Japan's consumer goods, such as automobiles.

What Kind of Government Does Japan Have?

Japan is a parliamentary democracy. Like Great Britain, Japan has a Parliament, called the **Diet,** and a prime minister. It also has a cabinet and a two-part legislature. The Japanese Diet holds the legislative power. It is made up of the House of Councilors and the House of Representatives. The country has an emperor, who has little power. The emperor is the symbol of the nation, much like the British monarch.

One part of the Japanese government that is much like the United States is the Japanese Supreme Court. It also has the power of judicial review, but over the years it has only named a few laws as unconstitutional.

What Are U.S.-Japanese Relations Like?

The U.S. has a good relationship with Japan. Japan is a small but wealthy country. It has a very stable economy. Japan manufactures a variety of consumer goods, including automobiles and all types of electronic equipment. About 90 percent of these goods are sold world wide. The United States buys about 30 percent of Japan's exports. The United States exports around 10 percent of its manufactured products to Japan. Japan also imports food, live animals, textiles, iron, steel, and wood from the United States. The trade policies and agreements between the United States and Japan are very important for both countries.

Foreign trade is essential to the Japanese economy. Japan must import much of the raw material on which its industries depend. It must export its manufactured goods. Japan uses the large profits it makes from trade to invest in foreign businesses and property.

SECTION 5 REVIEW On a separate sheet of paper, write the correct word to complete each sentence.

1) The People's Republic of China is governed by the (people, communists, Mao Tse-tung).

2) The highest ranking communist official is the (general secretary, Politburo, president).

3) China spends large amounts of money on (people's needs, nuclear weapons, a free press).

4) The leader of the Japanese government is the (king, prime minister, Supreme Court).

5) Japan imports (manufactured goods, raw materials, oil) from the United States.

What do you think

Japan has several auto manufacturing plants in the United States. What are some benefits of these plants for Japan? for the United States?

Words to Know

★**Blockade**
To use troops or ships to prevent movement of people or supplies

★**Constitutional democracy**
A government that has a written constitution and democratic policies

★**Federal republic**
A government in which supreme power is given to citizens who vote for government officials

Panama Canal
A canal built in Central America to connect the Atlantic and Pacific oceans

Western Hemisphere
The land and oceans around North and South America

The U.S. is in the **Western Hemisphere.** The Western Hemisphere includes North America, Central America, and South America. Many of the developing nations in the world are in the Western Hemisphere. In this section, we will describe governments of countries in the Western Hemisphere.

The United States has provided aid to many of these nations in developing their economies and maintaining democracy. Most of these countries are trying to build up their industries. They face problems of poverty, hunger, disease, and poorly educated citizens. The United States assists these countries with foreign aid. This can be in the form of money, equipment, or labor.

What Kind of Government Does Mexico Have?

In Mexico and most of the countries in Central and South America, the people speak Spanish. Mexico is a democratic country that has much in common with the United States. The two countries share a 2000-mile border and have close economic ties. Both countries are part of NAFTA.

Mexico is a **federal republic.** It has thirty-one states and one federal district. The federal district is much like the District of Columbia of the United States. Mexico's government has three branches. Mexico's president is elected by the people to a six-year term and cannot be re-elected. The congress has a senate and a chamber of deputies. It has the power to make laws, set the national budget, and raise taxes. Mexico's president is the most powerful official in the country. The president appoints the leaders and suggests much of the legislation.

Mexico has a poor economy. It has a rapidly growing population. Mexico has a high unemployment rate—many people do not have jobs. Over 33 percent of its people live

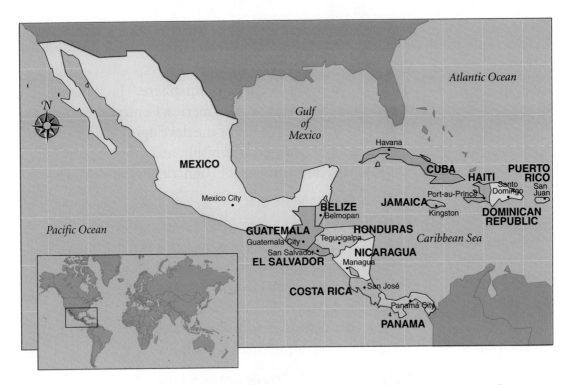

in poverty. Rural areas often have food shortages. The capital, Mexico City, is one of the most populated cities in the world. Because of overcrowding and poverty, many Mexicans come into the United States to seek a better life.

What Are the Countries of Central America?

Central America is between Mexico and South America. It includes Guatemala, El Salvador, Honduras, Nicaragua, Costa Rica, Panama, and Belize.

Panama is a long, narrow Central American country that connects Central America to South America. It is a **constitutional democracy.** The people elect a president and two vice presidents to five-year terms. Panama's legislature is called the National Assembly. Fifty-three deputies are elected to the National Assembly. Each deputy represents 15,000 people. Panama is divided into nine provinces. The president appoints the governors of the provinces.

In the early 1900s, the United States built the **Panama Canal** to connect the Atlantic and Pacific oceans. A 1903 treaty between the U.S. and Panama gave the U.S. the rights to operate the canal. In 1979, another agreement between the U.S. and Panama returned the control of the canal to Panama in 1999.

Why Does Cuba Have a Communist Government?

Cuba is a communist country. It is governed by Fidel Castro who is a dictator. Castro overthrew the Cuban government in 1959. In 1961, Castro declared Cuba a communist nation and stopped holding free elections. The Cuban government seized American-owned property in Cuba. Cuba received military and economic aid from other communist countries for many years. Since the communists lost power in the former Soviet Union, Cuba receives less help from other communist countries. Many Cuban people have come to the United States to find better living conditions.

Cuba is in the Caribbean Sea about 90 miles from Florida. In the early 1960s Cuba built missile sites with the help of Russia. The missiles could have been used against the United States. The U.S. **blockaded** Cuba to prevent Russian ships from bringing more military supplies to Cuba. The Russian ships turned back rather than start a military conflict with U.S. ships. This "Cuban missile crisis" happened in October, 1962.

What Kind of Government Does Brazil Have?

Brazil is the largest country in South America and the fifth largest country in the world. Brazil is a federal republic. It has twenty-six states and a federal district. It is the only Portuguese-speaking country in South America. Brazil was ruled by military leaders for many years. Today it has a democratic government with many political parties. Brazil's president and vice president are elected by the people to five-year terms. Its National Congress has a senate and chamber of deputies. Three senators are elected from each state and from the federal district. The number

of deputies from each state varies depending on the population. There are at least three deputies from each state. Brazil also has a system of regional parliaments.

Brazil is trying to improve its economy by increasing trade with other countries. Brazil depends on economic aid from the United States and Japan.

What Kind of Government Does Argentina Have?

Argentina is a federal republic. Its government has executive, legislative, and judicial branches. The president and vice president are elected by the people. Its president is elected to a six-year term. The Argentine congress has a senate and chamber of deputies. Argentina has twenty-two provinces, an island territory, and a federal district. Members of Argentina's senate are elected by the provincial legislatures.

Argentina has two major political parties. The Justicialist party, also called the Perónist party, supports the policies of a former president, Juan Perón. These policies call for heavy government spending and a strong nationalist feeling. Most of the labor unions back this party. Another major party is the Radical Civic Union. This is a somewhat conservative party. There are also a number of smaller parties.

Argentina has moved from being an agricultural country to a highly developed industrialized nation. It is an active member of the United Nations.

SECTION 6 REVIEW On a separate sheet of paper, answer the following questions using complete sentences.

1) What is the name of the trade agreement that the United States, Canada, and Mexico have signed?

2) What type of government does Mexico have?

3) What is the largest country in South America?

4) Which South American country has developed its industries?

5) What kind of government does Cuba have?

6) Where is Panama located?

What do you think

How does providing economic aid to South American countries help the United States?

Government Leaders in the Movies

Sometimes the lives of political people are featured in Hollywood movies. Stories about two U.S. Presidents—John Kennedy and Richard Nixon—have been featured in popular movies. The movie *JFK* is about the assassination of President John F. Kennedy in Dallas, Texas, in 1963. *Nixon* is about the presidency of Richard Nixon.

The Broadway musical and movie *Evita* tell about the life of Eva Duarte de Perón. She was a colorful Argentinian political figure. Eva was born near Buenos Aires, the capital of Argentina. Her family was very poor. When she was fifteen, Eva went to Buenos Aires to become an actress. About ten years later, when she was a successful radio actress, she met and married Juan Perón. Eva helped Perón campaign for president of Argentina. He was elected president in

1946. Perón appointed Eva to serve as his contact with the country's labor unions. In 1948, Eva established a women's branch of her husband's political party.

In 1951, Eva tried to run for vice president. Military leaders who were afraid Eva might eventually become president stopped her from running. Because Eva was an actress, many people didn't take her seriously as a politician. Eva died over forty years ago. Her story is still being told in a successful play and movie. "Don't Cry for Me, Argentina" is a well-known song from *Evita* by Andrew Lloyd Weber.

Review

1) When people see a movie about a public figure, do you think they believe everything in the movie is true?

2) Why might a movie producer want to make changes in a story about a politician's life?

3) Do you think movie producers should be allowed to change the facts of a political person's life? Give reasons for your answer. What First Amendment freedom could be affected here?

Words to Know

★Knesset
Israel's legislative body

★Mullah
A religious leader

Organization of Petroleum Exporting Countries (OPEC)
An organization of major oil producing countries formed in 1960

★Theocracy
A government run by religious leaders

The United States has friendly relations with many nations in the Middle East. The U.S. depends on these countries for oil. In 1960, the major oil producing countries formed the **Organization of Petroleum Exporting Countries (OPEC).** OPEC meets to set prices for the oil that it sells to the rest of the world. The United States imports about 53 percent of its oil from OPEC.

The United States also has close ties to Israel. Israel was created as a Jewish state in 1948 following World War II. There has been much conflict between Israel and the Arab countries of the Middle East. The Arab countries include Egypt, Lebanon, Syria, Saudi Arabia, Jordan, and Iraq. In recent years the leaders of the Arab countries and Israel have worked to agree on a peaceful way to live together.

Egypt and Israel are two important Middle Eastern countries that have a strong relationship with the United States.

What Kind of Government Does Israel Have?

Israel has a parliamentary form of government similar to Great Britain and Japan. There is a one-house parliament called the **Knesset.** The members are elected by popular vote. The entire country votes for lists of candidates from each political party. The members of the Knesset represent the country as a whole. They do not represent one state as members of Congress in the United States do.

Israel has no written constitution. It follows laws passed by the Knesset. Israel's president is elected by the Knesset for a five-year term. The president's role is mostly ceremonial.

The Israeli government is headed by a prime minister. The prime minister is usually the leader of the party that controls the most seats in the Knesset. In order to stay in office, the prime minister must have support from the majority of the Knesset.

The major political parties in Israel are the *Labor* and *Likud* parties. The Labor party wants the government to control the economy, with limited free enterprise. The Labor party is in favor of a negotiated peace settlement with the Arab countries. The Likud party wants limited government involvement in the economy. It does not favor a peace settlement with Arab countries.

What Types of Government Do Other Middle Eastern Countries Have?

Egypt is an Arabic-speaking republic in northeast Africa. It has a president and prime minister. The legislative branch of Egyptian government is called the People's Assembly. The president is nominated by one-third of the members of the People's Assembly. The president is then confirmed by two-thirds of the members. Candidates are elected into office by public referendum. Only one candidate is presented. The president can serve for an unlimited number of six-year terms. The president appoints one or two vice presidents.

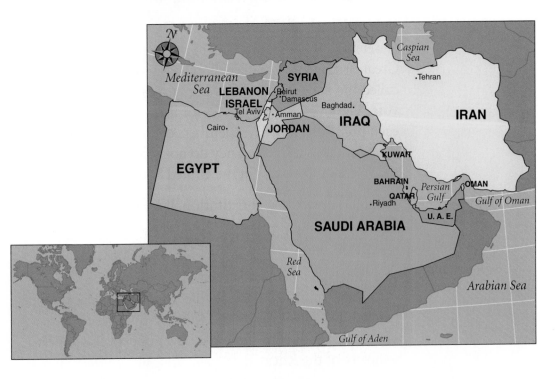

Oil tankers such as this one ship oil to countries around the world that need it.

The People's Assembly is made up of 444 people elected by voters. The president may appoint ten more members to five-year terms. The largest political party is the National Democratic party. It supports both private and public ownership. The National Democratic party has a friendly relationship with Europe and the United States. Egypt supported the United States in the Desert Storm operation after Iraq invaded Kuwait in 1991.

Saudi Arabia is a large country with huge oil and gas reserves. It is a leader among the Arab states. Saudi Arabia is governed by a monarchy with strong religious values. The king and royal family run the government. Weekly councils are held where citizens can ask the royal family for help. Often large amounts of money are given out at these meetings. Saudi Arabia has a friendly relationship with the United States.

Jordan is a constitutional monarchy. King Hussein has ruled Jordan since 1952. However, most of the country's political power is held by a prime minister. The prime minister heads the cabinet. The king can veto laws made by the legislative branch, the National Assembly. The National Assembly can override the king's veto. Jordan has a stable economy. Jordan and the United States have had a friendly relationship.

Iran is a Middle Eastern country that is a **theocracy.** A theocracy is led by religious leaders. These leaders, called **mullahs,** control the government. The leaders believe that people's religious values are most important. The people of Iran are poor. Economic growth is very slow.

Iraq is an Arab country that is ruled by Saddam Hussein. Hussein has attempted to control the oil supplies in the Persian Gulf. Since the early 1990s, the U.S. has been involved in conflicts with Hussein and Iraq. Iraq's economy is weak. Iraq and Iran are not friendly toward the United States. They are not friendly toward one another, either.

SECTION 7 REVIEW On a separate sheet of paper, write the correct word to complete each sentence.

1) The United States depends on the countries of the Middle East for (money, produce, oil).

2) (Iran, Egypt, Israel) was created as a Jewish state in 1948, following World War II.

3) (Egypt's, Israel's, Jordan's) president can appoint ten members to the legislative branch.

4) A theocracy is a kind of government that is led by (a president, an assembly, religious leaders).

5) Saudi Arabia is governed by a (Knesset, monarchy, prime minister).

What do you think **?** Why do you think the creation of Israel as a Jewish state has caused conflict?

Governments of the World

	Country	Type of Government	Chief Executive	Legislative Body
	Argentina	Federal Republic	President	Congress
	Brazil	Federal Republic	President	National Congress
	China	Communist	President	National People's Congress
	Cuba	Communist	President	National Assembly
	Egypt	Republic	President	People's Assembly
	France	Republic	President	Parliament
	Great Britain	Constitutional Monarchy	Prime Minister	Parliament
	Iran	Theocracy	President	Parliament
	Iraq	Republic	President	National Council
	Israel	Republic	Prime Minister	Knesset
	Japan	Parliamentary Democracy	Prime Minister	Diet
	Jordan	Constitutional Monarchy	King	National Assembly
	Mexico	Federal Republic	President	Congress
	Panama	Constitutional Democracy	King	National Assembly
	Russia	Republic	Prime Minister	Parliament
	Saudi Arabia	Monarchy	King	Council of Ministers
	United States of America	Federal Republic	President	Congress

Nelson Mandela, an African Leader

Nelson Mandela has spent most of his life fighting for racial justice in his country, the Republic of South Africa.

Mandela was born in 1918. He received a law degree from the University of South Africa in 1942. In 1944 he joined the African National Congress (ANC), a political group. In 1948, the South African government began a policy of segregation

called *apartheid*. The ANC openly resisted this policy.

In 1962, Mandela was sentenced to life in prison. He was charged with working to overthrow the white minority government. Mandela was released from prison in 1990. Following his release, he worked to gain political power for blacks by peaceful means. He negotiated with white leaders to end apartheid and set up a nonracial system of government.

In 1993, Mandela and the president of South Africa, F. W. de Klerk, received the Nobel Peace Prize for their work to end apartheid. Mandela was elected president of the Union of South Africa in 1994. He is the first black president of South Africa. He was elected in the first open elections in which people of all races could vote.

Review

1) What sacrifices did Nelson Mandela make for his country?

2) Why do you think the white minority government of South Africa established apartheid?

CHAPTER SUMMARY

* The goals of United States foreign policy are to keep the country safe, to maintain good relationships with other countries, and to carry out trade policies.

* The North American Free Trade Agreement (NAFTA) encourages trade between the United States, Mexico, and Canada by eliminating tariffs.

* The United Nations was formed to protect world peace and promote human rights.

* Great Britain and France are democratic countries that have friendly relations with the United States.

* The European Economic Community (EEC) is a common market agreement between European countries.

* The North Atlantic Treaty Organization (NATO) is an organization of sixteen countries that was formed after World War II for defense reasons.

* The Commonwealth of Independent States is the new name for the eleven republics and Russia that were part of the Soviet Union. They are no longer ruled by communism.

* China is the largest communist country in the world.

* Japan is a wealthy Asian country that is a leader in world trade and business.

* Many Central and South American countries have democratic governments.

* Cuba is the only communist country in the Western Hemisphere.

* The United States helps developing countries by providing foreign aid.

* The United States depends on the Middle East for oil.

* Israel was created as a democratic Jewish state following World War II.

Comprehension: Identifying Facts

On a separate sheet of paper, write the correct word or words from the Word Bank to match each statement below.

WORD BANK

China

constitutional monarchy

Cuba

Cuban missile crisis

Diet

European Economic Community

foreign policy

free trade

Knesset

North American Free Trade Agreement

Panama

prime minister

republic

State Department

United Nations

1) The United States' plan of action for working with other countries.

2) Department that maintains embassies in many countries.

3) Largest communist country in the world.

4) Trade between countries without legal barriers on imports or exports.

5) An agreement that lowers tariffs between Mexico, the United States, and Canada.

6) An organization that promotes peace and human welfare.

7) A country that connects Central and South America.

8) An organization to increase trade between European nations.

9) The parliament of Israel.

10) A dispute between the United States and Cuba.

11) France's government.

12) Chief executive of Great Britain.

13) Japan's parliament.

14) Communist country close to the U.S.

15) Jordan's government.

Comprehension: Understanding Main Ideas

On a separate sheet of paper, write the answers to the following questions using complete sentences.

1) Name one way the government of Russia has changed.

2) Why did the Commonwealth of Independent States form?

3) Who runs the government in the People's Republic of China?

4) What is the relationship between Taiwan and the People's Republic of China?

5) What products does Japan export? What products does Japan import?

6) Describe the government of Mexico.

7) How many candidates are there in Egypt's elections?

8) What country has a council in which citizens speak to government leaders?

9) Which countries are permanent members of the United Nations Security Council?

Critical Thinking: Write Your Opinion

Do you think the United States should be involved in so many peacekeeping missions in foreign countries? Give reasons for your answer.

> **Test Taking Tip** Always read directions more than once. Underline words that tell *how many* examples or items you must provide.

The Declaration of Independence

Adopted in Congress July 4, 1776
The Unanimous Declaration of the
Thirteen United States of America

When, in the course of human events, it becomes necessary for one people to dissolve the political bands which have connected them with another, and to assume among the powers of the earth, the separate and equal station to which the laws of nature and of nature's God entitle them, a decent respect to the opinions of mankind requires that they should declare the causes which impel them to the separation.

We hold these truths to be self-evident, that all men are created equal, that they are endowed by their Creator with certain unalienable rights, that among these are life, liberty, and the pursuit of happiness. That to secure these rights, governments are instituted among men, deriving their just powers from the consent of the governed. That whenever any form of government becomes destructive of these ends, it is the right of the people to alter or to abolish it, and to institute new government, laying its foundation on such principles and organizing its powers in such form, as to them shall seem most

La Declaración de Independencia

En el Congreso, 4 de Julio de 1776
Declaración Unánime de los Trece
Estados Unidos de América

Cuando, en el curso de los acontecimientos humanos, se hace necesario para un pueblo disolver las ligas políticas que lo han unido con otro, y asumir, entre las potencias de la tierra, un sitio separado e igual, al cual tiene derecho según las leyes de la naturaleza y el Dios de la naturaleza; el respeto debido a las opiniones del género humano exige que se declaren las causas que obligan a ese pueblo a la separación.

Sostenemos como verdades evidentes que todos los hombres nacen iguales, que están dotados por su Creador de ciertos derechos inalienables, entre los cuales se cuentan el derecho a la vida, a la libertad y al alcance de la felicidad; que, para asegurar estos derechos, los hombres instituyen gobiernos, derivando sus justos poderes del consentimiento de los gobernados; que cuando una forma de gobierno llega a ser destructora de estos fines, es un derecho del pueblo cambiarla o abolirla, e instituir un nuevo gobierno, basado en esos principios y organizando su autoridad en la forma

likely to effect their safety and happiness. Prudence, indeed, will dictate that governments long established should not be changed for light and transient causes; and accordingly all experience hath shown that mankind are more disposed to suffer, while evils are sufferable, than to right themselves by abolishing the forms to which they are accustomed. But when a long train of abuses and usurpations, pursuing invariably the same object evinces a design to reduce them under absolute despotism, it is their right, it is their duty, to throw off such government, and to provide new guards for their future security.

Such has been the patient sufferance of these colonies; and such is now the necessity which constrains them to alter their former systems of government. The history of the present King of Great Britain is a history of repeated injuries and usurpations, all having in direct object the establishment of an absolute tyranny over these states. To prove this, let facts be submitted to a candid world.

He has refused his assent to laws, the most wholesome and necessary for the public good.

que el pueblo estime como la más conveniente para obtener su seguridad y su felicidad. En realidad, la prudencia aconsejará que los gobiernos erigidos mucho tiempo atrás no sean cambiados por causas ligeras y transitorias; en efecto, la experiencia ha demostrado que la humanidad está más bien dispuesta a sufrir, mientras los males sean tolerables, que a hacerse justicia aboliendo las formas de gobierno a las cuales se halla acostumbrada. Pero cuando una larga cadena de abusos y usurpaciones, que persiguen invariablemente el mismo objetivo, hace patente la intención de reducir al pueblo a un despotismo absoluto, es derecho del hombre, es su obligación, arrojar a ese gobierno y procurarse nuevos guardianes para su seguridad futura.

Tal ha sido el paciente sufrimiento de estas colonias; tal es ahora la necesidad que las obliga a cambiar sus antiguos sistemas de gobierno. La historia del actual Rey de la Gran Bretaña es una historia de agravios y usurpaciones repetidas, que tienen como mira directa la de establecer una tirania absoluta en estos estados. Para demostrar lo anterior, presentamos los siguientes hechos ante un mundo que no los conoce:

El Rey se ha negado a aprobar las leyes más favorables y necesarias para el bienestar público.

He has forbidden his governors to pass laws of immediate and pressing importance, unless suspended in their operation till his assent should be obtained; and when so suspended, he has utterly neglected to attend to them.

He has refused to pass other laws for the accommodation of large districts of people, unless those people would relinquish the right of representation in the legislature, a right inestimable to them and formidable to tyrants only.

He has called together legislative bodies at places unusual, uncomfortable, and distant from the depository of their public records, for the sole purpose of fatiguing them into compliance with his measures.

He has dissolved representative houses repeatedly, for opposing with manly firmness his invasions on the rights of the people.

He has refused for a long time, after such dissolutions, to cause others to be elected; whereby the legislative powers, incapable of annihilation, have returned to the people at large for their exercise; the state remaining in the mean time exposed to all the dangers of invasion from without, and convulsions within.

He has endeavored to prevent the population of these states; for that purpose obstructing the laws for naturalization

Ha prohibido a sus gobernadores sancionar leyes de importancia immediata y apremiante, a menos que su ejecución se suspenda hasta obtener su asentimiento; y, una vez suspendidas, se ha negado por completo a prestarles atención.

Se ha rehusado a aprobar otras leyes convenientes a grandes comarcas pobladas, a menos que esos pueblos renuncien al derecho de ser representados en la legislatura; derecho que es inestimable para el pueblo y terrible sólo para los tiranos.

Ha convocado a los cuerpos legislativos en sitios desusados, incómodos y distantes del asiento de sus documentos públicos, con la sola idea de fatigarlos para cumplir con sus medidas.

En repetidas ocasiones ha disuelto las cámaras de representantes, por oponerse con firmeza viril a sus intromisiones en los derechos del pueblo.

Durante mucho tiempo, y después de esas disoluciones, se ha negado a permitir la elección de otras cámaras; por lo cual, los poderes legislativos, cuyo aniquilamiento es imposible, han retornado al pueblo, sin limitación para su ejercicio; permaneciendo el Estado, mientras tanto, expuesto a todos los peligros de una invasión exterior y a convulsiones internas.

Ha tratado de impedir que se pueblen estos estados; dificultando, con ese propósito las leyes de naturalización

of foreigners; refusing to pass others to encourage their migrations hither, and raising the conditions of new appropriations of lands.

He has obstructed the administration of justice, by refusing his assent to laws for establishing judiciary powers.

He has made judges dependent on his will alone, for the tenure of their offices, and the amount and payment of their salaries.

He has erected a multitude of new offices, and sent hither swarms of officers to harass our people, and eat out their substance.

He has kept among us, in times of peace, standing armies without the consent of our legislatures.

He has affected to render the military independent of and superior to the civil power.

He has combined with others to subject us to a jurisdiction foreign to our constitution, and unacknowledged by our laws; giving his assent to their acts of pretended legislation:

For quartering large bodies of armed troops among us:

For protecting them, by a mock trial, from punishment for any murders which they should commit on the inhabitants of these states:

de extranjeros; rehusando a aprobar otras para fomentar su immigración y elevando las condiciones para las nuevas adquisiciones de tierras.

Ha entorpecido la administración de justicia al no aprobar las leyes que establecen los poderes judiciales.

Ha hecho que los jueces dependan solamente de su voluntad, para poder desempeñar sus cargos y en cuanto a la cantidad y pago de sus emolumentos.

Ha fundado una gran diversidad de oficinas nuevas, enviando a un enjambre de funcionarios que acosan a nuestro pueblo y menguan su sustento.

En tiempo de paz, ha mantenido entre nosotros ejércitos permanentes, sin el consentimiento de nuestras legislaturas.

Ha influido para que la autoridad militar sea independiente de la civil y superior a ella.

Se ha asociado con otros para someternos a una jurisdicción extraña a nuestra constitución y no reconocida por nuestras leyes; aprobando sus actos de pretendida legislación:

Para acuartelar, entre nosotros, grandes cuerpos de tropas armadas:

Para protegerlos, por medio de un juicio ficticio, del castigo por los asesinatos que pudieren cometer entre los habitantes de estos estados:

For cutting off our trade with all parts of the world:

For imposing taxes on us without our consent:

For depriving us in many cases, of the benefits of trial by jury:

For transporting us beyond seas to be tried for pretended offenses:

For abolishing the free system of English laws in a neighboring province, establishing therein an arbitrary government, and enlarging its boundaries so as to render it at once an example and fit instrument for introducing the same absolute rule into these colonies:

For taking away our charters, abolishing our most valuable laws, and altering fundamentally the forms of our governments:

For suspending our own legislatures, and declaring themselves invested with power to legislate for us in all cases whatsoever.

He has abdicated government here, by declaring us out of his protection and waging war against us.

He has plundered our seas, ravaged our coasts, burned our towns, and destroyed the lives of our people.

Para suspender nuestro comercio con todas las partes del mundo:

Para imponernos impuestos sin nuestro consentimiento:

Para privarnos, en muchos casos, de los beneficios de un juicio por jurado:

Para transportarnos más allá de los mares, con el fin de ser juzgados por supuestos agravios:

Para abolir en una provincia vecina el libre sistema de las leyes inglesas, estableciendo en ella un gobierno arbítrario y extendiendo sus límites, con el objeto de dar un ejemplo y disponer de un instrumento adecuado para introducir el mismo gobierno absoluto en estas colonias:

Para suprimir nuestras cartas constitutivas, abolir nuestras leyes más valiosas y alterar en su esencia las formas de nuestros gobiernos:

Para suspender nuestras propias legislturas y delcararse investido con facultades para legislarnos en todos los casos, cualesquiera que éstos sean.

Ha abdicado de su gobierno en estos territorios al declarar que estamos fuera de su protección y al emprender una guerra contra nosotros.

Ha saqueado nuestros mares, asolado nuestras costas, incendiado nuestras ciudades y destruido la vida de nuestro pueblo.

He is at this time transporting large armies of foreign mercenaries to complete the works of death, desolation and tyranny, already begun with circumstances of cruelty and perfidy scarcely paralleled in the most barbarous ages, and totally unworthy the head of a civilized nation.

He has constrained our fellow citizens taken captive on the high seas to bear arms against their country, to become the executioners of their friends and brethren, or to fall themselves by their hands.

He has excited domestic insurrections amongst us, and has endeavored to bring on the inhabitants of our frontiers, the merciless Indian savages, whose known rule of warfare, is an undistinguished destruction of all ages, sexes, and conditions.

In every stage of these oppressions we have petitioned for redress in the most humble terms: our repeated petitions have been answered only by repeated injury. A prince, whose character is thus marked by every act which may define a tyrant is unfit to be the ruler of a free people.

Nor have we been wanting in attentions to our British brethren. We have warned them from time to time of attempts by their legislature to extend

Al presente, está transportando grandes ejércitos de extranjeros mercenarios para completar la obra de muerte, desolación y tirania, ya iniciada en circunstancias de crueldad y perfidia que apenas se encuentran paralelo en las épocas más bárbaras, y por completo indignas del jefe de una nación civilizada.

Ha obligado a nuestros conciudadanos, aprehendidos en alta mar, a que tomen armas contra su país, convirtiéndolos así en los verdugos de sus amigos y hermanos, o a morir bajo sus manos.

Ha provocado insurrecciones intestinas entre nosotros y se ha esforzado por lanzar sobre los habitantes de nuestras fronteras a los imisericordes indios salvajes, cuya conocida disposición para la guerra se distingue por la destrucción de vidas, sin considerar edades, sexos ni condiciones.

En todas las fases de estos abusos, hemos pedido una reparación en los términos más humildes; nuestras súplicas constantes han sido contestadas solamente con ofensas repetidas. Un príncipe, cuyo carácter está marcado, en consecuencia, por todas las acciones que definen a un tirano, no es el adecuado para gobernar a un pueblo libre.

Tampoco hemos incurrido en faltas de atención con nuestros hermanos británicos. Los hemos enterado, oportunamente, de los esfuerzos de

an unwarrantable jurisdiction over us. We have reminded them of the circumstances of our emigration and settlement here. We have appealed to their native justice and magnanimity, and we have conjured them by the ties of our common kindred to disavow these usurpations, which would inevitably interrupt our connections and correspondence. They too have been deaf to the voice of justice and of consanguinity. We must, therefore, acquiesce in the necessity, which denounces our separation, and hold them, as we hold the rest of mankind, enemies in war, in peace friends.

We, therefore, the representatives of the United States of America, in General Congress, assembled, appealing to the Supreme Judge of the world for the rectitude of our intentions, do, in the name, and by authority of the good people of these colonies, solemnly publish and declare, that these united colonies are, and of right ought to be free and independent states; that they are absolved from all allegiance to the British Crown, and that all political connection between them and the state of Great Britain, is and ought to be totally dissolved; and that as free and independent states, they have full power to levy war, conclude peace, contract alliances, establish commerce, and to do all other acts and things which independent states may of right

su legislatura para extender una autoridad injustificable sobre nosotros. Les hemos recordado las circunstancias de nuestra emigración y colonización en estos territorios. Hemos apelado a su justicia y magnanimidad naturales, y los hemos conjurado, por los lazos de nuestra común ascendencia, a que repudien esas usurpaciones, las cuales, inevitablemente, llegarán a interrumpir nuestros nexos y correspondencia. Ellos también se han mostrado sordos a la voz de la justicia y de la consanguinidad. Por tanto, aceptamos la necesidad que proclama nuestra separación, y en adelante los consideramos como al resto de la humanidad: enemigos en la guerra, amigos en la paz.

En consecuencia, nosotros, los representantes de los Estados Unidos de América, reunidos en Congreso General, y apelando al Juez Supremo del Mundo en cuanto a la rectitud de nuestras intenciones, en el nombre, y por la autoridad del buen pueblo de estas colonias, solemnemente publicamos y declaramos, que estas colonias unidas son, y de derecho deben ser, estados libres e independientes; que se hallan exentos de toda fidelidad a la Corona Británica, y que todos los lazos políticos entre ellos y el Estado de la Gran Bretaña son y deben ser totalmente disueltos; y que, como estados libres e independientes, tienen poderes suficientes para declarar la guerra, concertar la paz, celebrar alianzas, establecer el comercio y para efectuar

do. And for the support of this declaration, with a firm reliance on the protection of Divine Providence, we mutually pledge to each other our lives, our fortunes, and our sacred honor.

Signed by John Hancock of Massachusetts as President of the Congress and by the fifty-five other Representatives of the thirteen United States of America:

todos aquellos actos y cosas que los estados independientes pueden, por su derecho, llevar a cabo. Y, en apoyo de esta declaración, confiando firmemente en la protección de la Divina Providencia, comprometemos mutuamente nuestras vidas, nuestros bienes, y nuestro honor sacrosanto.

New Hampshire (Nueva Hampshire)
Josiah Bartlett
William Whipple
Matthew Thornton

Connecticut
Roger Sherman
Samuel Huntington
William Williams
Oliver Wolcott

Massachusetts Bay
Samuel Adams
John Adams
Robert Treat Paine
Elbridge Gerry

Rhode Island
Stephen Hopkins
William Ellery

Pennsylvania (Pensilvania)
Robert Morris
Benjamin Rush
Benjamin Franklin
John Morton
George Clymer
James Smith

George Taylor
James Wilson
George Ross

Delaware
Caesar Rodney
George Read
Thomas M'Kean

New York (Nueva York)
William Floyd
Philip Livingston
Francis Lewis
Lewis Morris

Virginia
George Wythe
Richard Henry Lee
Thomas Jefferson
Benjamin Harrison
Thomas Nelson, Jr.
Francis Lightfoot Lee
Carter Braxton

North Carolina (Carolina del Norte)
William Hooper
Joseph Hewes
John Penn

South Carolina (Carolina del Sur)
Edward Rutledge
Thomas Heyward, Jr.
Thomas Lynch, Jr.
Arthur Middleton

Georgia
Button Gwinnett
Lyman Hall
George Walton

Maryland
Samuel Chase
William Paca
Thomas Stone
Charles Carroll of
    Carrollton

New Jersey (Nueva Jersey)
Richard Stockton
John Witherspoon
Francis Hopkinson
John Hart
Abraham Clark

The Constitution of the United States

Preamble

We the people of the United States, in order to form a more perfect Union, establish justice, insure domestic tranquility, provide for the common defense, promote the general welfare, and secure the blessings of liberty to ourselves and our posterity, do ordain and establish this Constitution for the United States of America.

Article I
The Legislative Branch*

Congress

Section 1 All legislative powers herein granted shall be vested in a Congress of the United States, which shall consist of a Senate and House of Representatives.

The House of Representatives

Section 2 (1) The House of Representatives shall be composed of members chosen every second year by the people of the several states, and the electors in each state shall have the qualifications requisite for electors of the most numerous branch of the state legislature.

(2) No person shall be a representative who shall not have attained to the age of twenty-five years, and been seven years a citizen of the United States, and

Constitución de Los Estados Unidos

Preámbulo

Nosotros, el pueblo de los Estados Unidos, a fin de formar una Unión más perfecta, establecer la justicia, garantizar la tranquilidad nacional, atender a la defensa común, fomentar el bienestar general y asegurar los beneficios de la libertad para nosotros y para nuestra posteridad, por la presente promulgamos y establecemos esta Constitución para los Estados Unidos de América.

Artículo I

Sección 1 Todos los poderes legislativos otorgados por esta Constitución residirán en un Congreso de los Estados Unidos que se compondrá de un Senado y de una Cámara de Representantes.

Sección 2 (1) La Cámara de Representantes se compondrá de miembros elegidos cada dos años por el pueblo de los distintos estados y los electores en cada estado cumplirán con los requisitos exigidos a los electores de la cámara más numerosa de la asamblea legislativa de dicho estado.

(2) No podrá ser representante ninguna persona que no haya cumplido veinticinco años de edad, que no haya sido

who shall not, when elected, be an inhabitant of that state in which he shall be chosen.

(3) Representatives and direct taxes shall be apportioned among the several states which may be included within this Union, according to their respective numbers, [which shall be determined by adding to the whole number of free persons, including those bound to service for a term of years, and excluding Indians not taxed, three-fifths of all other persons]. The actual enumeration shall be made within three years after the first meeting of the Congress of the United States, and within every subsequent term of ten years, in such manner as they shall by law direct. The number of representatives shall not exceed one for every thirty thousand, but each state shall have at least one representative; [and until such enumeration shall be made, the state of New Hampshire shall be entitled to choose 3, Massachusetts 8, Rhode Island and Providence Plantations 1, Connecticut 5, New York 6, New Jersey 4, Pennsylvania 8, Delaware 1, Maryland 6, Virginia 10, North Carolina 5, South Carolina 5, and Georgia 3].

(4) When vacancies happen in the representation from any state, the executive authority thereof shall issue writs of election to fill such vacancies.

durante siete años ciudadano de los Estados Unidos y que al tiempo de su elección no resida en el estado que ha de elegirlo.

(3) Tanto los representantes como las contribuciones directas se prorratearán entre los diversos estados que integren esta Unión, en relación al número respectivo de sus habitantes, el cual se determinará añadiendo al número total de personas libres, en el que se incluye a las que estén obligadas al servicio por determinado número de años y se excluye a los indios que no paguen contribuciones, las tres quintas partes de todas las demás. Se efectuará el censo dentro de los tres años siguientes a la primera reunión del Congreso de los Estados Unidos, y en lo sucesivo cada diez años, en la forma en que éste lo dispusiere por ley. No habrá más de un representante por cada treinta mil habitantes, pero cada estado tendrá por lo menos un representante. En tanto se realiza el censo, el estado de Nueva Hampshire tendrá derecho a elegir tres representantes; Massachusetts, ocho; Rhode Island y las Plantaciones de Providence, uno; Connecticut, cinco; Nueva Jersey, cuatro; Pensilvania, ocho; Delaware, uno; Maryland, seis; Virginia, diez; Carolina del Norte, cinco; Carolina del Sur, cinco, y Georgia, tres.

(4) Cuando ocurrieren vacancias en la representación de cualquier estado, la autoridad ejecutiva de éste ordenará celebración de elecciones para cubrirlas.

(5) The House of Representatives shall choose their speaker and other officers; and shall have the sole power of impeachment.

The Senate

Section 3 (1) The Senate of the United States shall be composed of two senators from each state, [chosen by the legislature thereof,] for six years; and each senator shall have one vote.

(2) Immediately after they shall be assembled in consequence of the first election, they shall be divided as equally as may be into three classes. The seats of the senators of the first class shall be vacated at the expiration of the second year, of the second class at the expiration of the fourth year, and of the third class at the expiration of the sixth year, so that one-third may be chosen every second year; [and if vacancies happen by resignation, or otherwise, during the recess of the legislature of any state, the executive thereof may make temporary appointments until the next meeting of the legislature, which shall then fill such vacancies].

(3) No person shall be a senator who shall not have attained to the age of thirty years, and been nine years a citizen of the United States, and who shall not, when elected, be an inhabitant of that state for which he shall be chosen.

(5) La Cámara de Representantes elegirá su presidente y demás funcionarios y sólo ella tendrá la facultad de iniciar procedimientos de residencia.

Sección 3 (1) El Senado de los Estados Unidos se compondrá de dos senadores por cada estado, elegidos por sus respectivas asambleas legislativas por el término de seis años. Cada senador tendrá derecho a un voto.

(2) Tan pronto como se reúnan en virtud de la primera elección, se les dividirá en tres grupos los más iguales posible. El término de los senadores del primer grupo expirará al finalizar el segundo año; el del segundo grupo al finalizar el cuarto año y el del tercer grupo al finalizar el sexto año, de forma que cada dos años se renueve una tercera parte de sus miembros. Si ocurrieren vacancias, por renuncia o por cualquier otra causa, mientras esté en receso la Asamblea Legislativa del estado respectivo, la autoridad ejecutiva del mismo podrá hacer nombramientos provisionales hasta la próxima sesión de la asamblea legislativa, la que entonces cubrirá tales vacancias.

(3) No podrá ser senador quien no haya cumplido treinta años de edad, no haya sido durante nueve años ciudadano de los Estados Unidos y no resida, en la época de su elección, en el estado que ha de elegirlo.

(4) The Vice President of the United States shall be president of the Senate, but shall have no vote, unless they be equally divided.

(5) The Senate shall choose their other officers, and also a president pro tempore, in the absence of the Vice President, or when he shall exercise the office of President of the United States.

(6) The Senate shall have the sole power to try all impeachments. When sitting for that purpose, they shall be on oath or affirmation. When the President of the United States is tried, the Chief Justice shall preside: and no person shall be convicted without the concurrence of two-thirds of the members present.

(7) Judgment in cases of impeachment shall not extend further than to removal from office, and disqualification to hold and enjoy any office of honor, trust, or profit under the United States: but the party convicted shall nevertheless be liable and subject to indictment, trial, judgment, and punishment, according to law.

Organization of Congress

Section 4 (1) The times, places, and manner of holding elections for senators and representatives, shall be prescribed in each state by the legislature thereof; but the Congress may at any time by law make or alter such regulations, [except as to the places of choosing senators].

(4) El Vicepresidente de los Estados Unidos será presidente del Senado, pero no tendrá voto excepto en caso de empate.

(5) El Senado eligirá sus demás funcionarios así como también un presidente pro témpore en ausencia del Vicepresidente o cuando éste desempeñare el cargo de Presidente de los Estados Unidos.

(6) Tan sólo el Senado podrá conocer de procedimientos de residencia. Cuando se reúna para este fin, los senadores prestarán juramento o harán promesa de cumplir fielmente su cometido. Si se residenciare al Presidente de los Estados Unidos, presidirá la sesión el Juez Presidente del Tribunal Supremo. Nadie será convicto sin que concurran las dos terceras partes de los senadores presentes.

(7) La sentencia en procedimientos de residencia no podrá exceder de la destitución del cargo e inhabilitación para obtener y desempeñar ningún cargo de honor, de confianza o de retribución en el gobierno de los Estados Unidos; pero el funcionario convicto quedará, no obstante, sujeto a ser acusado, juzgado, sentenciado y castigado con arreglo a derecho.

Sección 4 (1) La asamblea legislativa de cada estado determinará la fecha, lugar y modo de celebrar las elecciones de senadores y representantes; pero el Congreso podrá en cualquier momento mediante legislación adecuada aprobar

(2) The Congress shall assemble at least once in every year, [and such meeting shall be on the first Monday in December,] unless they shall by law appoint a different day.

Rules and Procedures

Section 5 (1) Each house shall be the judge of the elections, returns and qualifications of its own members, and a majority of each shall constitute a quorum to do business; but a smaller number may adjourn from day to day, and may be authorized to compel the attendance of absent members, in such manner, and under such penalties as each house may provide.

(2) Each house may determine the rules of its proceedings, punish its members for disorderly behavior, and, with the concurrence of two-thirds, expel a member.

(3) Each house shall keep a journal of its proceedings, and from time to time publish the same, excepting such parts as may in their judgment require secrecy; and the yeas and nays of the members of either house on any question shall, at the desire of one-fifth of those present, be entered on the journal.

(4) Neither house, during the session of Congress, shall, without the consent of the other, adjourn for more than three days, nor to any other place than that in which the two houses shall be sitting.

o modificar tales disposiciones, salvo en relación al lugar donde se habrá de elegir a los senadores.

(2) El Congreso se reunirá por lo menos una vez al año y tal sesión comenzará el primer lunes de diciembre, a no ser que por ley se fije otro día.

Sección 5 (1) Cada cámara será el único juez del las elecciones, resultado de las mismas y capacidad de sus propios miembros; y la mayoría de cada una de ellas constituirá un quorum para realizar sus trabajos; pero un número menor podrá recesar de día en día y estará autorizado para compeler la asistencia de los miembros ausentes, en la forma y bajo las penalidades que cada cámara determinare.

(2) Cada cámara adoptará su reglamento, podrá castigar a sus miembros por conducta impropia y expulsarlos con el voto de dos terceras partes.

(3) Cada cámara tendrá un diario de sesiones, que publicará periódicamente, con excepción de aquello que, a su juicio, deba mantenerse en secreto; y siempre que así lo pidiere la quinta parte de los miembros presentes, se harán constar en dicho diario los votos afirmativos y negativos de los miembros de una u otra cámara sobre cualquier asunto.

(4) Mientas el Congreso estuviere reunido, ninguna cámara podrá, sin el consentimiento de la otra, levantar sus

Payment and Privileges

Section 6 (1) The senators and representatives shall receive a compensation for their services, to be ascertained by law, and paid out of the treasury of the United States. They shall in all cases, except treason, felony, and breach of the peace, be privileged from arrest during their attendance at the session of their respective houses, and in going to and returning from the same; and for any speech or debate in either house, they shall not be questioned in any other place.

(2) No senator or representative shall, during the time for which he was elected, be appointed to any civil office under the authority of the United States, which shall have been created, or the emoluments whereof shall have been increased during such time; and no person holding any office under the United States, shall be a member of either house during his continuance in office.

How a Bill Becomes a Law

Section 7 (1) All bills for raising revenue shall originate in the House of Representatives; but the Senate may propose or concur with amendments as on other bills.

(2) Every bill which shall have passed the House of Representatives and the Senate, shall, before it becomes a law, be presented to the President of the United States; if he approve he shall sign it, but if not he shall return it,

sesiones por más de tres días ni reunirse en otro lugar que no sea aquel en que las dos estén instaladas.

Sección 6 (1) Los senadores y representantes recibirán por sus servicios una remuneración fijada por ley y pagadera por el Tesoro de los Estados Unidos. Mientras asistan a las sesiones de sus respectivas cámaras, así como mientras se dirijan a ellas o regresen de las mismas, no podrán ser arrestados, excepto en casos de traición, delito grave o alteración de la paz. Tampoco podrán ser reconvenidos fuera de la cámara por ninguno de sus discursos o por sus manifestaciones en cualquier debate en ella.

(2) Ningún senador o representante, mientras dure el término por el cual fue elegido, será nombrado para ningún cargo civil bajo la autoridad de los Estados Unidos, que hubiere sido creado o cuyos emolumentos hubieren sido aumentados durante tal término; y nadie que desempeñe un cargo bajo la autoridad de los Estados Unidos podrá ser miembro de ninguna de las cámaras mientras ocupe tal cargo.

Sección 7 (1) Todo proyecto de ley para imponer contribuciones se originará en la Cámara de Representantes; pero el Senado podrá proponer enmiendas o concurrir en ellas como en los demás proyectos.

(2) Todo proyecto que hubiere sido aprobado por la Cámara de Represen-

with his objections to that house in which it shall have originated, who shall enter the objections at large on their journal, and proceed to reconsider it. If after such reconsideration two-thirds of that house shall agree to pass the bill, it shall be sent, together with the objections, to the other house, by which it shall likewise be reconsidered, and if approved by two-thirds of that house, it shall become a law. But in all such cases the votes of both houses shall be determined by yeas and nays, and the names of the persons voting for and against the bill shall be entered on the journal of each house, respectively. If any bill shall not be returned by the President within ten days (Sundays excepted) after it shall have been presented to him, the same shall be a law, in like manner as if he had signed it, unless the Congress by their adjournment prevent its return, in which case it shall not be a law.

(3) Every order, resolution, or vote to which the concurrence of the Senate and House of Representatives may be necessary (except on a question of adjournment) shall be presented to the President of the United States; and before the same shall take effect, shall be approved by him, or being disapproved by him, shall be repassed by two-thirds of the Senate and House of Representatives, according to the rules and limitations prescribed in the case of a bill.

tantes y Senado será sometido al Presidente de los Estados Unidos antes de que se convierta en ley. Si el Presidente lo aprueba, lo firmará. De lo contario, lo devolverá con sus objeciones a la cámara en donde se originó el proyecto, la que insertará en su diario las objeciones integramente y rocederá a reconsideralo. Si despúes de tal reconsideración dos terceras partes de dicha cámara convinieren en aprobar el proyecto, éste se enviará, junto con las objeciones, a la otra cámara, la que también lo reconsiderará y si resultare aprobado por las dos terceras partes de sus miembros, se convertirá en ley. En tales casos la votación en cada cámara será nominal y los votos en pro y en contra del proyecto así como los nombres de los votantes se consignarán en el diario de cada una de ellas. Si el Presidente no devolviere un proyecto de ley dentro de los diez días (excluyendo los domingos), después de haberle sido presentado, dicho proyecto se convertirá en ley, tal cual si lo hubiere firmado, a no ser que, por haber recesado, el Congreso impida su devolución. En tal caso el proyecto no se convertirá en ley.

(3) Toda orden, resolución o votación que requiera la concurrencia del Senado y de la Cámara de Representantes (salvo cuando se trate de levantar las sesiones) se presentará al Presidente de los Estados Unidos; y no tendrá efecto hasta que éste la apruebe o, en caso de ser desaprobada por él, hasta que dos terceras partes del Senado y de la

Powers Granted to Congress

Section 8 The Congress shall have power:

(1) To lay and collect taxes, duties, imposts, and excises, to pay the debts and provide for the common defense and general welfare of the United States; but all duties, imposts, and excises shall be uniform throughout the United States;

(2) To borrow money on the credit of the United States;

(3) To regulate commerce with foreign nations, and among the several states, and with the Indian tribes;

(4) To establish a uniform rule of naturalization, and uniform laws on the subject of bankruptcies throughout the United States;

(5) To coin money, regulate the value thereof, and of foreign coin, and fix the standard of weights and measures;

(6) To provide for the punishment of counterfeiting the securities and current coin of the United States;

(7) To establish post offices and post roads;

(8) To promote the progress of science and useful arts, by securing for limited times to authors and inventors the exclusive right to their respective writings and discoveries;

Cámara de Representantes la aprueben nuevamente, conforme a las reglas y restricciones prescritas para los proyectos de ley.

Sección 8 El Congreso tendrá facultad:

(1) para imponer y recaudar contribuciones, derechos, impuestos y arbitrios; para pagar las deudas y proveer para la defensa común y el bienestar general de los Estados Unidos; pero todos los derechos, impuestos y arbitrios serán uniformes en toda la nación;

(2) Para tomar dinero a préstamo con cargo al crédito de los Estados Unidos;

(3) Para reglamentar el comercio con naciones extranjeras, así como entre los estados y con las tribus indias;

(4) Para establecer una regla uniforme de naturalización y leyes uniformes de quiebras para toda la nación;

(5) Para acuñar moneda, reglamentar el valor de ésta y de la moneda extranjera, y fijar normas de pesas y medidas;

(6) Para fijar penas por la falsificación de los valores y de la moneda de los Estados Unidos;

(7) Para establecer oficinas de correo y vías postales;

(8) Para fomentar el progreso de la ciencia y de las artes útiles, garantizando por tiempo limitado a los autores e inventores el derecho exclusivo a sus respectivos escritos y descubrimientos;

(9) To constitute tribunals inferior to the Supreme Court;

(10) To define and punish piracies and felonies committed on the high seas, and offenses against the law of nations;

(11) To declare war, grant letters of marque and reprisal, and make rules concerning captures on land and water;

(12) To raise and support armies, but no appropriation of money to that use shall be for a longer term than two years;

(13) To provide and maintain a navy;

(14) To make rules for the government and regulation of the land and naval forces;

(15) To provide for calling forth the militia to execute the laws of the Union, suppress insurrections and repel invasions;

(16) To provide for organizing, arming, and disciplining, the militia, and for governing such part of them as may be employed in the service of the United States, reserving to the states respectively, the appointment of the officers, and the authority of training the militia according to the discipline prescribed by Congress;

(17) To exercise exclusive legislation in all cases whatsoever, over such district

(9) Para establecer tribunales inferiores al Tribunal Supremo;

(10) Para definir y castigar la piratería y los delitos graves cometidos en alta mar, así como las infracciones del derecho internacional;

(11) Para declarar la guerra, conceder patentes de corso y represalia y establecer reglas relativas a capturas en mar y tierra;

(12) Para reclutar y mantener ejércitos; pero ninguna asignación para este fin lo será por un período mayor de dos años;

(13) Para organizar y mantener una armada;

(14) Para establecer reglas para el gobierno y reglamentación de las fuerzas de mar y tierra;

(15) Para dictar reglas par llamar la milicia a fin de hacer cumplir las leyes de la Unión, sofocar insurrecciones y repeler invasiones;

(16) Para proveer para la organización, armamento y disciplina de la milicia y el gobierno de aquella parte de ella que estuviere al servicio de los Estados Unidos, reservando a los estados respectivos el nombramiento de los oficiales y la autoridad para adiestrar a la milicia de acuerdo con la disciplina prescrita por el Congreso;

(17) Para ejercer el derecho exclusivo a legislar en todas las materias

(not exceeding ten miles square) as may, by cession of particular states, and the acceptance of Congress, become the seat of the government of the United States, and to exercise like authority over all places purchased by the consent of the legislature of the state in which the same shall be, for the erection of forts, magazines, arsenals, dockyards, and other needful buildings; —And

(18) To make all laws which shall be necessary and proper for carrying into execution the foregoing powers, and all other powers vested by this Constitution in the government of the United States, or in any department or officer thereof.

Powers Denied Congress

Section 9 (1) The migration or importation of such persons as any of the states now existing shall think proper to admit, shall not be prohibited by the Congress prior to the year one thousand eight hundred and eight, but a tax or duty may be imposed on such importation, not exceeding ten dollars for each person.

(2) The privilege of the writ of habeas corpus shall not be suspended, unless when in cases of rebellion or invasion the public safety may require it.

(3) No bill of attainder or ex post facto law shall be passed.

concernientes a aquel distrito (cuya superficie no excederá de diez millas en cuadro) que, por cesión de algunos estados y aceptación del Congreso, se convirtiere en la sede del gobierno de los Estados Unidos; y para ejercer igual autoridad sobre todas aquellas tierras adquiridas con el consentimiento de la asamblea legislativa del estado en que radicaren, con el fin de construir fuertes, almacenes, arsenales, astilleros y otras edificaciones que fueren necesarias;

(18) Para aprobar todas las leyes que fueren necesarias y convenientes para poner en práctica las precedentes facultades, así como todas aquellas que en virtud de esta Constitución puedan estar investidas en el gobierno de los Estados Unidos o en cualquiera de sus departamentos o funcionarios.

Sección 9 (1) El Congreso no podrá antes del año 1808 prohibir la immigración de aquellas personas cuya admisión considere conveniente cualquiera de los estados existentes; pero se podrá imponer un tributo o impuesto al tal importación que no excederá de diez dólares por persona.

(2) No se suspenderá el privilegio del auto de hábeas corpus, salvo cuando en casos de rebelión o invasión la seguridad pública así lo exija.

(3) No se aprobará ningún proyecto para condenar sin celebración de juicio ni ninguna ley ex post facto.

(4) No capitation, [or other direct,] tax shall be laid, unless in proportion to the census or enumeration herein before directed to be taken.

(5) No tax or duty shall be laid on articles exported from any state.

(6) No preference shall be given by any regulation of commerce or revenue to the ports of one state over those of another: nor shall vessels bound to, or from, one state, be obliged to enter, clear, or pay duties in another.

(7) No money shall be drawn from the treasury, but in consequence of appropriations made by law; and a regular statement and account of the receipts and expenditures of all public money shall be published from time to time.

(8) No title of nobility shall be granted by the United States: And no person holding any office of profit or trust under them, shall, without the consent of the Congress, accept of any present, emolument, office, or title, of any kind whatever, from any king, prince, or foreign state.

Powers Denied the States
Section 10 **(1)** No state shall enter into any treaty, alliance, or confederation; grant letters of marque and reprisal; coin money; emit bills of credit; make anything but gold and silver coin a tender in payment of debts; pass any bill of attainder, ex

(4) No se impondrá capitación u otra contribución directa, sino en proporción al censo o enumeración que esta Constitución ordena se lleve a efecto.

(5) No se impondrán contribuciones o impuestos sobre los artículos que se exporten de cualquier estado.

(6) No se dará preferencia, por ningún reglamento de comercio o de rentas internas, a los puertos de un estado sobre los de otro. Tampoco podrá obligarse a las embarcaciones que se dirijan a un estado o salgan de él, que entren, descarguen o paguen impuestos en otro.

(7) No se podrá retirar cantidad alguna del Tesoro sino a virtud de asignaciones hechas por ley; y periódicamente se publicará un estado completo de los ingresos y egresos públicos.

(8) Los Estados Unidos no concederán títulos de nobleza; y ninguna persona que desempeñe bajo la autoridad del Gobierno un cargo retribuído o de confianza podrá aceptar, sin el consentimiento del Congreso, donativo, emolumento, empleo o título, de clase alguna, de ningún rey, príncipe o nación extranjera.

Sección 10 **(1)** Ningún estado celebrará tratado, alianza o confederación alguna; concederá patentes de corso y represalia; acuñará moneda; emitirá cartas de crédito; autorizará el pago de deudas en otro numerario que no sea oro y plata; aprobará ningún proyecto para

post facto law, or law impairing the obligation of contracts, or grant any title of nobility.

(2) No state shall, without the consent of the Congress, lay any imposts or duties on imports or exports, except what may be absolutely necessary for executing its inspection laws: and the net produce of all duties and imposts, laid by any state on imports or exports, shall be for the use of the treasury of the United States; and all such laws shall be subject to the revision and control of the Congress.

(3) No state shall, without the consent of Congress, lay any duty of tonnage, keep troops, or ships of war in time of peace, enter into any agreement or compact with another state, or with a foreign power, or engage in war, unless actually invaded, or in such imminent danger as will not admit of delay.

ARTICLE II
The Executive Branch

The President
Section 1 (1) The executive power shall be vested in a President of the United States of America. He shall hold his office during the term of four years, and, together with the Vice President, chosen for the same term, be elected, as follows:

(2) Each state shall appoint, in such manner as the legislature thereof may direct, a number of electors, equal to

condenar sin celebración de juicio, ley ex post facto o que menoscabe la obligación de los contratos, ni concederá títulos de nobleza.

(2) Ningún estado podrá, sin el consentimiento del Congreso, fijar impuestos o derechos sobre las importaciones o exportaciones, salvo cuando fuere absolutamente necesario para hacer cumplir sus leyes de inspección; y el producto neto de todos los derechos e impuestos que fijare cualquier estado sobre las importaciones o exportaciones, ingresará en el Tesoro de los Estados Unidos. Todas esas leyes quedarán sujetas a la revisión e intervención del Congreso.

(3) Ningún estado podrá, sin el consentimiento del Congreso, fijar derecho alguno de tonelaje, ni mantener tropas o embarcaciones de guerra en tiempos de paz, ni celebrar convenios o pactos con otro estado o con potencias extranjeras, ni entrar en guerra, a menos que fuere de hecho invadido o estuviere en peligro tan inminente que su defensa no admita demora.

Artículo II

Sección 1 (1) El poder ejecutivo residirá en el Presidente de los Estados Unidos de América. Este desempeñará sus funciones por un término de cuatro años y se le eligirá, junto con el Vicepresidente, quien también desempeñará su cargo por un término similar, de la siguiente manera;

the whole number of senators and representatives to which the state may be entitled in the Congress: but no senator or representative, or person holding an office of trust or profit under the United States, shall be appointed an elector.

[The electors shall meet in their respective states, and vote by ballot for two persons, of whom one at least shall not be an inhabitant of the same state with themselves. And they shall make a list of all the persons voted for, and of the number of votes for each; which list they shall sign and certify, and transmit sealed to the seat of the government of the United States, directed to the president of the Senate. The president of the Senate shall, in the presence of the Senate and House of Representatives, open all the certificates, and the votes shall then be counted. The person having the greatest number of votes shall be the President, if such number be a majority of the whole number of electors appointed; and if there be more than one who have such majority, and have an equal number of votes, then the House of Representatives shall immediately choose by ballot one of them for President; and if no person have a majority, then from the five highest on the list the said House shall in like manner choose the President. But in choosing the President, the votes shall be taken by states, the representation from each state having one vote; a quorum for this purpose shall consist of a

(2) Cada estado designará, en la forma que prescribiere su asamblea legislativa, un número de compromisarios igual al número total de senadores y representantes que le corresponda en el Congreso, pero no será nombrado compromisario ningún senador o representante o persona alguna que ocupare un cargo de confianza o retribuído bajo la autoridad de los Estados Unidos.

Los compromisarios se reunirán en sus respectivos estados, y mediante votación secreta votarán por dos personas, de las cuales por lo menos una no será residente del mismo estado que ellos. Se hará una lista de todas las personas por quienes se hubiere votado así como del número de votos que cada una obtuviere. Los compromisarios firmarán y certificarán esta lista, y la remitirán sellada a la sede del gobierno de los Estados Unidos, dirigida al presidente del Senado. En presencia del Senado y de la Cámara de Representantes, el presidente del Senado abrirá todos los certificados y se procederá entonces a verificar el escrutinio. Será presidente la persona que obtuviere mayor número de votos si dicho número fuere la mayoría del número total de compromisarios designados. Si más de una persona obtuviere tal mayoría, entonces la Cámara eligirá en igual forma al Presidente de entre las cinco personas que hubieren obtenido más votos en la lista. Pero en la elección del Presidente, la votación será por

member or members from two-thirds of the states, and a majority of all the states shall be necessary to a choice. In every case, after the choice of the President, the person having the greatest number of votes of the electors shall be the Vice President. But if there should remain two or more who have equal votes, the Senate shall choose from them by ballot the Vice President.]

(3) The Congress may determine the time of choosing the electors, and the day on which they shall give their votes; which day shall be the same throughout the United States.

(4) No person except a natural-born citizen, or a citizen of the United States at the time of the adoption of this Constitution, shall be eligible to the office of President; neither shall any person be eligible to that office who shall not have attained to the age of thirty-five years, and been fourteen years a resident within the United States.

(5) In case of the removal of the President from office, or of his death, resignation, or inability to discharge the powers and duties of the said office, the same shall devolve on the Vice President, and the Congress may by law provide for the case of removal, death, or resignation or inability, both of the President and Vice President, declaring what officer shall then act as President, and such officer shall act accordingly, until the disability be removed, or a President shall be elected.

estados y la representación de cada estado tendrá derecho a un voto. Para este fin el quorum constará de uno o más miembros de las dos terceras partes de las representaciones de los estados, y para que haya elección será necesaria una mayoría de todos los estados. En cualquier caso, una vez elegido el Presidente, será Vicepresidente la persona que obtuviere el mayor número de votos de los compromisarios. Pero si hubiere dos o más con un número iqual de votos, el Senado, por votación secreta, elegirá entre ellas al Vicepresidente.

(3) El Congreso determinará la fecha de seleccionar los compromisarios y el día en que habrán de votar, que serán los mismos en toda la Nación.

(4) No será elegible para el cargo de Presidente quien no fuere ciudadano por nacimiento o ciudadano de los Estados Unidos al tiempo in que se adopte esta Constitución. Tampoco lo será quien no hubiere cumplido treinta y cinco años de edad y no hubiere residido catorce años en los Estados Unidos.

(5) En caso de destitución, muerte, renuncia o incapacidad del Presidente para desempeñar las funciones de su cargo, le sustituirá el Vicepresidente. En caso de destitución, muerte, renuncia o incapacidad tanto del Presidente como del Vicepresidente, el Congreso dispondrá mediante legislación quién desempeñará presidencia y tal funcionario ejercerá el cargo hasta que cese la incapacidad o se elija un nuevo presidente.

(6) The President shall, at stated times, receive for his services, a compensation, which shall neither be increased or diminished during the period for which he shall have been elected, and he shall not receive within that period any other emolument from the United States, or any of them.

(7) Before he enter on the execution of his office, he shall take the following oath or affirmation: —"I do solemnly swear (or affirm) that I will faithfully execute the office of President of the United States, and will to the best of my ability, preserve, protect, and defend the Constitution of the United States."

Powers of the President
Section 2 (1) The President shall be commander in chief of the Army and Navy of the United States, and of the militia of the several states, when called into the actual service of the United States; he may require the opinion, in writing, of the principal officer in each of the executive departments, upon any subject relating to the duties of their respective offices, and he shall have power to grant reprieves and pardons for offenses against the United States, except in cases of impeachment.

(2) He shall have power, by and with the advice and consent of the Senate, to make treaties, provided two-thirds of the senators present concur; and he shall nominate, and by and with the advice and consent of the Senate, shall

(6) Como remuneración por sus servicios el Presidente recibirá, en las fechas que se determinen, una compensación que no podrá ser aumentada ni disminuida durante el término para el cual se le eligió, y no recibirá durante dicho término ningún otro emolumento de los Estados Unidos ni de ninguno de los estados.

(7) Antes de comenzar a desempeñar su cargo, el Presidente prestará el siguiente juramento o promesa: "Juro (o prometo) solemnemente que desempeñaré fielmente el cargo de Presidente de los Estados Unidos y que de la mejor manera a mi alcance guardaré, protegeré y defenderé la Constitución de los Estados Unidos."

Sección 2 (1) El Presidente será jefe supremo del Ejército y de la Armada de los Estados Unidos, así como de la milicia de los distintos estados cuando ésta fuere llamada al servicio activo de la nación. Podrá exigir opinión por escrito al jefe de cada departamento ejecutivo sobre cualquier asunto que se relacione con los deberes de sus respectivos cargos y tendrá facultad para suspender la ejecución de sentencias y para conceder indultos por delitos contra los Estados Unidos, salvo en casos de residencia.

(2) Con el consejo y consentimiento del Senado tendrá poder para celebrar tratados, siempre que en ellos concurran los dos terceras partes de los senadores presentes. Asimismo, con el consejo y

appoint ambassadors, other public ministers and consuls, judges of the Supreme Court, and all other officers of the United States, whose appointments are not herein otherwise provided for, and which shall be established by law: but the Congress may by law vest the appointment of such inferior officers, as they think proper, in the President alone, in the courts of law, or in the heads of departments.

(3) The President shall have power to fill up all vacancies that may happen during the recess of the Senate, by granting commissions which shall expire at the end of their next session.

Duties of the President

Section 3 He shall from time to time give to the Congress information of the state of the Union, and recommend to their consideration such measures as he shall judge necessary and expedient; he may, on extraordinary occasions, convene both houses, or either of them, and in case of disagreement between them, with respect to the time of adjournment, he may adjourn them to such time as he shall think proper; he shall receive ambassadors and other public ministers; he shall take care that the laws be faithfully executed, and shall commission all the officers of the United States.

consentimiento del Senado, nombrará embajadores, otros ministros y cónsules públicos, los jueces del Tribunal Supremo y todos los demás funcionarios de los Estados Unidos cuyos cargos se establezcan por ley y cuyos nombramientos esta Constitución no prescriba. Pero el Congreso podrá por ley, confiar el nombramiento de aquellos funcionarios subalternos que creyere prudente, al presidente únicamente, a los tribunales de justicia o a los jefes de departamento.

(3) El Presidente tendrá poder para cubrir todas las vacancias que ocurrieren durante el receso del Senado, extendiendo nombramientos que expirarán al finalizar la próxima sesión del Senado.

Sección 3 El Presidente informará periódicamente al Congreso sobre el estado de la Unión y le recomendará aquellas medidas que él estime necesarias y convenientes. Podrá, en ocasiones extraordinarias, convocar a ambas cámaras si no estuvieren de acuerdo con relación a la fecha para recesar, el Presidente podrá fijarla según lo juzgue conveniente. El Presidente recibirá a los embajadores y demás ministro públicos. Velará por el fiel cumplimiento de las leyes y extenderá los nombramientos de todos los funcionarios de los Estados Unidos.

Impeachment

Section 4 The President, Vice President, and all civil officers of the United States, shall be removed from office on impeachment for, and conviction of, treason, bribery, or other high crimes and misdemeanors.

ARTICLE III
The Judicial Branch

Federal Courts and Judges

Section 1 The judicial power of the United States, shall be vested in one Supreme Court, and in such inferior courts as the Congress may from time to time ordain and establish. The judges, both of the Supreme and inferior courts, shall hold their offices during good behavior, and shall, at stated times, receive for their services, a compensation, which shall not be diminished during their continuance in office.

Jurisdiction of United States Courts

Section 2 (1) The judicial power shall extend to all cases, in law and equity, arising under this Constitution, the laws of the United States, and treaties made, or which shall be made, under their authority; — to all cases affecting ambassadors, other public ministers and consuls; — to all cases of admiralty and maritime jurisdiction; — to controversies to which the United States shall be a party; — to controversies between two or more states; — [between a state and citizens of another state;] —

Sección 4 El Presidente, el Vicepresidente y todos los funcionarios civiles de los Estados Unidos serán destituídos de sus cargos mediante procedimiento de residencia, previa acusación y convictos que fueren de traición, cohecho u otros delitos graves y menos graves.

Artículo III

Sección 1 El poder judicial de los Estados Unidos residirá en un Tribunal Supremo y en aquellos tribunales inferiores que periódicamente el Congreso creare y estableciere. Los jueces, tanto del Tribunal Supremo como de tribunales inferiores, desempeñarán sus cargos mientras observen buena conducta y en determinadas fechas recibirán por sus servicios una compensación que no será rebajada mientras desempeñen sus cargos.

Sección 2 (1) El poder judicial se extenderá a todo caso que en derecho y equidad surja de esta Constitución, de las leyes de los Estados Unidos, así como de los tratados celebrados o que se celebraren bajo su autoridad; a todas los casos que afecten a embajadores y otros ministros y cónsules públicos; a todos los casos de almirantazgo y jurisdicción marítima; a todas las controversias en que los Estados Unidos sean parte; a las controversias entre dos o más estados; entre un estado y los ciudadanos de otro estado; entre los ciudadanos de diferentes estados; entre los ciudadanos del mismo estado que

between citizens of different states; — between citizens of the same state claiming lands under grants of different states, and between a state, or the citizens thereof, and foreign states, [citizens or subjects].

(2) In all cases affecting ambassadors, other public ministers and consuls, and those in which a state shall be party, the Supreme Court shall have original jurisdiction. In all the other cases before mentioned, the Supreme Court shall have appellate jurisdiction, both as to law and fact, with such exceptions, and under such regulations as the Congress shall make.

(3) The trial of all crimes, except in cases of impeachment, shall be by jury; and such trial shall be held in the state where the said crimes shall have been committed; but when not committed within any state, the trial shall be at such place or places as the Congress may by law have directed.

Treason
Section 3 (1) Treason against the United States, shall consist only in levying war against them, or in adhering to their enemies, giving them aid and comfort. No person shall be convicted of treason unless on the testimony of two witnesses to the same overt act, or on confession in open court.

(2) The Congress shall have power to declare the punishment of treason, but no attainder of treason shall work cor-

reclamaren tierras en virtud de concesiones hechas por diversos estados, y entre un estado o sus ciudadanos y estados, ciudadanos o súbditos extranjeros.

(2) El Tribunal Supremo tendrá jurisdicción original en todos los casos que afectaren a embajadores, ministros y cónsules públicos, y en aquellos en que un estado fuere parte. De todos los demás casos antes mencionados conocerá el Tribunal Supremo en apelación, tanto sobre cuestiones de derecho como de hecho, con las excepciones y bajo la reglamentación que el Congreso estableciere.

(3) Se juzgarán ante jurado todas las causas criminales, excepto las que den lugar al procedimiento de residencia; y el juicio se celebrará en el estado en que se cometió el delito. Si no se cometiere en ningún estado, se celebrará el juicio en el sitio o en los sitios que el Congreso designare por ley.

Sección 3 (1) El delito de traición contra los Estados Unidos consistirá solamente en tomar las armas contra ellos o en unirse a sus enemigos, dándoles ayuda y facilidades. Nadie será convicto de traición sino por el testimonio de dos testigos del hecho incriminatorio o por confesión en corte abierta.

(2) El Congreso tendrá poder para fijar la pena correspondiente al delito de traición; pero la sentencia por traición

ruption of blood, or forfeiture except during the life of the person attainted.

ARTICLE IV
The States and the Federal Government

State Acts and Records
Section 1 Full faith and credit shall be given in each state to the public acts, records, and judicial proceedings of every other state. And the Congress may by general laws prescribe the manner in which such acts, records, and proceedings shall be proved, and the effect thereof.

Rights of Citizens
Section 2 (1) The citizens of each state shall be entitled to all privileges and immunities of citizens in the several states.

(2) A person charged in any state with treason, felony, or other crime, who shall flee from justice, and be found in another state, shall on demand of the executive authority of the state from which he fled, be delivered up, to be removed to the state having jurisdiction of the crime.

(3) [No person held to service or labor in one state, under the laws thereof, escaping into another, shall, in consequence of any law or regulation therein, be discharged from such service or labor, but shall be delivered up on claim of the party to whom such service or labor may be due.]

no alcanzará en sus efectos a los herederos del culpable ni llevará consigo la confiscación de sus bienes salvo durante la vida de la persona sentenciada.

Artículo IV

Sección 1 Se dará entera fe y crédito en cada estado a los actos públicos, documentos y procedimientos judiciales de los otros estados. El Congreso podrá prescribir mediante leyes generales la manera de probar tales actos, documentos y procedimientos así como los efectos que deban surtir.

Sección 2 (1) Los ciudadanos de cada estado disfrutarán de todos los privilegios e immunidades de los ciudadanos de otros estados.

(2) Toda persona acusada de traición, delito grave o de cualquier otro delito, que huyere del estado en donde se le acusa y fuere hallada en otro estado, será, a solicitud de la autoridad ejecutiva del estado de donde se fugó, entregada a dicha autoridad para ser devuelta al estado que tuviere jurisdicción para conocer del delito.

(3) Ninguna persona obligada a servir o trabajar en un estado, a tenor con las leyes allí vigentes, que huyere a otro estado, será dispensada de prestar dicho servicio o trabajo amparándose en leyes o reglamentos del estado al cual se acogiere, sino que será entregada a petición de la parte que tuviere derecho al susodicho servicio o trabajo.

New States and Territories

Section 3 (1) New states may be admitted by the Congress into this Union; but no new state shall be formed or erected within the jurisdiction of any other state; nor any state be formed by the junction of two or more states, or parts of states, without the consent of the legislatures of the states concerned as well as of the Congress.

(2) The Congress shall have power to dispose of and make all needful rules and regulations respecting the territory or other property belonging to the United States; and nothing in this Constitution shall be so construed as to prejudice any claims of the United States, or of any particular state.

Protection of States Guaranteed

Section 4 The United States shall guarantee to every state in this Union a republican form of government, and shall protect each of them against invasion; and on application of the legislature, or of the executive (when the legislature cannot be convened) against domestic violence.

ARTICLE V
Amending the Constitution

The Congress, whenever two-thirds of both houses shall deem it necessary, shall propose amendments to this Constitution, or, on the application of the legislatures of two-thirds of the several states, shall call a convention for proposing amendments, which, in

Sección 3 (1) El Congreso podrá admitir nuevos estados a esta Unión; pero no se formará o establecerá ningún estado nuevo dentro de la jurisdicción de ningún otro estado. Tampoco se formará ningún estado por unión de dos o más estados, o partes de estados, sin el consentimiento tanto de las asambleas legislativas de los estados en cuestión como del Congreso.

(2) El Congreso podrá disponer de o promulgar todas las reglas y reglamentos necesarios en relación con, el territorio o cualquier propiedad perteneciente a los Estados Unidos. Ninguna disposición de esta Constitución se interpretará en forma tal que pudiere perjudicar cualesquiera reclamaciones de los Estados Unidos o de algún estado en particular.

Sección 4 Los Estados Unidos garantizarán a cada estado de esta Unión una forma republicana de gobierno y protegerán a cada uno de ellos contra toda invasión; y cuando lo solicitare la asamblea legislativa o el ejecutivo (si no se pudiere convocar la primera), le protegerá contra desórdenes internos.

Artículo V

El Congreso propondrá enmiendas a esta Constitución, siempre que dos terceras partes de ambas cámaras lo estimen necesario; o, a petición de las asambleas legislativas de dos terceras partes de los estados, convocará una convención para proponer enmiendas,

either case, shall be valid to all intents and purposes, as part of this Constitution, when ratified by the legislatures of three-fourths of the several states, or by conventions in three-fourths thereof, as the one or the other mode of ratification may be proposed by the Congress; provided [that no amendment which may be made prior to the year one thousand eight hundred and eight shall in any manner affect the first and fourth clauses in the ninth section of the first article; and] that no state, without its consent, shall be deprived of its equal suffrage in the Senate.

ARTICLE VI
General Provisions

(1) All debts contracted and engagements entered into, before the adoption of this Constitution, shall be as valid against the United States under this Constitution, as under the Confederation.

(2) This Constitution, and the laws of the United States which shall be made in pursuance thereof; and all treaties made, or which shall be made, under the authority of the United States, shall be the supreme law of the land; and the judges in every state shall be bound thereby, anything in the constitution or laws of any state to the contrary notwithstanding.

las cuales, en uno u otro caso, serán válidas para todos los fines y propósitos, como parte de esta Constitución, cuando las ratifiquen las asambleas legislativas de las tres cuartas partes de los estados, o las convenciones celebradas en las tres cuartas partes de los mismos, de acuerdo con el modo de ratificación propuesto por el Congreso; disponiéndose, que ninguna enmienda hecha antes del año mil ochocientos ocho afectara en modo alguno los incisos primero y cuarto de la novena sección del primer artículo; y que no se privará a ningún estado, sin su consentimiento, de la igualdad de sufragio en el Senado.

Artículo VI

(1) Todas las deudas y obligaciones contraídas antes de promulgarse este Constitución serán tan válidas contra los Estados Unidos bajo esta Constitución como lo eran bajo la Confederación.

(2) La presente Constitución, las leyes de los Estados Unidos que en virtud de ella se aprobaren y todos los tratados celebrados o que se celebraren bajo la autoridad de los Estados Unidos serán la suprema ley del país. Los jueces de cada estado estarán obligados a observarla aun cuando hubiere alguna disposición en contrario en la Constitución o en las leyes de cualquier estado.

(3) The senators and representatives before mentioned, and the members of the several state legislatures, and all executive and judicial officers, both of the United States and of the several states, shall be bound by oath or affirmation, to support this Constitution; but no religious test shall ever be required as a qualification to any office or public trust under the United States.

ARTICLE VII
Ratifying the Constitution

The ratification of the conventions of nine states shall be sufficient for the establishment of this Constitution between the states so ratifying the same.

Done in convention by the unanimous consent of the states present the seventeenth day of September in the year of our Lord one thousand seven hundred and eighty-seven and of the independence of the United States of America the twelfth. In witness thereof we have hereunto subscribed our names.

(3) Los senadores y representantes antes mencionados, los miembros de las asambleas legislativas de los diversos estados, así como todos los funcionarios ejecutivos y judiciales, tanto de los Estados Unidos como de los diversos estados, se comprometerán bajo juramento o promesa a sostener esta Constitución; pero no existirá requisito religioso alguno para desempeñar ningún cargo o empleo, retribuído o de confianza, bajo la autoridad de los Estados Unidos.

Artículo VII

La ratificación de las convenciones de nueve estados será suficiente para que esta Constitución rija entre los estados que la ratificaren.

Dada en convención con el consentimiento unánime de los estados presentes, el día diecisiete de septiembre del año de Nuestro Señor mil setecientos ochenta y siete, duodécimo de la independencia de los Estados Unidos de América. En testimonio de lo cual suscribimos la presente.

George Washington —
President and deputy from Virginia (Presidente y Diputado por Virginia)

Delaware
George Read
Gunning Bedford, Jr.
John Dickinson
Richard Bassett
Jacob Broom

Maryland
James McHenry
Dan of St. Thomas Jenifer
Daniel Carroll

Virginia
John Blair
James Madison, Jr.

North Carolina (Carolina del Norte)
William Blount
Richard Dobbs Spaight
Hugh Williamson

South Carolina (Carolina del Sur)
John Rutledge
Charles Cotesworth Pinckney
Charles Pinckney
Pierce Butler

Georgia
William Few
Abraham Baldwin

New Hampshire (Nueva Hampshire)
John Langdon
Nicholas Gilman

Massachusetts
Nathaniel Gorham
Rufus King

Connecticut
William Samuel Johnson
Roger Sherman

New York (Nueva York)
Alexander Hamilton

New Jersey (Nueva Jersey)
William Livingston
David Brearley
William Paterson
Jonathan Dayton

Pennsylvania (Pensilvania)
Benjamin Franklin
Thomas Mifflin
Robert Morris
George Clymer
Thomas FitzSimons
Jared Ingersoll
James Wilson
Gouverneur Morris

Attest:
William Jackson, Secretary

* *Headings and paragraph numbers have been added to help the reader. The original Constitution has only the article and section numbers.*

Amendments to the Constitution

The Bill of Rights

AMENDMENT 1
Religious and Political Freedoms (1791)
Congress shall make no law respecting an establishment of religion, or prohibiting the free exercise thereof; or abridging the freedom of speech, or of the press; or the right of the people peaceably to assemble, and to petition the government for a redress of grievances.

AMENDMENT 2
Right to Bear Arms (1791)
A well-regulated militia, being necessary to the security of a free state, the right of the people to keep and bear arms shall not be infringed.

AMENDMENT 3
Housing of Soldiers (1791)
No soldier shall, in time of peace be quartered in any house, without the consent of the owner, nor in time of war, but in a manner to be prescribed by law.

AMENDMENT 4
Search and Arrest Warrants (1791)
The right of the people to be secure in their persons, houses, papers, and

Declaracion de Derechos

ENMIENDA 1
El Congreso no aprobará ninguna ley con respecto al establecimiento de religión alguna, o que prohiba el libre ejercicio de palabra o de prensa; o el derecho del pueblo a reunirse pacificamente y a solicitar del gobierno la reparación de agravios.

ENMIENDA 2
Siendo necesaria para la seguridad de un estado libre una milicia bien organizada, no se coartará el derecho de pueblo a tener y portar armas.

ENMIENDA 3
En tiempos de paz ningún soldado será alojado en casa alguna, sin el consentimiento del propietario, ni tampoco lo será en tiempos de guerra sino de la manera prescrita por ley.

ENMIENDA 4
No se violará el derecho del pueblo a la seguridad de sus personas, hogares, documentos y pertenencias, contra

effects, against unreasonable searches and seizures, shall not be violated, and no warrants shall issue, but upon probable cause, supported by oath or affirmation, and particularly describing the place to be searched, and the persons or things to be seized.

AMENDMENT 5
Rights in Criminal Cases (1791)

No person shall be held to answer for a capital, or otherwise infamous crime, unless on a presentment or indictment of a grand jury, except in cases arising in the land or naval forces, or in the militia, when in actual service in time of war or public danger; nor shall any person be subject for the same offense to be twice put in jeopardy of life or limb; nor shall be compelled in any criminal case to be a witness against himself, nor be deprived of life, liberty, or property, without due process of law; nor shall private property be taken for public use, without just compensation.

AMENDMENT 6
Rights to a Fair Trial (1791)

In all criminal prosecutions, the accused shall enjoy the right to a speedy and public trial, by an impartial jury of the state and district wherein the crime shall have been committed, which district shall have been previously ascertained by law, and to be informed of the nature and cause of the accusation; to be confronted with the witnesses against him; to have compulsory process for obtaining witnesses in his favor, and

registros y allanamientos irrazonables, y no se expedirá ningún mandamiento, sino a virtud de causa probable, apoyado por juramento o promesa, y que describa en detalle el lugar que ha de ser allanado y las personas o cosas que han de ser detenidas o incautadas.

ENMIENDA 5

Ninguna persona será obligada a responder por delito capital o infamante, sino en virtud de denuncia o acusación por un gran jurado, salvo en los casos que ocurran en las fuerzas de mar y tierra, o en la milicia, cuando se hallen en servicio activo en tiempos de guerra o de peligro público; ni podrá nadie ser sometido por el mismo delito dos veces a un juicio que pueda ocasionarle la pérdida de la vida o la integridad corporal; ni será compelido en ningún caso criminal a declarar contra sí mismo, ni será privado de su vida, de su libertad o de su propiedad, sin el debido procedimiento de ley; ni se podrá tomar propriedad privada para uso público, sin justa compensación.

ENMIENDA 6

En todas las causas criminales, el acusado gozará del derecho a un juicio rápido y público, ante un jurado imparcial del estado y distrito en que el delito haya sido cometido, distrito que será previamente fijado por ley; a ser informado de la naturaleza y causa de la acusación; a carearse con los testigos en su contra; a que se adopten medidas compulsivas para la comparecencia de

to have the assistance of counsel for his defense.

AMENDMENT 7
Rights in Civil Cases (1791)
In suits at common law, where the value in controversy shall exceed twenty dollars, the right of trial by jury shall be preserved, and no fact tried by a jury, shall be otherwise re-examined in any court of the United States, than according to the rules of the common law.

AMENDMENT 8
Bails, Fines, and Punishments (1791)
Excessive bail shall not be required, nor excessive fines imposed, nor cruel and unusual punishments inflicted.

AMENDMENT 9
Rights Retained by the People (1791)
The enumeration in the Constitution, of certain rights, shall not be construed to deny or disparage others retained by the people.

AMENDMENT 10
Powers Retained by the States and the People (1791)
The powers not delegated to the United States by the Constitution, nor prohibited by it to the states, are reserved to the states respectively, or to the people.

los testigos que cite a su favor y a la asistencia de abogado para su defensa.

ENMIENDA 7
En litigios en derecho común, en que el valor en controversia exceda de veinte dólares, se mantendrá el derecho a juicio por jurado, y ningún hecho fallado por un jurado, será revisado por ningún tribunal de los Estados Unidos, sino de acuerdo con las reglas del derecho común.

ENMIENDA 8
No se exigirán fianzas excesivas, ni se impondrán multas excesivas, ni castigos crueles e inusitados.

ENMIENDA 9
La inclusión de ciertos derechos en la Constitución no se interpretará en el sentido de denegar o restringir otros derechos que se haya reservado el pueblo.

ENMIENDA 10
Las facultades que esta Constitución no delegue a los Estados Unidos, ni prohiba a los estados, quedan reservadas a los estados respectivamente o al pueblo.

AMENDMENT 11
Lawsuits Against States (1795)

The judicial power of the United States shall not be construed to extend to any suit in law or equity, commenced or prosecuted against one of the United States by citizens of another state, or by citizens or subjects of any foreign state.

AMENDMENT 12
Election of the President and Vice President (1804)

The electors shall meet in their respective states and vote by ballot for President and Vice President, one of whom, at least, shall not be an inhabitant of the same state with themselves; they shall name in their ballots the person voted for as President, and in distinct ballots the person voted for as Vice President, and they shall make distinct lists of all persons voted for as President, and of all persons voted for as Vice President, and of the number of votes for each, which lists they shall sign and certify, and transmit sealed to the seat of the government of the United States, directed to the president of the Senate; — the president of the Senate shall, in the presence of the Senate and House of Representatives, open all the certificates and the votes shall then be counted; — the person having the greatest number of votes for President, shall be the President, if such number be a majority of the whole number of electors appointed; and if no person have such majority, then from the persons having the highest numbers not exceeding three on the list of those voted for as President, the House of Representatives shall choose immediately, by ballot, the President. But in choosing the President, the votes shall be taken by states, the representation from each state having one vote; a quorum for this purpose shall consist of a member or members from two-thirds of the states, and a majority of all the states shall be necessary to a choice. And if the House of Representatives shall not choose a President whenever the right of choice shall devolve upon them, [before the fourth day of March next following,] then the Vice President shall act as President, as in the case of the death or other constitutional disability of the President. — The person having the greatest number of votes as Vice President, shall be the Vice President, if such number be a majority of the whole number of electors appointed, and if no person have a majority, then from the two highest numbers on the list, the Senate shall choose the Vice President; a quorum for the purpose shall consist of two-thirds of the whole number of senators, and a majority of the whole number shall be necessary to a choice. But no person constitutionally ineligible to the office of President shall be eligible to that of Vice President of the United States.

AMENDMENT 13
Abolition of Slavery (1865)

Section 1 Neither slavery nor involuntary servitude, except as a punishment for crime whereof the party shall have been duly convicted, shall exist within the United States, or any place subject to their jurisdiction.

Section 2 Congress shall have power to enforce this article by appropriate legislation.

AMENDMENT 14
Civil Rights (1868)

Section 1 All persons born or naturalized in the United States, and subject to the jurisdiction thereof, are citizens of the United States and of the state wherein they reside. No state shall make or enforce any law which shall abridge the privileges or immunities of citizens of the United States; nor shall any state deprive any person of life, liberty, or property, without due process of law; nor deny to any person within its jurisdiction the equal protection of the laws.

Section 2 Representatives shall be apportioned among the several states according to their respective numbers, counting the whole number of persons in each state, [excluding Indians not taxed]. But when the right to vote at any election for the choice of electors for President and Vice President of the United States, representatives in Congress, the executive and judicial officers of a state, or the members of the legislature thereof, is denied to any of the male inhabitants of such state, being twenty-one years of age, and citizens of the United States, or in any way abridged, except for participation in rebellion, or other crime, the basis of representation therein shall be reduced in the proportion which the number of such male citizens shall bear to the whole number of male citizens twenty-one years of age in such state.

Section 3 No person shall be a senator or representative in Congress, or elector of President and Vice President, or hold any office, civil or military, under the United States, or under any state, who, having previously taken an oath, as a member of Congress, or as an officer of the United States, or as a member of any state legislature, or as an executive or judicial officer of any state, to support the Constitution of the United States, shall have engaged in insurrection or rebellion against the same, or given aid or comfort to the enemies thereof. But Congress may by a vote of two-thirds of each House, remove such disability.

Section 4 The validity of the public debt of the United States, authorized by law, including debts incurred for payment of pensions and bounties for services in suppressing insurrection or rebellion, shall not be questioned. But neither the United States nor any state shall assume or pay any debt or obligation incurred in aid of insurrection or rebellion against the United States, or any claim for the loss or emancipation of any slave; but all such debts, obligations, and claims shall be held illegal and void.

Section 5 The Congress shall have power to enforce, by appropriate legislation, the provisions of this article.

AMENDMENT 15
Right to Vote (1870)
Section 1 The right of citizens of the United States to vote shall not be denied or abridged by the United States or by any state on account of race, color, or previous condition of servitude.

Section 2 The Congress shall have power to enforce this article by appropriate legislation.

AMENDMENT 16
Income Taxes (1913)
The Congress shall have power to lay and collect taxes on incomes, from whatever source derived, without apportionment among the several states, and without regard to any census or enumeration.

AMENDMENT 17
Direct Election of Senators (1913)
(1) The Senate of the United States shall be composed of two senators from each state, elected by the people thereof for six years; and each senator shall have one vote. The electors in each state shall have the qualifications requisite for electors of the most numerous branch of the state legislatures.

(2) When vacancies happen in the representation of any state in the Senate, the executive authority of such state shall issue writs of election to fill such vacancies: provided, that the legislature of any state may empower the executive thereof to make temporary appointments until the people fill the vacancies by election as the legislature may direct.

(3) This amendment shall not be so construed as to affect the election or term of any senator chosen before it becomes valid as part of the Constitution.

AMENDMENT 18
Prohibition of Liquor (1919)
Section 1 After one year from the ratification of this article the manufacture, sale, or transportation of intoxicating liquors within, the importation thereof into, or the exportation thereof from the United States and all territory subject to the jurisdiction thereof for beverage purposes is hereby prohibited.

Section 2 The Congress and the several states shall have concurrent power to enforce this article by appropriate legislation.

Section 3 This article shall be inoperative unless it shall have been ratified as an amendment to the Constitution by the legislatures of the several states, as provided in the Constitution, within seven years from the date of the submission hereof to the states by the Congress.

AMENDMENT 19
Women's Suffrage (1920)

Section 1 The right of citizens of the United States to vote shall not be denied or abridged by the United States or by any state on account of sex.

Section 2 Congress shall have power to enforce this article by appropriate legislation.

AMENDMENT 20
Terms of the President and Congress (1933)

Section 1 The terms of the President and Vice President shall end at noon on the 20th day of January, and the terms of senators and representatives at noon on the third day of January, of the years in which such terms would have ended if this article had not been ratified; and the terms of their successors shall then begin.

Section 2 The Congress shall assemble at least once in every year, and such meeting shall begin at noon on the third day of January, unless they shall by law appoint a different day.

Section 3 If, at the time fixed for the beginning of the term of the President, the President elect shall have died, the Vice President elect shall become President. If a President shall not have been chosen before the time fixed for the beginning of his term, of if the President elect shall have failed to qualify, then the Vice President elect shall act as President until a President shall have qualified; and the Congress may by law provide for the case wherein neither a President elect nor a Vice President elect shall have qualified, declaring who shall then act as President, or the manner in which one who is to act shall be selected, and such person shall act accordingly until a President or Vice President shall have qualified.

Section 4 The Congress may by law provide for the case of the death of any of the persons from whom the House of Representatives may choose a President whenever the right of choice shall have devolved upon them, and for the case of the death of any of the persons from whom the Senate may choose a Vice President whenever the right of choice shall have devolved upon them.

Section 5 Sections 1 and 2 shall take effect on the 15th day of October following the ratification of this article.

Section 6 This article shall be inoperative unless it shall have been ratified as an amendment to the Constitution by the legislatures of three-fourths of the several states within seven years from the date of its submission.

AMENDMENT 21
Repeal of Prohibition (1933)

Section 1 The eighteenth article of amendment to the Constitution of the United States is hereby repealed.

Section 2 The transportation or importation into any state, territory, or possession of the United States for delivery or use therein of intoxicating liquors, in violation of the laws thereof, is hereby prohibited.

Section 3 This article shall be inoperative unless it shall have been ratified as an amendment to the Constitution by conventions in the several states, as provided in the Constitution, within seven years from the date of the submission hereof to the states by the Congress.

AMENDMENT 22
Limitation on Presidential Terms (1951)

Section 1 No person shall be elected to the office of the President more than twice, and no person who has held the office of President, or acted as President, for more than two years of a term to which some other person was elected President shall be elected to the office of the President more than once. But this article shall not apply to any person holding the office of President when this article was proposed by the Congress, and shall not prevent any person who may be holding the office of President, or acting as President, during the term within which this article becomes operative from holding the office of President or acting as President during the remainder of such term.

Section 2 This article shall be inoperative unless it shall have been ratified as an amendment to the Constitution by the legislatures of three-fourths of the several states within seven years from the date of its submission to the states by the Congress.

AMENDMENT 23
Suffrage in the District of Columbia (1961)

Section 1 The district constituting the seat of government of the United States shall appoint in such manner as the Congress may direct: A number of electors of President and Vice President equal to the whole number of senators and representatives in Congress to which the district would be entitled if it were a state, but in no event more than the least populous state; they shall be in addition to those appointed by the states, but they shall be considered, for the purposes of the election of President and Vice President, to be electors appointed by a state; and they shall meet in the district and perform such duties as provided by the twelfth article of amendment.

Section 2 The Congress shall have power to enforce this article by appropriate legislation.

AMENDMENT 24
Poll Taxes (1964)

Section 1 The right of citizens of the United States to vote in any primary or other election for President or Vice President, for electors for President or Vice President, or for senator or representative in Congress, shall not be denied or abridged by the United States or any state by reason of failure to pay any poll tax or other tax.

Section 2 The Congress shall have power to enforce this article by appropriate legislation.

AMENDMENT 25
Presidential Disability and Succession (1967)

Section 1 In case of the removal of the President from office or of his death or resignation, the Vice President shall become President.

Section 2 Whenever there is a vacancy in the office of the Vice President, the President shall nominate a Vice President who shall take office upon confirmation by a majority vote of both houses of Congress.

Section 3 Whenever the President transmits to the president *pro tempore* of the Senate and the Speaker of the House of Representatives his written declaration that he is unable to discharge the powers and duties of his office, and until he transmits to them a written declaration to the contrary, such powers and duties shall be discharged by the Vice President as acting President.

Section 4 Whenever the Vice President and a majority of either the principal officers of the executive departments or of such other body as Congress may by law provide, transmit to the president pro tempore of the Senate and the Speaker of the House of Representatives their written declaration that the President is unable to discharge the powers and duties of his office, the Vice President shall immediately assume the powers and duties of the office as acting President.

Thereafter, when the President transmits to the president pro tempore of the Senate and the speaker of the House of Representatives his written declaration that no inability exists, he shall resume the powers and duties of his office unless the Vice President and a majority of either the principal officers of the executive department or of such other body as Congress may by law provide, transmit within four days to the president pro tempore of the Senate and the Speaker of the House of Representatives their written declaration that the President is unable to discharge the powers and duties of his office. Thereupon Congress shall decide the issue, assembling within forty-eight hours for that purpose if not in session. If the Congress, within twenty-one days after receipt of the latter written declaration, or, if Congress is not in session, within twenty-one days after Congress is required to assemble, determines by two-thirds vote of both houses that the President is unable to discharge the powers and duties of his office, the Vice President shall continue to discharge the same as acting President; otherwise, the President shall resume the powers and duties of his office.

AMENDMENT 26
Suffrage for 18-Year-Olds (1971)
Section 1 The right of citizens of the United States, who are eighteen years of age or older, to vote shall not be denied or abridged by the United States or by any state on account of age.

Section 2 The Congress shall have power to enforce this article by appropriate legislation.

AMENDMENT 27
Congressional Pay (1992)
No law, varying the compensation for the services of the senators and representatives, shall take effect, until an election of representatives shall have intervened.

Presidents of the United States

1. George Washington
"Father of His Country"
Term of Office: 1789-1797
Elected From: Virginia
Party: None
Born: 1732   Died: 1799

2. John Adams
"Colossus of Debate"
Term of Office: 1797-1801
Elected From: Massachusetts
Party: Federalist
Born: 1735   Died: 1826

3. Thomas Jefferson
"Father of the Declaration of
   Independence"
Term of Office: 1801-1809
Elected From: Virginia
Party: Democratic-Republican
Born: 1743   Died: 1826

4. James Madison
"Father of the Constitution"
Term of Office: 1809-1817
Elected From: Virginia
Party: Democratic-Republican
Born: 1751   Died: 1836

5. James Monroe
"Era of Good Feeling President"
Term of Office: 1817-1825
Elected From: Virginia
Party: Democratic-Republican
Born: 1758   Died: 1831

6. John Quincy Adams
"Old Man Eloquent"
Term of Office: 1825-1829
Elected From: Massachusetts
Party: None
Born: 1767   Died: 1848

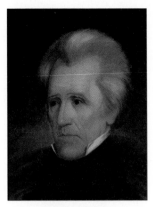

7. Andrew Jackson

"Old Hickory"
Term of Office: 1829-1837
Elected From: South Carolina
Party: Democratic
Born: 1767   Died: 1845

8. Martin Van Buren

"Young Hickory"
Term of Office: 1837-1841
Elected From: New York
Party: Democratic
Born: 1782   Died: 1862

9. William H. Harrison

"Old Tippecanoe"
Term of Office: 1841
Elected From: Virginia
Party: Whig
Born: 1773   Died: 1841

10. John Tyler

"Accidental President"
Term of Office: 1841-1845
Elected From: Virginia
Party: Whig
Born: 1790   Died: 1862

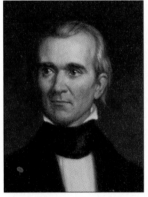

11. James K. Polk

"First Dark Horse"
Term of Office: 1845-1849
Elected From: Tennessee
Party: Democratic
Born: 1795   Died: 1849

12. Zachary Taylor

"Old Rough and Ready"
Term of Office: 1849-1850
Elected From: Virginia
Party: Whig
Born: 1784   Died: 1850

13. Millard Fillmore

"Wool-Carder President"
Term of Office: 1850-1853
Elected From: New York
Party: Whig
Born: 1800   Died: 1874

14. Franklin Pierce

"Handsome Frank"
Term of Office: 1853-1857
Elected From: New Hampshire
Party: Democratic
Born: 1804   Died: 1869

15. James Buchanan

"Bachelor President"
Term of Office: 1857-1861
Elected From: Pennsylvania
Party: Democratic
Born: 1791   Died: 1868

16. Abraham Lincoln

"Honest Abe"
Term of Office: 1861-1865
Elected From: Illinois
Party: Republican
Born: 1809   Died: 1865

17. Andrew Johnson

"King Andrew the First"
Term of Office: 1865-1869
Elected From: Tennessee
Party: Republican
Born: 1808   Died: 1875

18. Ulysses S. Grant

"American Caesar"
Term of Office: 1869-1877
Elected From: Ohio
Party: Republican
Born: 1822   Died: 1885

19. Rutherford B. Hayes
"Hero of '77"
Term of Office: 1877-1881
Elected From: Ohio
Party: Republican
Born: 1822   Died: 1893

20. James A. Garfield
"Preacher President"
Term of Office: 1881
Elected From: Ohio
Party: Republican
Born: 1831   Died: 1881

21. Chester A. Arthur
"America's First Gentleman"
Term of Office: 1881-1885
Elected From: New York
Party: Republican
Born: 1830   Died: 1886

22., 24. Grover Cleveland
"Perpetual Candidate"
Term of Office: 1885-1889,
   1893-1897
Elected From: New York
Party: Democratic
Born: 1837   Died: 1908

23. Benjamin Harrison
"Centennial President"
Term of Office: 1889-1893
Elected From: Indiana
Party: Republican
Born: 1833   Died: 1901

25. William McKinley
"Stocking-Foot Orator"
Term of Office: 1897-1901
Elected From: Ohio
Party: Republican
Born: 1843   Died: 1901

26. Theodore Roosevelt
"TR"
Term of Office: 1901-1909
Elected From: New York
Party: Republican
Born: 1858   Died: 1919

27. William H. Taft
"Big Chief"
Term of Office: 1909-1913
Elected From: Ohio
Party: Republican
Born: 1857   Died: 1930

28. Woodrow Wilson
"Professor"
Term of Office: 1913-1921
Elected From: New Jersey
Party: Democratic
Born: 1856   Died: 1924

29. Warren G. Harding
"Dark Horse Candidate"
Term of Office: 1921-1923
Elected From: Ohio
Party: Republican
Born: 1865   Died: 1923

30. Calvin Coolidge
"Silent Cal"
Term of Office: 1923-1929
Elected From: Massachusetts
Party: Republican
Born: 1872   Died: 1933

31. Herbert Hoover
"Grand Old Man"
Term of Office: 1929-1933
Elected From: California
Party: Republican
Born: 1874   Died: 1964

32. Franklin D. Roosevelt
"FDR"
Term of Office: 1933-1945
Elected From: New York
Party: Democratic
Born: 1882   Died: 1945

33. Harry S. Truman
"Man from Independence"
Term of Office: 1945-1953
Elected From: Missouri
Party: Democratic
Born: 1884   Died: 1972

34. Dwight D. Eisenhower
"Ike"
Term of Office: 1953-1961
Elected From: Kansas
Party: Republican
Born: 1890   Died: 1969

35. John F. Kennedy
"JFK"
Term of Office: 1961-1963
Elected From: Massachusetts
Party: Democratic
Born: 1917   Died: 1963

36. Lyndon B. Johnson
"LBJ"
Term of Office: 1963-1969
Elected From: Texas
Party: Democratic
Born: 1908   Died: 1973

37. Richard M. Nixon
"Embattled President"
Term of Office: 1969-1974
Elected From: California
Party: Republican
Born: 1913   Died: 1994

38. Gerald R. Ford

"Mr. Clean"
Term of Office: 1974-1977
Elected From: Michigan
Party: Republican
Born: 1913

39. James E. Carter

"Peanut Farmer"
Term of Office: 1977-1981
Elected From: Georgia
Party: Democratic
Born: 1924

40. Ronald W. Reagan

"Great Communicator"
Term of Office: 1981-1989
Elected From: California
Party: Republican
Born: 1911

41. George H.W. Bush

Term of Office: 1989-1993
Elected From: Texas
Party: Republican
Born: 1924

42. William J. Clinton

Term of Office: 1993-2001
Elected From: Arkansas
Party: Democratic
Born: 1946

Glossary

Absentee ballot — A ballot that is mailed in before an election (p. 218)

Acceptance speech — A speech agreeing to accept a nomination (p. 211)

Adjourn — To bring a meeting to an end (p. 67)

Administrate — To manage or direct (p. 120)

Admit — To allow or permit to enter (p. 72)

Adviser — A person who gives information, advice, or help (p. 80)

Aeronautics — The science of designing, building, and flying aircraft (p. 126)

Affirmative action — A policy to increase employment for minorities (p. 221)

Agency — A division within the executive branch that serves a special purpose (p. 80)

Alien — A person who lives in a country but is a citizen of another country (p. 232)

Ally – A country joined to another country by a treaty or agreement (p. 247)

Alternate — Someone who is appointed to substitute for a delegate at a political convention (p. 208)

Ambassador — A person appointed by the President to represent the United States in a foreign country (p. 41)

Amendment — A change or correction made by a certain process (p. 43)

Ancient — Many years ago; belonging to early history (p. 3)

Anti-Federalist — A person who favored state and individual rights (p. 32)

Appoint — To name or choose a person for an office, but not by election (p. 5)

Apportion — To divide and assign something according to a plan (p. 143)

Appropriations bill — A bill that gives government agencies money to operate (p. 93)

Article — One of the parts of a written document (p. 40)

Assassinate — To kill a politically important person (p. 91)

Assemble — To come together as a group (p. 47)

Assembly — A group gathered to discuss and pass laws (p. 4)

Assessor — A person who sets the value of property (p. 184)

Authority — The power or right to command or make final decisions (p. 32)

Bankrupt — Without money; declared legally unable to pay one's bills (p. 128)

Bill — A proposed new law (p. 68)

Blockade — To use troops or ships to prevent movement of people or supplies (p. 265)

Borough — Name for local government in Alaska (p. 157)

Brief — A document that describes the main arguments with supporting statements and evidence (p. 142)

Budget — A plan for how money will be taken in and spent (p. 90)

Bureaucracy — A group of non-elected government officials or offices (p. 120)

Cabinet — Group of advisers to a head of state (p. 100)

Campaign — To work on activities connected to getting elected to a political office (p. 82)

Candidate — A person who hopes to be elected to a public office (p. 54)

Challenge — To question the truth or accuracy of something (p. 141)

Charter — A document that states a group's purpose and plan (p. 154)

Checks and Balances — A plan to keep any part of government from becoming too powerful (p. 29)

Circuit — An assigned district or territory (p. 139)

Circulate — To pass from person to person (p. 220)

Circumstance — An event or condition (p. 166)

Citizen — A person given certain rights, duties, and privileges because he or she was born in, or chooses to live in, a city, state, or country (p. 64)

Civil — Having to do with citizens; a civil law case does not involve a crime (p. 52)

Civilian — A person not in the military or naval service (p. 111)

Coalition — A group of several parties (p. 200)

Colonist — Person that settles in a new country (p. 2)

Combination — A grouping of people, things, or ideas that are joined together for a special reason (p. 2)

Commander — A person who has full control of a group (p. 88)

Common law — Group of laws based on customs (p. 251)

Common market — A group of countries that has come together to remove trade restrictions (p. 252)

Communication satellites — Manufactured objects that travel around the earth in outer space; they are used to send information (p. 123)

Communism — A plan for government that seeks to eliminate private property (p. 255)

Community — The people living together in an area; a group of people who have a common interest (p. 2)

Complicated — Difficult (p. 2)

Compromise — A settlement of differences in which each side gives up some of its demands (p. 27)

Compulsory referendum — A referendum that requires voter approval (p. 220)

Congress — The legislative branch of the United States government; it includes the Senate and House of Representative (p. 40)

Conservation — The care and protection of natural resources (p. 107)

Conservative — A person who opposes or resists change (p. 203)

Consider — To examine or think over carefully (p. 3)

Constituent — A member of an office holder's voting district (p. 204)

Constitution — A plan for government (p. 10)

Constitutional democracy — A government that has a written constitution and democratic policies (p. 264)

Consul — A person who is appointed to represent the commercial interests of United States citizens in a foreign country (p. 103)

Consulate — The building where a consul works (p. 103)

Consumers — Persons who use goods and services (p. 100)

Contract — An agreement made by two or more persons (p. 10)

Controversy — Discussion between people who hold opposite views (p. 128)

Convention — A formal meeting called for a special purpose (p. 43)

Convict — To find guilty of crime (p. 51)

Cooperative — Willing to work together (p. 246)

Coroner — Official who looks into the cause of a person's death (p. 182)

Correctional — Intended to improve or to set right (p. 162)

Cosmetics — Materials containing chemicals people use to improve their appearance (p. 113)

Counterfeit — Imitation or fake (p. 104)

County seat — Place where county offices are located (p. 180)

Criticize — To put down or find fault with (p. 11)

Cultural — Having to do with the values, attitudes, and customs of people in a community (p. 183)

Custom — A common practice observed by many people (p. 2)

D

Debate — An argument or discussion between persons with different views (p. 55)

Decision — Act of making up one's mind; judgment (p. 6)

Dedicated — Devoted to; to give one's full attention to (p. 196)

Defend — To protect from attack or harm (p. 72)

Defendant — A person accused of doing something that is not legal (p. 136)

Delegate — A person chosen to speak or act for another person or group (p. 22)

Democracy — A form of government in which citizens take part (p. 4)

Democratic party — U.S. political party that stands for protecting rights of the individual (p. 196)

Deport — To send away or order to leave a country (p. 232)

Dictator — A person ruling with total control, power, and authority (p. 4)

Diet — Japan's legislative body (p. 258)

Diplomat — A person appointed to represent his or her country in another country (p. 88)

Diplomatic relations — When a country sends an ambassador to another country (p. 260)

Direct democracy — Form of government in which all voters gather to conduct town business (p. 187)

Direct primary — Kind of primary where voters choose a candidate to support (p. 206)

Disabled — To be physically or mentally handicapped (p. 113)

Disagreement — A quarrel; a difference of opinion (p. 137)

Discrimination — Treating people unfairly because of their race, sex, or age (p. 109)

Dishonorable discharge — To be put out of the armed forces for shameful or disgraceful reasons (p. 216)

Disobey — To do something that is against the rules (p. 136)

Disorderly conduct — Disturbing public peace (p. 170)

Domestic relations court — A court that hears home and family disputes (p. 170)

Donation — A gift or contribution (p. 212)

Due process — Right to a fair trial according to rules and procedures (p. 52)

E

Economical — Operating with little waste of money (p. 112)

Economy — The system of handling money and business in a country (p. 94)

Efficient — Well-run or operating smoothly (p. 112)

Elastic clause — A part of the Constitution that gives Congress power to make laws as needed (p. 73)

Electoral College — A group of people chosen by political parties to vote for the President and Vice President (p. 82)

Eligible — Someone who qualifies to do something (p. 216)

Embassy — A country's headquarters in a foreign country (p. 247)

Endowment — A gift given to a person or organization to provide income (p. 127)

Enforce — To see that a rule or law is obeyed (p. 101)

Environment — Having to do with the climate, soil, and preservation of natural resources (p. 94)

Equality — Having the same rights as others (p. 236)

Essays — Short compositions on special subjects (p. 32)

European Economic Community (EEC) —
A group of twelve European nations that
is becoming a common market (p. 252)

Evidence — The objects and statements
gathered and used to judge a person of a
crime (p. 51)

Exception — A case in which a rule does not
apply or is not followed (p. 163)

Executive — A person or group having the
power to carry out the plans and duties of
a group; for example, a president (p. 24)

Exports — Goods sold and shipped to
foreign countries (p. 28)

Express — To make known one's thoughts,
ideas, or feelings; to put an idea into words
(p. 46)

F

Famine — A shortage of food so severe that
people may starve (p. 228)

Federal — A system of government in which
power is divided between a central
government and state governments (p. 24)

Federalist — A person who favored the
Constitution (p. 32)

Federal republic — A government in which
supreme power is given to citizens who
vote for government officials (p. 263)

Fee — A sum paid or charged for a service
(p. 159)

Felony — A serious crime (p. 171)

Financial — Having to do with money (p. 22)

Flexible — Capable of being bent or changed
(p. 73)

Foreign policy — The plan a country follows
in dealing with other countries (p. 103)

Free enterprise — Freedom of private
businesses to operate without government
interference (p. 123)

Free trade — Trade between countries
without legal barriers on imports or
exports (p. 248)

Frequency — The location on the airwaves
that a radio or television station uses
(p. 123)

Function — The act or operation expected of
a person or group (p. 72)

Fund raiser — An activity held to raise
money (p. 204)

Funds — Sums of money set aside for a
particular purpose (p. 158)

G

Gamble — To play a game for money or
property (p. 128)

Generation — The people in each stage or
step in a family's history. For example, a
grandfather, a father, and a son are three
generations (p. 6)

Government — Laws and customs people
live by (p. 2)

Grand jury — A group of people who decide
if there is enough evidence against an
accused person to conduct a trial (p. 51)

Grant — A gift of money to be used for a
certain purpose (p. 127)

Guarantee — An agreement to protect a
possession or right (p. 32)

H

Humanities — Study of human thought
and experience in literature, history,
music, and art (p. 127)

Humanitarian — Having to do with
promoting human welfare and social
reform (p. 249)

I

Illegal — Against the law (p. 104)

Immigrant — A person who comes to live
in a new country (p. 228)

Impeach — To accuse or charge a public
official of misconduct (p. 141)

Imports — Goods brought from foreign
countries (p. 28)

Incompetent — Lacking qualities needed
to do something (p. 216)

Incumbent — A person who holds an office
(p. 204)

Indict — To accuse or charge with a crime, usually done by a grand jury (p. 51)

Indirect primary — Kind of primary where delegates choose candidates (p. 206)

Initiative — The process of proposing a law through a petition and then voting on it (p. 221)

Insurance — To buy protection from an unplanned loss of property (p. 108)

Interfere — To meddle in the business of others (p. 14)

Interpret — To explain or tell the meaning of something (p. 139)

Interstate — Between or connecting two or more states (p. 27)

J

Joint Committee — A committee that includes members of both houses of Congress (p. 69)

Judicial — Having to do with courts of law and justice (p. 29)

Jury — A group of citizens chosen in a court to listen to both sides in a case and to make a decision (p. 7)

Justice — Fair and equal treatment under the law; the use of authority to uphold what is right and lawful (p. 22)

Juvenile Court — A court that hears cases of young people (p. 170)

K

Keynote address — A speech that presents the main issues of interest and promotes enthusiasm and party unity (p. 208)

Kidnap — To seize and hold someone for ransom (p. 136)

Knesset — Israel's legislative body (p. 269)

L

Labor — Human activity that provides goods or services (p. 94)

Lawsuit — A question or case that is decided in a court of law (p. 6)

Legal document — An official paper having to do with rules and laws (p. 14)

Legislator — A person who makes or passes laws (p. 90)

Legislature — A group of people in a country or state with power to make laws (p. 7)

Liberal — A person whose political views are open to change and who supports individual rights (p. 203)

Limited — Restricted; kept within a boundary (p. 22)

Limited Government — All parts of government must obey the law (p. 29)

Lottery ticket — A ticket that gives someone a chance to win money (p. 128)

Loyal — Faithful; true to a country or belief (p. 10)

M

Magistrate — A minor law official similar to a justice of the peace (p. 170)

Maintenance — Repair or upkeep of property or equipment (p. 188)

Majority — The greater number or part of something; more than one-half of the total (p. 43)

Mediator — A person or group who talks with people on both sides of an argument to settle differences (p. 250)

Medicare — Government medical insurance for people over 65 (p. 127)

Military — Having to do with war or the armed forces (p. 72)

Militia — An organized group of citizens who serve as soldiers during times of state or national emergency (p. 47)

Minimum — The smallest number or quantity possible (p. 109)

Minister — A person who is appointed to help an ambassador (p. 103)

Minority — A group that is a smaller part of something or that is different in some way (p. 66)

Minor party — A political party whose electoral strength is usually too small for it to gain control of the government (p. 200)

Minutemen — A group of armed men who fought in the Revolutionary War (p. 14)

Misdemeanor — A minor crime (p. 171)

Monarchy — Rule by a single person or family (p. 6)

Mullah — A religious leader (p. 272)

Multiparty — Many parties (p. 200)

Municipal court — A court that hears civil cases, minor criminal offenses, and probate (p. 170)

N

National — Having to do with the whole country or nation (p. 10)

National debt — Money borrowed by the federal government on which interest must be paid (p. 89)

Nationality — The state of belonging to a certain country (p. 230)

Native — A person who was born in the country where he or she lives (p. 232)

Natural resources — Raw materials from nature, such as water and soil (p. 94)

Naturalization — The act of giving full citizenship to a person born in a foreign country (p. 233)

Nominate — To select someone for a job or office (p. 200)

Nominee — A person who has been chosen to run for election (p. 208)

Nonpartisan primary — A primary not influenced by a particular political party (p. 206)

North American Free Trade Agreement (NAFTA) — An agreement that took affect in 1994 that lowers tariffs between North American countries (p. 247)

North Atlantic Treaty Organization (NATO) — An organization of sixteen nations joined together to create a common defense (p. 254)

Nuclear — Having to do with energy produced from atoms (p. 123)

O

Obstacle — Something that stands in the way (p. 201)

Opinion — A belief or judgment of an individual or group (p. 47)

Opposition party — A political party that does not have a majority in the government (p. 205)

Optional referendum — A referendum that a legislature sends to voters willingly (p. 220)

Organization — A group that carries out certain activities (p. 80)

Organization of Petroleum Exporting Countries (OPEC) — An organization of major oil producing countries formed in 1960 (p. 269)

Organize — To arrange or set up a group effort (p. 15)

Override — To reject or not accept (p. 165)

P

Pamphlet — A printed paper (p. 14)

Panama Canal — A canal built in Central America to connect the Atlantic and Pacific Oceans (p. 264)

Pardon — To release or excuse someone from jail or prison (p. 166)

Parish — Name for local government in Louisiana (p. 157)

Parliament — A legislative body in England and some other countries (p. 7)

Participate — To take part in (p. 246)

Patent — An official document granting the right to make and sell an invention (p. 108)

Patriotism — Love or devotion to one's country (p. 237)

Percent — A part of the whole assigned to profit, taxes, commission, or other division of the total (p. 158)

Permanent — Lasting a long time or forever (p. 69)

Persecution — The act of punishing people for their religious or political beliefs (p. 230)

Persuade — To urge someone to do or believe something by giving reasons (p. 32)

Petition — A written document or legal paper asking for a right or benefit from someone in authority (p. 7)

Petition referendum — A referendum that is placed on a ballot to protest a law (p. 220)

Platform — A statement of the ideas, policies, and beliefs of a political party in an election (p. 203)

Pocket veto — When a bill is dropped because the President does not act on it (p. 69)

Political asylum — A place where a person is safe from being mistreated by his or her own country or government (p. 234)

Politburo — The policy-making body of a communist government (p. 259)

Political — Having to do with government or the actions of the government (p. 3)

Political Action Committee (PAC) — A group that collects money to spend for political purposes (p. 213)

Poll — Place where people vote (p. 218)

Polling place — A place where people cast their votes (p. 82)

Pollution — A state of being unclean (p. 111)

Popular Sovereignty — People elect their leaders (p. 29)

Power — Authority to take action; the right to decide (p. 72)

Preamble — An introduction or short statement of purpose (p. 40)

Predict — State what will happen before it happens (p. 208)

Preference — Choice (p. 207)

Preside — To act as leader or official (p. 164)

Press — Newspapers, magazines, and the people who work for them (p. 11)

Primary election — An election to choose candidates or select delegates to a party convention (p. 206)

Prime minister — The chief executive in some countries (p. 251)

Principle — A basic truth, law, or ideal of behavior (p. 29)

Privacy — Being alone, where no one can observe you (p. 218)

Probate court — A municipal court that makes decisions about wills (p. 171)

Procedure — A series of steps followed in a regular order (p. 139)

Progressive — In favor of changing government (p. 200)

Prohibition — The Twenty-First Amendment to the Constitution; it made production and sale of alcoholic beverages illegal (p. 44)

Propaganda — Ideas, facts, or information spread deliberately to help or harm a cause (p. 215)

Prosecute — To bring legal action against (p. 182)

Prosper — To succeed, thrive, or gain wealth (p. 112)

Publicity — Information that is presented to call attention to a candidate's activities in order to get votes (p. 212)

Publish — Print information, such as a newspaper, magazine, or book (p. 11)

Puritan — A member of a religious group (p. 11)

Pyramid — A structure that has a large, square base in which each side meets at a point at the top (p. 120)

Q

Qualification — A skill or quality a person must have to fill a job or position (p. 82)

Quota — An assigned number (p. 230)

R

Radioactive material — Substances that release harmful radiation (p. 124)

Ratify — To approve (p. 32)

Recall — The process of removing a public official from office by voting (p. 221)

Redistricting — Changing the borders or boundaries of an area (p. 218)

Referendum — Having voters vote on a law proposed by popular demand or by a legislative body (p. 220)

Refuge — Protection or shelter (p. 228)

Refugee — A person who flees from a country to a safer place (p. 230)

Register — To fill out a form so one can vote (p. 216)

Regulate — To control or direct (p. 67)

Regulatory commission — An agency that enforces rules and regulations (p. 123)

Rehabilitation — To help build or restore a person's physical or mental health and abilities (p. 168)

Reject — To refuse to accept (p. 68)

Religious — Having to do with church practices (p. 10)

Representative — A government in which officials are elected by people (p. 5); also a member of the House of Representatives; a person who is given the power to act for others (p. 64)

Republic — A government in which citizens elect people to speak and act for them (p. 4)

Republican party — U.S. political party that stands for a limited government role in people's lives and limited change (p. 196)

Requirement — A quality that is needed or required (p. 72)

Reserved — Held aside for a special reason; for example, the states reserved some power for themselves (p. 156)

Resident — A person who lives in a place (p. 64)

Resign — To give up an office or job; to leave one's office (p. 91)

Resignation — An announcement that a person is leaving a job (p. 67)

Responsibility — An activity or task that is assigned to a person or group (p. 24)

Restrict — To limit (p. 72)

Reverse — To overturn or set aside (p. 140)

Revise — To improve; to bring up to date (p. 23)

Revolt — To take a stand against a government or a cause (p. 4)

Riot — A public disturbance by a group of people (p. 166)

Roll call — To call off the name of each state (p. 210)

S

Sanction — An action taken to force a country to obey a rule or law (p. 250)

Secret ballot — A ballot that contains candidates' names and is marked in a private voting booth (p. 82)

Security — Safety and protection (p. 93)

Segregate — To separate or set apart from others (p. 143)

Senate — A governing body that makes rules and laws (p. 5)

Seniority system — Appointing people to jobs based on years of service (p. 70)

Separation of Power — Government power is divided between the executive, legislative, and judicial branches (p. 29)

Serve — To spend a period of time carrying out a duty (p. 64)

Session — The period of time each year when Congress meets (p. 67)

Small claims court — A court that hears cases about small sums of money (p. 170)

Specific — Definite, accurate (p. 120)

Staff — A group of people who advise or assist a chief executive officer (p. 80)

Standard — A rule or model that is set to control quality, size, or how something is done (p. 72)

Statehood — The condition of being a state; having all the rights and benefits of belonging to the United States of America (p. 153)

Statistics — Numerical data gathered in order to present information (p. 113)

Strict — Stern; not changing (p. 10)

Sue — To bring legal action against a person to satisfy a claim or complaint (p. 54)

Supervise — To direct activities of a group or organization (p. 181)

Surplus — Amount over what is needed (p. 107)

T

Tariff — A charge for bringing products into a country (p. 247)

Tax evasion — Not paying taxes (p. 136)

Temporary — Lasting for a limited time (p. 33)

Term — A period of time for carrying out a duty (p. 64)

Territory — A part of the United States not included in any state but organized with a separate legislature (p. 137)

Theocracy — A government run by religious leaders (p. 272)

Third party — A major party that exists for a period of time in a nation or state that usually has a two-party system (p. 200)

Tories — Colonists loyal to the King of England (p. 196)

Traditional — An established or customary way of doing things (p. 203)

Treaty — An agreement between two or more countries or states about trade, peace, or other matters (p. 22)

Trustee — A person who is given power to act for others (p. 188)

U

Unconstitutional — Not following the Constitution (p. 31)

Unity — Having agreement of purpose and a feeling of oneness (p. 211)

Unpledged — Not promised to a particular candidate (p. 208)

Urban — Having to do with living in a city (p. 183)

Utilities — Companies that provide heat, telephones, electricity, or water to a community (p. 162)

V

Vary — To change (p. 139)

Verdict — The finding or judgment of a court (p. 140)

Veto — The power of a person or group of people to reject or forbid a rule or law (p. 5)

Violation — Breaking of a law or rule (p. 136)

Voting power — The right to vote (p. 24)

W

Ward — A political division in a city (p. 184)

Welfare — Programs set up to improve the lives of citizens who need special assistance (p. 168)

Western Hemisphere — The land and oceans around North and South America (p. 263)

Whigs — Colonists who wanted independence from England (p. 196)

Witness — Someone who has seen or heard something; a person who is called to testify, or tell what he or she knows, in court (p. 52)

X

Zoning — Dividing parts of a community according to how they may be used (p. 180)

Index

D

E